Putting on the Blitz

Our Breakthrough Methodology!

Janet Nadine Mort PhD

Printed by CreateSpace, An Amazon.com Company
ISBN-10: 1537490028
ISBN-13: 978-1537490021

Dedication

Dear Colleagues:

I take pleasure in introducing our three great grandchildren – Piper, Reid and Logan. Their innocence inspires me and I love them.

Piper and Reid are lucky in literacy: They were born into a literate family that understands the power of knowledge and the tools of learning. They represent the next generation: Like most other children their age, they will begin their career paths in about 2035.

I dedicate this book to the unlucky children in the past, who were born into poverty, adversity and other conditions outside their control and, therefore, did not learn to read and write. We thought then that they couldn't, that they had experiential gaps that could not be resolved within the school system. We know differently now!

I, therefore, also dedicate this book to you the teachers who – thanks to scientific advancements, and your determination - will change the lives and the trajectories of these children. Over 90% of them can now succeed regardless of their experience(s) prior to school. Thank you for your dedication, commitment and passion.

Piper and Reid.

Enjoy *Putting on the Blitz*!

Sincerely,

Janet

celebrating
Dr. Clyde
Hertzman

Table of Contents

Acknowledgements

I am exceedingly grateful to hundreds of teachers who have worked so hard to implement *Joyful Literacy Interventions* (2015). They took the most recent research available (the NELP Report) and implemented the heart of it with integrity and passion.

As a result we are categorically able to prove that we can change the trajectory of school success for young children when we do 'the right things' in the early years and close the experiential gaps. This book, *Putting on the Blitz*, documents the story. Specifically I want to thank Leslie Lambie, Superintendent of Schools, and the SD 59 Peace River South primary teachers who led the way and are now in the third year of implementation with demonstrable success - close to our 90% goal of success for all children. Shauna Lothrop, SD 28 Quesnel, has also been a 'shining star' in her own kindergarten classroom and at our Summits.

I also wish to thank the Lauwelnew Tribal School primary staff and their principal, Maryann Gladstone, now entering the third year of *Joyful Literacy Intervention* implementation. We now have proven that our aboriginal children can learn at the 90% success level just like everyone else - when teachers do 'the right things.'

Thirty-one teachers contributed their stories about Blitzing in Chapter One including 20 ideas for learning game activities, and three of them contributed instructions for 32 games that have worked so well for their children in Chapter Four. These wonderful teachers are personally acknowledged in each chapter.

Thank you as well to the Superintendent in School District No. 23 Central Okanagan for giving us permission to reprint some of the work from the primary *Early Learning Profiles* (2012), especially Director Clara Sulz, EL Coordinator Donna Kozak and SLP Pat Smith.

Thank you Gay Pringle for the excellent editing and book design!

Janet

The Joyful Literacy Series

1.
Joyful
Literacy
Interventions
Mort 2015
(BOOK)

2.
Putting on
the Blitz
Our Breakthrough
Methodology
Mort 2016
(BOOK)

(available Oct 2016
from Amazon.com)

5.
The Summit Series
(PROFESSIONAL
DEVELOPMENT)

Joyful
Literacy
Interventions
SERIES
JoyfulLiteracy.com

3.
Circle Charts:
The Assessment &
Tracking Tool
Foundational Skills
(Hard Copies)

4.
Circle Charts:
The Assessment &
Tracking Tool
Foundational
Skills app

(Available in Oct 2016)

(Reproducible copies are included
in the book *Putting on the Blitz*)

Joyful Literacy Interventions: PART ONE Early Learning Classroom Essentials

This is Janet's landmark book and the foundation of her intervention strategy. Based on recent international literacy research she describes how to organize classrooms using literacy centers and joyful activities to teach essential skills. Practicing classroom teachers provide hundreds of playful practice games and ideas that reinforce skills for struggling early learners. (Mort 2014)

Part Two - Putting on the Blitz: Our Breakthrough Methodology

Janet and her team invented the "blitz" as a powerful strategy that has proven to close the skill gap between struggling readers and those who learn readily. Classroom teachers describe how they have implemented blitzes in their classrooms. Teachers describe thirty blitz games that have been very successful in closing these gaps. The book also identifies all the essential skills and provides instructions for assessing them. (Mort 2016)

Available on Amazon in October 2016

Circle Charts: The Assessment and Tracking Tool for Foundational Skills

Dr. Mort invented this simple and elegant strategy for tracking all children in a class, documenting their progress with each essential skill - not yet learned, needing review, and mastery. This makes it possible for teachers to organize whole group, small-group and individual skill instruction accurately and efficiently. Hundreds of teachers have implemented the Circle Charts and love them!

Packaged with "Putting on the Blitz"

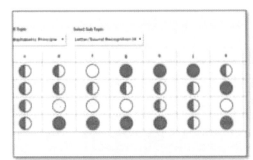

Joyful Literacy Online: The Digital Assessment and Tracking Tool for Foundational Skills

Once the paper version of the Circle Charts became popular, teachers everywhere requested that they be made available digitally. As a result, the online version of the Circle Charts is now available!

New! Joyful Literacy Online is an interactive web application for teachers to use the methods described in this book. Teachers can access the application at www.joyfulliteracy.com from any device with an internet connection - including desktop computers, laptops and tablets.

Once logged in, teachers can assess and track student progress on familiar Joyful Literacy Circle Charts with a click or a tap. Navigation between different Circle Charts is quick and easy, and all of the assessments you do on one device will automatically be saved. Next time you sign in, no matter from what device, your most recent assessments will be available.

Need to quickly figure out which skills to re-teach, or which students need help? Each Circle Chart makes this information quickly available, saving you hours of analysis each week. Need to print something out to hand to a parent? An export is just a click away.

The best part? We're using feedback from real teachers to make Joyful Literacy Online the best it can be. By the time you've read this, we've already improved the tool - and we'll continue to over the coming months and years!

Joyful Literacy's curriculum proves that students can read at grade level by grade two. Joyful Literacy Online helps teachers administer the curriculum quickly and easily, so they can focus on what they do best: student instruction.

The Summit Series (Professional Development)

For the past three years *Early Learning Inc.* (my company) has been sponsoring Summits in British Columbia, Alberta, Washington State and Oregon three times a year. The Summits bring together some of the finest experts in both countries to focus on vulnerable children and struggling readers with a goal of reaching 90% success for them by the end of grade two. You can visit the web site listed below to review details and upcoming Summits you may want to attend. You can register for Summits at joyfulliteracy.com.

Enjoy!!!

Janet N. Mort PhD
Let's connect!

www.joyfulliteracy.com
jnmort@shaw.ca
joyfulliteracy@shaw.ca

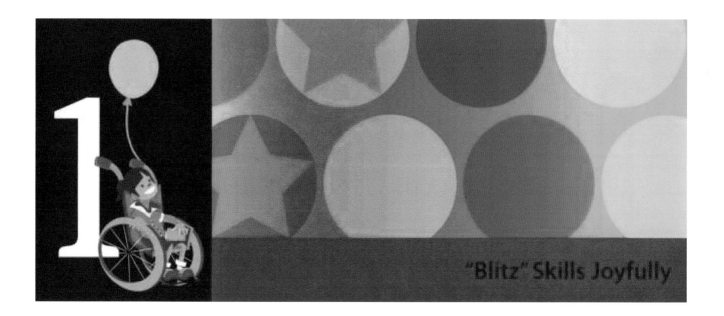

"Blitz" Skills Joyfully

The Birth of the "Blitz"

I had a theory; I found a strong research base that was not debatable; I analyzed school district results to determine why some districts were more successful in the Early Learning field than others; I invited school districts to engage with me to test my theories about our capacity to be successful with over 90% of all children regardless of their culture, ethnicity, lack of experience with literacy in the preschool years or even their socio-economic backgrounds – all believed to doom young children to an illiterate future and school challenges in my early years in the school system.

I was so fortunate to meet Leslie Lambie, Superintendent of School District 59 Peace River South, who shared my vision and passion. She expressed an interest in providing me with a forum and a partnership in her district to implement, test and measure my research-based theories and to work with approximately 60 volunteer teachers who were also hopeful and optimistic that we could do a better job than we had in the past.

I was to visit the district for two-day professional development sessions with this group – introducing them to the latest research, engaging them in discussion and planning activities for implementation and guiding them in adjusting and monitoring the proposed Joyful Literacy Intervention Strategy as the year progressed. My visits in August and November were exciting and rewarding, mostly because I found myself engaged with some of the most dedicated and determined primary teachers I have ever worked with – and I have worked with many over my 35 years of leadership in the school system.

My January visit was compelling and important to us all. Data collection was an expectation at the outset of the project and all staff had agreed to participate in collecting and submitting data to the central office to be compiled. In my view this reflected on the trust the staff had for their superintendent who promised that the data would be used respectfully and only to enhance district, school and individual practices. She also made it clear that the school was the entity for change and staff members were responsible collectively for considering results at the school level with the leadership of the principal.

The superintendent projected the data for the group to consider (Figure 1). Note that no schools were named or identified publicly. Schools, of course, were already in possession of their own data so could readily recognize where their data fit in the district picture. The room was still and silent as almost 100 staff members scanned the charted data. They were asked to identify anomalies in the data:

- What was surprising?
- What was worrisome?
- What trends could they see?
- Was there any data that raised questions?
- What were the questions they wanted to ask?

SD 59: Peace River South Project Data
Alphabet Knowledge and Phonological Awareness Progress: January to June 2014

School District 59
Peace River South

Kindergarten Results

January: 157 students
June: 164 students

Month	Alphabet Knowledge	Rhyme Discrimination	Rhyme Production	Isolation (Initial)	Blending Syllables	Segmentation Syllables	Deletion
January	13%	62%	47%	65%	69%	46%	62%
June	63%	79%	70%	82%	84%	67%	73%

Grade 1 Results

January: 191 students
June: 183 students

Month	Alphabet Knowledge	Isolation (Medial)	Isolation (Final)	Blending Syllables	Segmentation Syllables	Segmentation Phonemes
January	51%	54%	79%	68%	75%	51%
June	91%	83%	90%	83%	87%	81%

Figure 1

© Dr. Janet Mort 2014

The staff members were sitting in school groups at round tables with their principals. They were asked to discuss these questions among themselves then share their responses with the whole group. At this stage there was no effort to answer the questions. Groups were next asked to return to table discussions to speculate about what might have caused any trends in the data. Again we turned to the whole group to share some of the speculation. We had not intended to discuss individual schools at all but what happened next was remarkable.

Principals began to speak up identifying which school was theirs, explaining why the data appeared the way it was. Individual teachers spoke up and pointed out which data belonged to them and described why there were discrepancies from other schools. Influential factors included rate of attendance, cultural differences, second language issues, competing priorities, teacher illness and lack of resources. Where data was higher than normal professionals explained how they had achieved such successes and the factors that had contributed. This was unexpected but impressive.

It became apparent in the discussion that the issue of 'doses' arose. It became apparent that vulnerable children need more practice with new skills than children who learn a new skill after just one or two lessons. Teachers agreed that after they introduced the skill as many as 50% of the children mastered the skill with one or two practice activities, whereas many children needed as many as 10 to 20 experiences using the new skill in a variety of ways – kinesthetic, writing, reading, playing and celebrating final successes.

We decided to use the medical term 'doses' as a reference point for this concept. We concluded that we had to build in strategies that would give vulnerable children the opportunity for increased 'doses' immediately after instruction so they didn't fall behind their peers. This is why ongoing assessments are so important: To plan daily instruction and plan the 'doses' required teachers need to have an immediate tool to reference so they are able to organize groups with 'like-needs.' We decided to use the *Circle Charts* as our strategy for tracking each child's progress.

Learning the Alphabet four ways.

The initial focus for the first term was Alphabet Knowledge and Phonological Awareness. With respect to the alphabet one teacher pointed out that her results were low because she had spent the first term of the year focusing on Phonological Awareness, Print Concepts and establishing Practice Centers – all valid priorities in kindergarten; she expressed a desire to move forward with the alphabet quickly as she saw how many other classes had done so. (One of the stated goals was that all children know the alphabet four ways - the sound of the letter, the name of letter, the ability to find it in a book and to print it – in order for mastery to be recorded in the *Circle Charts.*)

We asked school groups, once again, to review their data; to decide if they were on target with the district goals; to make a plan for how to reach the district goals; and totake responsibility as a whole school for ensuring that children in the early years would achieve at grade level by the end of grade two. We asked them to brainstorm creative ways of achieving this by reconsidering how they might re-deploy school-based resources in innovative ways.

As groups reported back it became apparent that the need for increased 'doses' had to be part of the solution. The immediate backlash from the entire group was that we CANNOT resort to any type of 'skill and drill.' Young children thrive when engaging in playful activities; when they laugh, they're excited, they achieve, they wonder, they experiment. How could we create an experience for these vulnerable children where they could have many playful practice 'doses' and love the experience? We set about to create it and implement it. I consider the "Blitz" to be one of the most innovative and successful strategies I have been part of inventing along with our team of teachers in Peace River South – true out-of-the-box thinking.

What is a "Blitz"?

To put it simply, **A BLITZ IS AN INTENTIONAL STRATEGY DESIGNED FOR A GROUP OF TARGETED CHILDREN WHO HAVE SIMILAR SKILL NEEDS.**

Let's dig into the meaning of this. 'Similar skill needs' are key words in this definition. In order to conduct a Blitz we need to be able to identify (at a moment's glance) which of the children have similar skill needs. The *Circle Charts* have been our most effective way to do this. We encourage you, if you don't use the *Circle Charts*, to create your own system that identifies each essential skill and where each child is in terms of progress.

How urgent is the urgency?

Interesting question! Just as I was writing this part of the book I received the following email (excerpt). *"About a year or two ago, my wife came back home from one of your conferences and the word that she dropped in my soul from you was that the work that we ought to do on vulnerable readers is that 'urgent' and in multiple 'doses.' This has had a great influence on my thinking and performance in the classroom. When you have a bit of time, please drop me a note. I would like to hear directly from you. How urgent is the urgency?"*

The answer: There can be no greater urgency when it comes to literacy for struggling and vulnerable children. These are the unlucky children – maybe not unlucky in loving families – but unlucky in families who **are not literate**.

When do we use a Blitz?
Which children belong in a Blitz?

A Blitz is used when there is a need to accelerate learning in a specific skill. You cannot have a successful Blitz unless your children are grouped effectively. If they don't require additional 'doses' of skill practice then we are wasting their time. If they do require additional 'doses' of the skill then they have an opportunity to work with their peers who have similar needs, can support each other together and can celebrate as a group as they achieve mastery.

How do we decide which children belong in a Blitz?

We will only know through detailed skill assessments. We recommend that assessments in kindergarten be completed in September and October or as soon as possible so that needy children can be targeted as soon as possible. In kindergarten, Phonological Awareness and Alphabet knowledge are most important as well as Print Concepts. Print Concepts, however, can be introduced and assessed on an ongoing basis during morning messages and shared reading. This is not an overwhelming task: Assess Alphabet knowledge in September and move to Phonological Awareness in October.

Approach your principal or other members of staff to cover your class during PE, center play time, or propose that some classes be combined to give you private time to get these assessments completed. Assessments typically take only 5 minutes per child in the beginning. Later in the year, assessments can be kept up-to-date during quick personal assessments during daily work with guided reading, center time and other quiet times in the classroom. Once we have the assessments completed we are in a position to identify key skills where gains can be made quickly by identifying groups who have the same skill need and would be served well by a Blitz.

How long should a Blitz last?

You will hear stories in the next section of this chapter from different schools that have used the Blitz, and they each have used the Blitz as it was meaningful to them – and that's the way it should be. Overall, however, we have found that an effective Blitz needs only to last – at the most – 2 to 3 weeks. The reason: After 20 to 30 experiences with practicing the skills they have learned through the Blitz, most children are ready to 'graduate.' They have learned the skills, know how to apply them and are ready to take the next steps. They may not be involved in a Blitz again – or – they may be involved again when there is another skill that they have not mastered. Some children, unfortunately, do not achieve mastery through the Blitz.

We do not continue this strategy for them; rather we seek individual support for them through professional specialists – hearing, eyesight, psychology, learning, emotional or physical issues – children who may have special conditions that need a special diagnosis. We do not want to waste time if these children need extra-special services. One Blitz is enough before we start to look for other more serious issues that may be impeding learning when we find a child who is not making progress through the Blitz. This is a powerful and instant way to find the Tier 3 children who require different services quickly before it is too late for interventions.

How frequently do vulnerable children experience the Blitz in a week or a month or a year?

In our stories you will find that the decisions vary and you should make your own choices based on your circumstances. My best experience was in the Tribal School where the Blitz was held four times a week from 1:00 pm to 2:15 pm – Monday to Thursday. This left Friday for classroom special events and planning time for the Blitz team. The important impact, from my perspective, is that the children had almost daily 'doses' with little time to forget the skill message and apply it in their daily work in the classroom. You will hear other rationales in the Blitz stories in other sites and I believe they are also legitimate. DO WHAT WORKS FOR YOU!

What does a Blitz look like?

A Blitz can happen in an empty classroom, in a play space, outdoors or in an individual classroom – anywhere – where there is space for four groups of children who want to play a game. We recommend that there be only three or four centers for the Blitz, each one featuring a different way of, and a different approach to Blitzing the skill. Children usually only participate in the Blitz for about 70 minutes, spending about 15 minutes in each center before rotating to the next center. We recommend an adult at each center – older students, Teacher Assistants, the principal, the Learning Assistance teacher, volunteer parents – anyone who has been **trained** in how to work with struggling learners – trained in how to motivate them, how to praise them and reinforce them, how to play the games and how to lead the activities.

What does a Blitz look like? It looks like a child's party. The games are fun. The children collaborate and celebrate each other. They beam with pride. They laugh when they achieve success. They poke each other and then collaborate. They celebrate each other's success. They collect stickers, pats on the back and delight from the people who lead their game or activity. They **glow**. They object when they 'graduate' after two weeks and don't get to come back tomorrow. The Blitz experience is a place of joy and celebration.

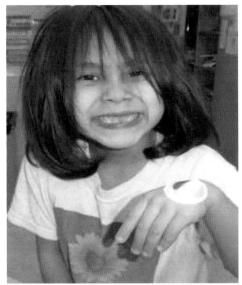

Rewards are fun!

How do we assess the children's progress?

We recommend that the Learning Assistance teacher lead the Blitz organization and implementation. In our Tribal School Nancy Eassie (the Learning Assistance teacher) is the person who analyses the progress of the children in multi-grade classrooms and designs the Blitz to reflect the similar needs of the children so that the

Nancy, professional in charge

Blitz can be targeted to like-skill-needs. She trains the individuals who work with the children at each center but most importantly she receives the children at the last center of the day and assesses whether they have mastered the targeted skills. This often takes the full two weeks but it is Nancy who makes the final call and informs the classroom teacher of the mastery.

While I emphasize the importance of professional leadership in the Blitz program I cannot underestimate the importance of the communication between the Blitz program and the classroom teacher. The classroom teacher must be the team leader for the children. The teacher assesses the skills; the classroom teacher maintains the ongoing monitoring of the *Circle Chart* or other tracking mechanisms. The classroom teacher consults with the Blitz leader over the selection of the children. The Blitz leader stays in close touch with the classroom teacher and finally provides the teacher with mastery results or recommendations for other approaches if the Blitz has not proven to be effective.

Putting the Blitz into Action

The Blitz has been implemented in over one hundred classrooms for over three years. As teachers have become familiar with the Blitz they have adapted it to suit their own needs. We encourage this adaptation, as no two schools or classrooms are alike.

Ten features of blitzing are not negotiable from our experience and research-based expertise:

1. Assessments must be conducted prior to the design of the Blitz and the design must be the source of all decisions related to the Blitz.

2. Games and activities used in the Blitz must be playful, joyful, and be constructed so that children experience multiple ways of applying the skills.

3. The skills must be "essential skills" based on research as described in the *Circle Charts*.

4. Children are engaged in the Blitz only until skill mastery is achieved; then they graduate from the Blitz process.

5. If the Blitz does not appear to work for a child after multiple 'doses' professional staff need to plan for more individualized interventions.

6. Children must see blitzing as a joyful experience; otherwise change your strategy or provide resistant children with a different experience.

7. The Blitz does not replace the classroom teacher who has prime responsibility for each child's growth. Intense communication between the Blitz program and the classroom teacher is essential. The teacher must ultimately be responsible for the growth and development of each child, supported and enhanced by the Blitz program.

8. Table activity leaders in the Blitz program, whether they be older children, paraprofessionals or volunteers, must be trained by professionals so that their interactions with children are supportive and consistent with the goals of the Blitz.

9. The leader of the Blitz program must be a professional staff member trained in intervention strategies.

10. Only children with similar needs are organized as part of a Blitz. Some children may never participate if they do not have a need.

Teachers' Blitz Stories

1 **Parkland Elementary School**
   SD 59 Peace River South

Sharlene Weingart (K/1 teacher)

Our Blitz!

1. How do you assess and track skills before you begin a Blitz?

I start the year assessing Phonological Awareness skills, Alphabet Knowledge and Sight Words. My first Blitz is generally on Phonological Awareness skills. Once those are mastered or well underway, I move into Alphabet and finally Sight Words. Once we are approaching mastery, we have a fluency Blitz with choral readings and readers' theatre. My class is a split grade, so it's important to do an initial assessment early on so that I am able to use student time effectively. I individualize what they are working on for each Blitz. In some cases, where students are meeting all the skills already, they become the models in the groups.

2. When in the year do you first establish blitzing?

Initially I started blitzing at the very beginning of the school year. Upon reflection, I will be focusing first on self-regulation and classroom routines before I begin a Blitz. My goal for the coming year is to start blitzing in October. We do a series of Blitzes during the year. I assess once a week at one of the Blitz stations so that I can determine whether we are making gains or need to adjust our methods. This is also how I individualize for students every week. I should be clear though that I start assessment right away because that is what influences my planning and teaching from the start.

3. Describe how you organize your blitzing.

To organize a Blitz, I start by assessing the children's skills. I track their progress on a *Circle Chart* and use this information to form multi-ability groups. I don't want kids who are

Mixed ability groups provide opportunities for teaching each other.

learning the same skills in the same group because they need models of what they are going to learn. During the Blitz process, my focus is on the most vulnerable children. Mixed groups work because the students have individual goals (word lists, alphabet letters) in the group, but they play the same game. So, if one child doesn't know how to read a word, there is someone in the group who can help. They always have someone they can ask or look to as a model. Mixed ages and abilities have worked well in this case.

Students have a folder that I load with their individual sight words or alphabet letters each Monday. They carry this with them and keep any game boards in it. It shows me what they have accomplished and keeps them accountable. I have been able to show the student a correlation between the work they did (or didn't) do and their graph progress. It keeps us all focused on the goals for each child.

I use the assessment data I collect using the *Circle Charts* to form multi-ability groups. The groups are flexible and I change them regularly to allow kids to work with new people. On Thursdays, the center I lead becomes the assessment center, so each group just rotates through as one of their regular stops.

My very first assessment is done in one color, in this case green. I check them with a pen or pencil as I assess them and then color them in afterwards to save time. The 'x' means I went back and checked in a later week and they didn't have the word, so the word went back in their list to work on. I don't have them reread all the words every week, just the new ones, but about once a month, for kids I'm not sure about, I'll go back and double check all the words.

Thursday: Assessment Day

Each week I choose a different color. This allows me to see the growth. When I see a week or more without significant improvement, I know I need to change what I was planning for the sight-word centers, or have individual conversations with students who weren't putting in an effort, based on what I see in their results and their folders. I choose the words for each child based on this chart as well. Student #3 on this list would have two words from this page and then I would flip to the next page to get the next words. I generally choose 10 words a week as a focus.

I use this format each week to outline what will take place at each center and who will lead it, and to organize the groups. Each adult has a copy along with one group member.

4. Who is involved in implementing the Blitz?

We have combined classrooms during Blitzes, so we have had two teachers and the principal along with any support staff who may be available. We have had as many as 35-40 children and two to five staff members at any given time. When we haven't had adults available to run centers, we ensure that some centers encourage kids to be independent. Teaming up really works well because it gives you the most teacher/student time at more centers.

5. How many children have been engaged over the past year?

We had about 35 children involved during the past year in grades K-4.

6. What skills have your Blitzes focused on?

We start the year with Phonological Awareness skills. From there we move into Alphabet knowledge and then into Sight Words. My class this year was a K/1 so some kids might be working on Sight Words at a center while others are working on the alphabet. We included printing formation and fluency in our Blitz centers. We found that when children had to write the word or letter as part of the game they remembered the item better.

Literacy Groups Week of : Insert Dates Here		
Start at the Center with the same number as your group. Centers will be 15 minutes each.		
I recommend mixed ability groups so that students support and teach each other at independent centers. These groups also allow for focus on the most vulnerable students at teacher led centers.		
Group 1	Group 2	Group 3
Group 4	Group 5	Group 6
Group 7		

Centers and Leaders		
Highlight and change to meet your needs.		
Center & Leader	Location	Supplies
Shared Reading Mrs. Weingart	Carpet	Clifford's Family
1. Mini Journals Mrs. Dueck	Rainbow Table	Mini-Journals, pencils
2. Roll A Word Mrs. Smith	Table 1	Dice, Templates, Word/letter lists, pencils
3. ABC Reading	Blue Table	ABC Charts, Books, Glasses, Pointers
4. Stamping Names, Sight Words	Table 2	Letter stamps, ink pad
5. Candy Land Sight Words	Table 3	Board Game, Mini White Boards, Dry erase markers
6. Reading Mrs. Wright	Carpet	Book boxes, Leveled PM books
7. Read to Self		
This is where I include notes for the week. This form is provided to all staff and volunteers.		

7. Describe the kind of activities children engage in, in a Blitz. Provide a few examples.

Before every Blitz we start with shared reading to bring our focus back to the big picture. We are doing the blitzing to learn what we need to know to help us read books. It is important to teach the reason we are learning the alphabet in four ways or with sight words. It all helps students become better readers and writers. We think of it as a whole-part-whole model so that the children aren't just getting buckets of information that are not related to anything or not useful outside centers.

We started with centers that were very playful (musical chair sight words) but we found that the children were not retaining the information; they were vulnerable kids from older grades leading centers. We thought that they would learn along with the others, but we found that they were "flat-lined" in our data collection. They needed to be part of a group with their own individualized list of words to work on.

We added a writing component to each center and saw a huge increase in retention. For example, we had **Sight Word Tic-Tac-Toe** where they had to place a marker over the words and read them. When we changed it to writing their word in the box, the retention and fluency of printing the word increased. So, rather than working on a worksheet, writing became part of a game with a purpose. It makes it fun!

Brothers at Tic-Tac Sight Word

Roll-a-Sight-Word was another popular game and brought a number-sense skill into the time. Students had a game board filled in for them ahead of time (individualized to the words he/she was learning) and then rolled the die. They wrote the word in the column for the number they rolled to see which word would reach the top first.

The children enjoyed **Go Fish** and would read and write down the word of the fish they caught. I found that these centers worked well for grade one and up. For the kindergarten children, I found that they needed to experience the sight words in a book before it was meaningful for them to practice. For them, it worked well if we learned a sight word in a choral poem or a story and then searched for the word and wrote it down on a clipboard. Again, the whole-part-whole is so important! 3D movie glasses without the lenses made this fun.

8. Can you provide hard data that show blitzing makes a difference (graphs, numbers, etc.)?

Acceleration … as I was tracking the data on the *Circle Charts*, I noticed something shocking. Kids were making huge gains. This is when I actually sat down and graphed the data.

Sight Word Progress May 7: Three Months

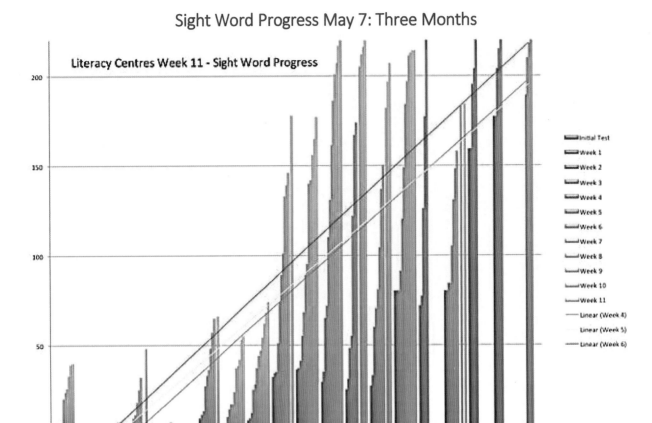

Figure 2

This was the acceleration curve we were learning to aim for in Reading Recovery and I was seeing it occur across the class. This result motivated me to keep going with planning, individualizing, etc.

It can look messy, and it can be kind of loud, but the data shows it is working! This is a combined k/1/2/3.

ABC Upper and Lowercase Four Ways

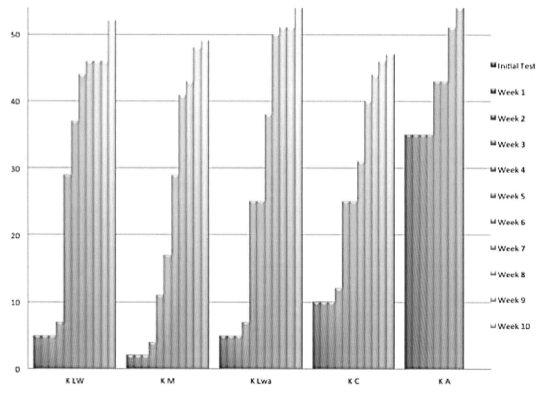

Kindergarten Alphabet Literacy Group 10 Weeks

Figure 3

This group of kindergarten students was not progressing with their Alphabet Knowledge and would likely have gone into grade one without knowing the alphabet four ways based on their progress. Now it's easier to count the letters they don't know four ways! They will master this and will be learning to read alongside their peers. One of these students is ESL. Two of them joined our class during the second term of school. I have nine students in kindergarten, but this represents only the ones who had not attained the alphabet goal as of January 15th.

The following chart (Figure 4) shows the progress of the kindergarten group from the first year in the Sight Word and Alphabet data. This is what they were able to accomplish in grade one. Their Sight Word data are shown on the bar graph along with the text box that shows their end-of-year reading level using unseen text. I am so proud of these kids! This is the progress we can see with targeted instruction and a growth

Sight word fluency, reading and writing in kindergarten.

mindset. Every child deserves our best and they can all learn. We just have to do what works. If we concentrate on the skills they are missing, we can give them the very best start.

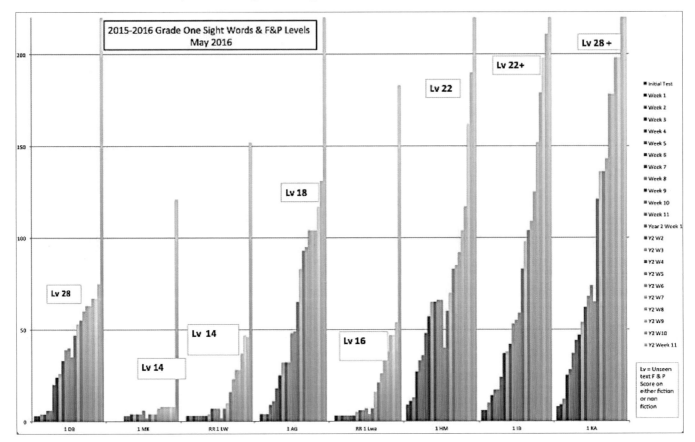

Figure 4

9. What were the biggest speed bumps you faced?

Our biggest challenge was getting and keeping staff on board and keeping track of data every week. Actually graphing the data to show the growth made participating hard to argue with. Our data showed accelerated growth across the class. It was worth the time and effort to plan, individualize and get others on board where necessary. Supporting each other and sharing ideas based on weekly data made a huge difference in overcoming obstacles. When we slowed down on weekly meetings, we saw deterioration in teamwork. The weekly meeting, bringing the data from the week, keeps the focus on the kids and what they need next. I highly recommend meeting each week and sharing the workload.

10. What were your greatest achievements?

Our greatest achievement was the progress made by our most vulnerable children. Many were at least a year behind in reading. They not only caught up to grade level, but in some cases exceeded grade level. This year we have grade one students reading at or above grade level, along with many kindergarten students. This success allows us to focus on the kids who need the most attention. We know that we can make a huge difference for them by targeting the skills they need. I feel confident that we can make a difference for every child, not just the ones who are easy to teach.

Teachers' Blitz Stories

2   Little Prairie School
SD 59 Peace River South

Diane Bassendowski (coach mentor)
Katie Sanford (K teacher)
Christi Munch (K/1 teacher and vice principal)

Putting on the Blitz!

1. How do you assess and track skills before you begin a Blitz?

We assess all primary students using Janet Mort's Dolch Sight Word lists to determine which words each student will work on. We assess each student using the *Circle Charts* to determine the greatest need in terms of skills. From this data, we choose a skill to focus on for two or three weeks. At the end of our timeframe, we re-assess the students.

2. When in the year do you first establish blitzing?

We begin the first week of October.

3. Describe how you organize your blitzing.

I am going to paint a picture of a typical Blitz in our school. Every Friday from 11:00-12:00 we have a Blitz with all primary students. Students gather in our pod (which is a big open area between classrooms) and we always begin with the question: "Why do we have a literacy Blitz?" The kids shout out: "So we can be readers and writers!" They know our goal of having every child reading at grade level by grade 3. We also go over our promise. We put our hands on our hearts and say: "I promise to listen to the mini teachers (our grade 4/5 helpers) and the big teachers (us)." Each mini teacher and teacher holds up a sign with their group number and students go to their group. We organize the students into ability groups. I call out the names of students and off they go to

Mini-teachers (grade 4/5 helpers) guide the students.

begin their first station. Stations run for about 8-12 minutes. We start with 8 minutes in the first month and increase it as the weeks go by. The timekeeper (a grade 4/5 student) rings the chime and kids rotate to the next station. At 12:00 we meet back in our pod and celebrate by making five book draws. At every Blitz we draw five names and the winners can choose a brand new book to take home.

4. Who is involved in implementing the Blitz?

We involve classroom teachers, the aboriginal support worker, a coach mentor, administrators and our amazing grade 4/5 "mini teachers." (These are grade 4/5 students who are leaders and have been trained by staff to coach the youngest students.) We also collaborate with the Reading Recovery teacher leader.

5. How many children have been engaged over the past year?

We have involved about 70 students.

6. What skills have your Blitzes focused on?

We have focused on sight words, rhyming, segmenting, writing, deletion, reading, isolating sounds and blending.

7. Describe the kind of activities children engage in, in a Blitz. Provide a few examples.

Our mini teachers run Sight Word centers. Each student has their own sight-word ring with the words they are learning to master, for example, "FEED THE MONSTER." Students say the word, write it on a whiteboard, then run to the monster (which is a box that looks like a monster with a slot for a mouth). The key is to keep the word in their head while running to the monster. They write the word again on a slip of paper and feed the monster. All the while, the mini teachers are cheering them on and checking their words. The kids LOVE this station. Our mini teachers know that research tells us it's important for kids to see it, say it, write it, hold it and move, then write it again. All the Sight Word stations have the above elements except for the "SIGHT WORD DETECTIVES," which is where they use magnifying glasses to find sight words in text. We want kids to make the connections between sight words and text.

Practicing sight words.

The teachers do not run Sight Word stations. We look at our data and blitz a skill. The student data drive and dictate our teaching. For example, we might notice a gap in rhyming. We also differentiate the teacher-run stations based on the group's needs. For example, if I am running a station about isolating sounds, I may have one group doing beginning sounds, while others are working on middle or end sounds. The data tell us which kids need to work on which skills.

I should also note that students who are high achieving and do not need the Blitz intervention either became mini teachers or worked with one of the teachers for a reading and writing project.

8. Can you provide hard data that show blitzing makes a difference (graphs, numbers, etc.)?

We have our *Circle Charts* and use the Fountas & Pinnell (2011) measurement tool. The Circle Charts show a clear picture of students' progress. Every single kindergarten student is currently reading at the Fountas & Pinnell grade level!

9. What were the biggest speed bumps you faced?

Some of the biggest challenges have been grouping the students. Sometimes students that are in similar ability groups don't always work well together, so we have to do a mixed-ability group, which made it harder to plan stations. Another challenge was that kids were able to read and remember some sight words but they didn't always remember them later. What we discovered was students need to see it, say it, write it, hold it in your head, move your body, then write it again at every Sight Word station. Once we made this adjustment we saw a huge increase in students' progress.

10. What were your greatest achievements?

Definitely a high level of engagement! The kids were having fun while learning! We saw students make giant leaps after only a few weeks of blitzing. Also, the leadership skills from our mini teachers have played a HUGE role in the Blitz. Our mini teachers can tell you why we have the Blitz and are personally invested in helping us reach our goal of having "90% of our students reading at grade level by the end of grade 3." Another great achievement is our regular collaboration to discuss current data. We do a tremendous amount of learning together as professionals through the Blitz.

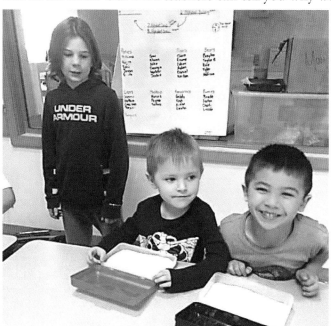

Learn letters and write them!

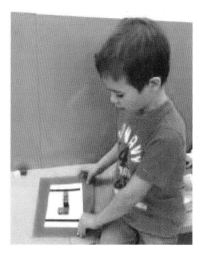

Learning sight words.

Teachers' Blitz Stories

3

Tumbler Ridge Elementary
SD 59 Peace River South

Kim Ferguson (Principal)
Karen Edwards (Literacy support teacher)
Stacie Gruntman (Grade 1/2 teacher)
Julie Tobin (K teacher)
Cristal Bertrand (Learning assistance, literacy support and reading recovery

1. How do you assess and track skills before you begin a Blitz?

Karen: Although I do not decide when blitzes occur, I pay attention to which of the blitz skills are present/not present during my literacy work with learners. I also check with educators and the database re: *Circle Chart* skills acquired or yet to be acquired. Communication with classrooms teachers is critical.

Cristal: I look at the data, connect with teachers and Educational Assistants (EAs). I facilitate with educational assistants about ways they could help. I use Kindergarten Screens, Speech and Language assessments and shared teacher data and recommendations.

Julie: I use the *Circle Charts*, meeting with teachers and Learning Assistant Teachers, and Literacy Support teachers to establish groupings related to results from the Phonological Awareness App.

Stacie: *Circle Charts* and observations during guided reading are a key component for me to know which skills need to be worked on. I also look at trends with the Phonological Awareness app as well for my grade ones.

2. When in the year do you first establish blitzing?

Karen: This is up to the classroom teacher, however it is also discussed during Coach Mentor and Collaboration Meetings.

Cristal: I start after all the assessments have been completed.

I use screening devices, consult with the Speech Language Pathologist, reference the *Circle Charts* and count on discussions and decisions made during Student Based Team Meetings.

Julie: After all the assessments have been completed and I see a need to begin a Blitz on a specific topic, I meet with other teachers to consider their needs as well as talk about the needs of students during Coach Mentor and Collaboration Meetings, and Student Based Team Meetings. I usually will begin blitzing after Spring Break.

Stacie: I count on informal conversations with colleagues, and planned collaborative meetings have been helpful to decide on when to Blitz.

3. Describe how you organize your blitzing?

Karen: I blend it in and integrate it during guided reading time and lessons, or scheduling blitzing as a literacy time on my schedule. I also meet with the teachers involved in blitzing.

Cristal: I meet with Education Assistants (EAs) and teachers about data from the Kindergarten screen for Phonological Awareness groups, and *Circle Chart* data. I make sure EAs have resources to do blitzing (if not directly led by the classroom teacher). I blend targeted areas (*Circle Charts* and district data) with guided reading in literacy groups and Reading Recovery lessons.

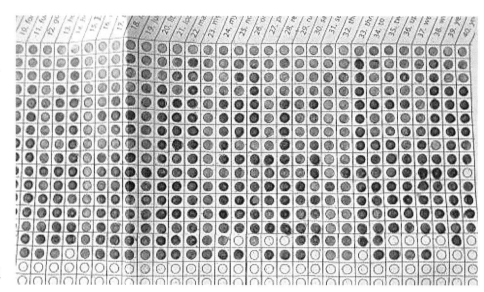

Circle Chart Sight Words, Pre-Primer.

Julie: I look at areas of weaknesses on *Circle Charts* and the Phonological Awareness app to see what skills are missing. Then, I get together with colleagues to group similar students and look at the EA schedule to see where extra help is available. I organize around teacher and class schedules, usually scheduled for 45 minutes twice a week.

Stacie: I do something similar to Julie, but as a ½ split with 2 or 3 teachers, our time goes longer; when we did the Blitz this year, it was for 1 hour and 15 minutes. I personally like to have small groups in centers for the skills I focus on during the Blitz.

Kim: As an administrator I give release time for teachers to meet or they meet on their own.

4. Who is involved in implementing the Blitz?

Karen: I count on classroom teachers, the literacy support teacher, the Learning Assistance teacher.

Cristal: I also use Educational Assistants.

Julie: I also rely on Educational Assistants, the Principal and high school students.

Stacie: As well, on occasion I ask parents to come in and assist at a center.

5. How many children have been engaged over the past year?

All Staff: All primary students have been involved in one form or another.

6. What skills have your Blitzes focused on?

Karen: I focused on segmenting, rhyming, the Alphabet and Sight Words.

Cristal: In my one-on-one or small group interventions (I used support from EAs) – primarily in Phonological Awareness skills, working memory, letter identification and letter formation.

Julie: I also focus on isolation, deletion, Alphabet Knowledge (and essentially all *Circle Chart* items).

Stacie: In one Blitz (grades 2/3) we focused on vowel combinations (ee, ea, ou, ai, etc), while others have focused on the areas mentioned above.

7. Describe the kinds of activities children engage in, in a Blitz.

Karen: Sight Word games, Elkonin boxes, looking at literature, puppets to review sight words, memory style type games, and writing (various forms).

Julie: I included modification of existing games and board games and kinesthetic activities as well as on-line ideas.

Practicing Sight Words.

Cristal: In my small group or one-on-one I use blended and guided reading, and Reading Recovery. I focus on Phonological Awareness work and a "try it" page for skills application, Elkonin boxes, magnetic letters, framing words and linking these tasks all within literature and context of reading and writing.

Stacie: I do the same as Cristal.

8. Can you provide hard data that shows blitzing makes a difference (graphs, numbers, etc.)?

All Staff: This is available through the school district and is collected in January and June.

Janet's Comments

Data-driven graphs are displayed throughout Joyful Literacy Interventions Part One: Early Learning Classroom Essentials, as well as in this book, *Putting on the Blitz*.

Janet

9. What were the biggest speed bumps you faced?

Karen: Scheduling was difficult but it can be accomplished with communication and flexibility with all staff as critical to the process.

Cristal: We need time to connect with other staff, plan, and coordinate so we can orchestrate the Blitz.

Julie: Scheduling!

Stacie: Scheduling!

10. What were your greatest achievements?

Karen: Being a part of the process and team; flexibility and communication.

Cristal: Being part of the process and being involved in the PLC (Professional Learning Community), being a part of Reading Recovery. While there is still a need for Reading Recovery that need has been reduced in number by our work. We have all really come together to demonstrate group achievement.

Julie: I love seeing the children's success and their growth on the *Circle Charts* over time.

Taking ownership of learning.

Stacie: I loved seeing the students work together to learn! Most groupings were multi-age so it was also wonderful to see students take on leadership roles. Watching them 'get it' is always satisfying as a teacher.

Kim (Principal): Seeing the overall school success — enthusiasm for love of learning of both teachers and students.

Teachers' Blitz Stories

4

Lauwelnew Tribal School
Saanich, British Columbia

Nancy Eassie (Learning Assistance Teacher)

Janet's Comments

Nancy Eassie addresses the same questions as the other contributors but chose to use an essay format. She tells us her story …

Janet

When I was first introduced to Dr. Janet Mort, she was excited about how to help us implement quick recall of sight words and how students needed these words to become successful readers. Then she showed our staff members her *Circle Charts* and the implications thereof, and so began my love-hate relationship with the data and the analysis of the *Circle Charts*. I will admit I was resistant, only because I knew that responsibility would come to me and making the *Circle Charts* work as an assessment tool to help me find where the gaps were and get those students help as soon as possible.

I am the Learning Assistance teacher at my school. I have been a classroom teacher in many grades but have settled into a position that allows me to help as many students as my day permits. Having the *Circle Charts* makes me, and helps me, narrow down that list and pinpoint exactly where I need to be and with whom. For that I am grateful, as I don't feel like I just running from one student to the next and spinning my wheels hoping I am giving them what they need but actually knowing that I am!

To lead the Blitz within our school, I quickly grabbed my resources of flash cards of alphabet and sight words containing Pre-primer, Primer, Grade 1/2/3 Sight Words. For each student to show knowledge of the alphabet, they had to be able to identify each letter (upper and lower case), able to tell the sound of each letter, and give a word beginning with a letter. For example: Bb says 'b', bubble. Sight Word knowledge is being able to read the words and have an understanding of them in context. After filling out the *Circle Charts* with each student's name (in our school's case) we started with all the grade 2s, grade 1s, and the alphabet with the kindergarten children.

Once I was able to sit and assess each student it was time to organize the 'Blitz.'

I perused the data and organized a system that worked for me. I was able to create a chart that let me see and gather all the students that were missing similar letters and sight words. It is very important to spend the time to find how you are going to use the information provided by the *Circle Charts*, sort the information, and share the information. Once I had the information at hand, I was able to approach each teacher and explain who was going to be with me during a daily RTI (Response To Intervention) session. In our school's situation, it was scheduled for Monday through Thursday from 1 pm – 2pm. I had full support from our Principal and with some flexibility with staff, I was able to get the assistance of three other para-professional staff members. In our case they were teacher assistance staff members.

After collaborating with the staff, explaining our plan, and getting them excited about it, our team was set; off we went to create games and gather resources that made filling the skill gaps fun … in other words, play-based learning! It had to be specific and very goal oriented. Once I had the names of the students and pinpointed their needs, I made a list of who and what the gap was. It is very important to share this information, otherwise your team for RTI quickly disintegrates into a waste of time for students, staff and resources. With names and games in hand, four of us set up in a nursery classroom not being used in the afternoon and set up a timer with 15 minutes on the clock. Twelve students were separated into three groups and each adult worked

with each group until the time was up and then we rotated. Each staff member was given a different task during the centers. One staff member did spelling, one did word sort, another did context in books and I did quick recall. All of these were done in a game setting. All of these were ideas from the staff members and they took ownership so they were invested. They were invested in the students, their time being well utilized, and shared the same goal of getting the students to read at grade level.

Learning Assistance Leadership.

To date we have probably had about 60 students being assessed and probably half of that number put through our primary-aged blitz. I will say, however, that guilt quickly set in for me and I wanted to do the same program for our grade 3, 4 and 5 students. I knew there were kids that needed help and I didn't want them left behind. So I loosely say that 60 students had experienced the assessment process. We have 120-plus students in intermediate and after assessing those that I knew were well below grade level, I set up a separate RTI time and did small groups on my own on a rotation basis.

The graphs you see here are of my intermediate students that had huge gaps. I find these compelling. I know you will see the data and the percentages from the primary students but it is important to see that progress can be made in the intermediate grades at well. Some of these students have diagnosed learning challenges, some are not yet diagnosed, some have intense attendance issues, and some move to and from our school during the school year.

These assessments and Blitzes help me help these students no matter where they are and how often they come to school.

If we look at the graphs, Alphabetic Principle, Pre-Primer, Primer, Grade1, Grade 2, and Grade 3, you can see the students gain as the assessments continued. It is important to remember that you must not continue on with the next set of sight words if the previous ones have not been mastered.

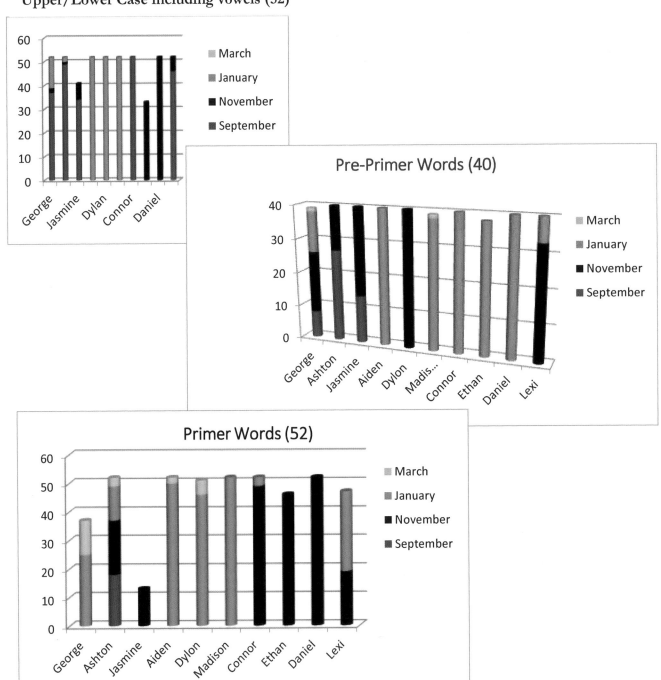

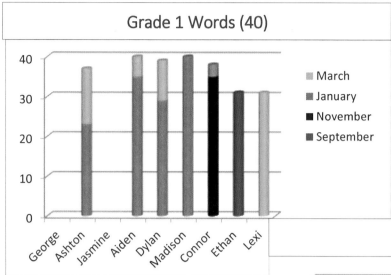

For example, if we look at George, you can see that in September, he was missing 13 out of the 52 letters in the Alphabetic Principle. He did get them by the end of March along with his Pre-Primer words. As you look at the following list words you will notice that he has not mastered the next list so he has no data and now we know where to start in the new school year.

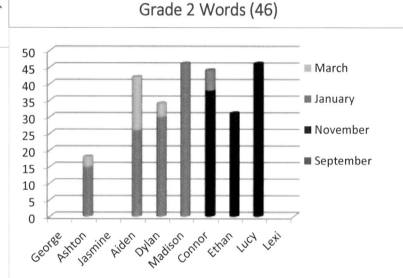

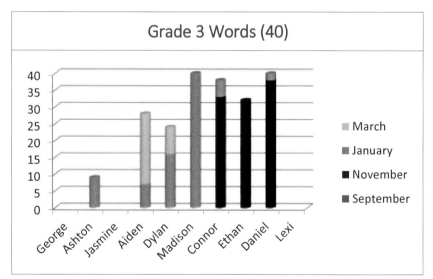

Now let's look at Jasmine. What do you see? Jasmine came to us with the 'want to read' and you can see her growth from September to November. There are huge jumps in her mastery. Then nothing occurs after November. What happened? She moved and our only hope now is that her current school is able to grab on to her 'want to read' and continue her reading success. On a positive note, if and when she comes back to our school, it will be quick and easy to reassess her and get her back on our system of mastery.

One last example is Lexi. If you notice, Lexi came to us missing the Alphabetic Principle. She worked hard and was able to gain her missing concepts. Many of her strides occurred between the months of September and November, then again in March. How did she not gain mastery of anything in January? Once again, Lexi came and went from our school, but with the Blitz, we were able to pick up where we left off and continue to help her on her journey. Lexi came to us sounding out every word she reads. I am not exaggerating. She had very little recall when it came to sight words. For example, words like 'and, it, how, is' she sounded out every word and it made reading very difficult as she spent so much time sounding out that she had no connection to the written word or comprehension of what she was reading. We have spent a lot of time having Lexi remember words and have a quick recall. Lexi has taught me how important recall is. Without quick recall and mastery reading words in a sentence are just that: reading words.

Any platform that one might choose to utilize and believe in will have challenges. Having to Blitz an entire school, one challenge will be the 'buy in.' This term means having to convince others around you that this is IT. This IS what will make reading easier. This IS what will help our students succeed. This IS what play based learning is. This IS how to use *Circle Charts* to your advantage. This IS how to show growth to parents, students, and peers.

Pride in progress!

Our school's biggest achievement is making our way to having almost 90% reading at grade level with our kindergarten students entering grade 1 with all the Alphabet Principle and the first 40 Sight Words.

If I were to be honest, my biggest personal achievement is gaining leadership skills and not taking NO for an answer. I have been upfront with my co-workers and really believe that it's a 'not personal, it's business' conversation. RTI can be rather intrusive to some teachers who dislike the pull outs. I myself dislike pull-outs as a classroom teacher. It is important to remember though that if one continues to do rotations of RTI now, the hope is that the evolution of mastery will wean RTI out. The goal is to not have Response To Intervention and have very few students that have gaps. On a comic side to this, I realize as I write this that my current job description is to slowly wean myself out of a job.

Every teacher and school will need to carve out their own roads for the journey and write their own stories. This is just a small example of what might work for you and yours. Remember that there will always be nay-sayers; those that don't like change; those that are content with being stagnant; and others that seem to support you up front but purse their lips behind your back. Blitzing is not for the faint of heart. It is a long, tedious, eye opening, heart wrenching, bare facts, emotional roller coaster with honest data. It is our job as professionals to try our best. If we make a mistake, we pick ourselves up, dust ourselves off and push forward with optimism for vulnerable children.

"My teacher thought I was smarter than I was – so I was." (Six-year-old)

5 Riverview School
SD 28 Quesnel

Shauna Lothrop (K Teacher)

Putting on the Blitz

Prior to starting any Blitz it is essential to have strong, up-to-date assessment data that will guide what skills certain students require extra instruction in and practice with. By completing the assessment in a one-on-one situation I gain further knowledge and understanding of each student's level of development. I know whether they are just starting to develop an awareness of the concept and would benefit from further targeted instruction (like a Blitz situation) or if perhaps they require more practice in order to gain mastery of the concept (possibly a short term Blitz but definitely practice opportunities provided during Practice Centers).

I start 'blitzing' early in the year. After all, there's no time to waste!! As the beginning of the year is the time when I am establishing my initial assessment baseline, it is the perfect time to start giving a 'leg-up' to those students who are showing signs of struggling. Seeing these students in a 'blitzing' situation also provides me with the added benefit of more time to build a relationship with them. If these students are struggling a strong, personal connection will be needed in order for them to trust me and take risks in their learning later on.

I have used a variety of 'blitzing' formats in the past. If I am lucky enough to have any Learning Assistance (LA) teacher time assigned to my class I will use that time to blitz groups of students on the skills and concepts they are experiencing difficulty with. I will group the students together based on my assessment results. I'll inform the LA teacher which students, what skill or concept they will be targeting and an approximate timeline (2 weeks initially), then if we are not seeing progress we need to re-group and come up with a different plan). I'll sit down and share with the LA teacher how I introduce, teach, and practice that

Alphabet Knowledge Literacy Station

skill in class so that the students are hearing the same language for that skill/concept. The LA teacher may teach the skill or concept differently than me but the foundation of how I explain it to the students, and what I expect the students to be able to do would be similar between the two of us. I communicate regularly with the LA teacher and as she is seeing growth towards mastery she'll communicate that to me and I can sit down for a quick assessment with the student(s).

As students reach mastery they leave the group and I may replace them with another student who would benefit from just the extra practice with the LA teacher. Some skills and concepts require a longer period of time with the LA teacher (Alphabetic Knowledge, letter/sound correspondence). Some are better suited to

Practicing rhyming words.

being broken down into smaller skills and 'blitzed' several times through the year. (The first step in rhyming might be just to hear rhymes, then later in the year we might blitz on producing rhyming words.)

If my class isn't targeted for Learning Assistance teacher time then I need to approach 'blitzing' from within my classroom. I need to find the time to meet with an identified group and provide them with extra instruction and practice with the skill or concept they are struggling with. I can accomplish this in a variety of ways. First, I look at my schedule for each day. I try to find 15 minutes where I could pull a small group while the others are engaged in an activity. For me, first thing in the morning is a prime opportunity since our routine is to come in each morning and engage in an activity for 20 minutes or so before we gather together for formal instruction.

I've set up the routine that if there is no activity for them at their table space then the students know they are going to meet me at the 'rainbow table' for their activity. I settle the class and ensure that they are started on their task then meet my small group at the rainbow table for a short session of targeted instruction and practice. As one group reaches skill mastery I go back to my assessment date and target another group of students with another skill and start working with them. In this way 'Blitzing' becomes part of my everyday practice and is very fluid and responsive to students' needs. This type of system requires clear expectations for those working at their tables. Before I start to take a group we have practiced the morning routine many times and the students require little intervention from me in order to be successful.

Another way that I provide groups of students with 'an extra dose' of instruction and/or guided practice is by scheduling a group to work with me twice during our Practice Centers time. I can manipulate the group rotation schedule during Practice Centers to have a certain group visit me twice in a day. I would try to space the two visits apart, allowing for some practice time in between.

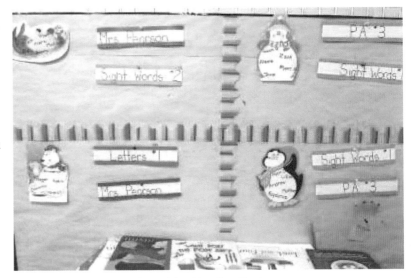

Organizing Practice Centers.

If I have a group of students who would benefit from extra practice (not instruction) guided by an adult I make use of any Education Assistant (EA) time that is assigned to my class. I will sit down with my EA and share the list of students, the skill or concept, and the activity I'd like them to engage in. I let the EA know about appropriate times when the students can be pulled over to work with her. Depending on the skill the EA may work with students independently or in small groups.

I have also used 'Big Buddies' for the same purpose. I have 'Big Buddy' time scheduled twice a week for 20 minutes. The buddies are trained to come in, find an activity or game in the assigned bucket that has a list of students' names attached, call that group together, and take them in the hall to play the game. My responsibility is to have games ready and labeled with student names that target the students' specific needs.

Organizing activities and games for practice centers.

Early in the year we focus on Alphabet Knowledge and letter/sound association. Later in the year the 'Big Buddies' are able to provide support to my students with learning their sight words by playing games with them. It's amazing to see the older students start to take interest in their 'little buddy's' learning. They will often come up to me and share successes with me or share if they have a worry that one student is not progressing as fast as another. This is great information for me to hear!

Big Buddy Blitzing

Every 'blitzing' situation is centered around using games to practice the targeted concept or some other activity that involves fun, motivating materials for students to use to practice the skill or concept. I always have hands-on materials available for the students to use because this raises their interest level, which impacts their time on task and motivation, and results in more engagement in the activity. I have a variety of forms of alphabet letters available to use (magnet, plastic, fabric, beads, foam), a variety of materials to make letters with (pipe cleaners, wiki stiks, stir sticks, string, white boards), and other materials that the students love to use (bingo dobbers, Play-Doh, smelly markers, large die, special pens, pointers). Many practice center activities start out as small group instruction activities. Once I have introduced the activity to the group of students and we have practiced with the game/materials (some times over several targeted sessions) that activity can be moved over and used as a practice center.

Read, write and smell.

At the kindergarten level my Blitzes usually focus on alphabetic knowledge, letter/sound correspondence, and phonemic awareness skills. After all, these are the building blocks to later reading and writing success. I try to incorporate a written element for each of these skills and concepts because I do not want students to just be able to orally name the letters of the alphabet. I also want them to be able to find that letter in text and form it themselves. Reinforcing the reading/writing connection is important for their overall development.

One of my biggest hurdles was learning to break apart skills and concepts into small incremental steps in order to provide students with a path that would clearly lead them to success. Students who are struggling to correctly identify and name the letters of the alphabet will see far more success when they are presented with just a few, meaningful letters to learn at a time. Their practice opportunities must be organized so that they experience a lot of success and become to feel confident about themselves as learners.

Initially finding ideas and materials for students to practice skills/concepts in new and novel ways was difficult. Years ago, I may have thought that the only way to teach segmenting and blending sounds was with Elkonin boxes. Now, we tap and swipe sounds, hop and jump sounds together, use little cars to drive sounds together, use magnet wands to swipe sounds together. My best resources were other teachers (reading blogs, talking with and listening to teachers at Professional Development events), Pinterest, and my classroom supply shelves. Over time as I began to explore the ideas that I was encountering I began to see materials in my classroom differently and started to wonder, "How could I use this (e.g. a magnet wand) to engage students in blending sounds?"

The 'detective' finds the missing letters!

As I largely need to rely on 'blitzing' to happen within my own classroom, I am finding now that I do not view 'blitzing' as an extra event added to my day but instead it is simply being responsive to student needs. My ultimate goal is to develop strong learners who believe in themselves and find joy in exploring and creating the world around themselves. The more responsive I am to each students' needs, the more success they will see, and they will view learning more positively because they will be able to experience learning in steps that are successful for them.

McLeod Elementary School
SD 59 Peace River South

Kristy Lineham (K/1 teacher)

1. How do you assess and track skills before you begin a Blitz?

Let me use Sight Words as an example. Each classroom teacher meets with students to read over the Dolch list. I created a leveled list with about 10 words per level. Words are arranged by top 25, followed by Pre-Primer, Primer, Grades one, two and three. See below for what I have created. Each level is also given a color to help keep organization simple (i.e., top 25 are green, Pre-Primer are white, etc.). When students start to miss words in a level they stay at that level. I did this during my guided reading time. Students read words on the list; if they could read it within 3 seconds, it was highlighted. Once they had about 10 words unknown, I would stop. Most times I could get through all 16 students and have a bit of time left to read with some of my struggling students who need it the most.

2. When in the year do you first establish blitzing?

We usually establish blitzing in the first term as soon as all assessments are done and we know what their needs are. This would be the latter part of October in order to get a Blitz in before the Christmas break.

We usually conduct a 6-week Blitz per term.

3. Describe how you organize your blitzing?

We have mostly done a Sight Word and Alphabet Blitz. Once the students are assessed, I take all the students levels and group them accordingly to try to make groups of reasonable sizes. Then we set up 6-7 stations per rotation. One teacher would prepare 3 stations and the other teacher would prepare 4. If there were 6 stations we ran them for 10 minutes each (60 minutes in total). If there were 7 stations we ran them for 8 minutes each (56 minutes). We ran the blitz once per week. It is important that you have one person who is the timekeeper and keeps everyone moving on time. Throughout the rest of the week each classroom would continue to have students work on their word lists and each teacher retested the Sight Words or Alphabet every Friday. Please see Figure 7 to see the seven rotating centers and Figure 8 for the teacher assignments and scheduling plan.

4. Who is involved in implementing the Blitz?

One other classroom teacher and I ran the Blitz. We also were fortunate enough to have our support staff run one station and our PREP coverage teacher run another station.

5. How many children have been engaged over the past year?

This past year, there were 30 students engaged in the Blitzes we ran. This involved our K/1 Class (16) and our 2/3 class and some intermediate students needing intervention (14).

6. What skills have your Blitzes focused on?

The Blitzes focused on mainly Sight Words this year. We tried to have a balance of stations requiring writing of sight words, reading of sight words, tactile experiences (sand, playdough), movement and music. Some stations also worked on the lists of words students were currently working on (their 10 words) and some stations used full sections of words (Pre-Primer). For those students not ready for sight words, they worked on the alphabet as they rotated around to the stations. Some stations focused on the general alphabet and some stations worked on specific letters students had been assigned.

Alphabet letters create sight words!

Throughout the year, in my class for ½ hour, 4-5 times a week, I do intervention groups. During this time I worked with specific groups of students or individuals requiring extra practice with a skill such as Phonological Awareness or the Alphabet. I would work with them until I felt they were successful at the task.

At the end of the year our support staff (who is trained), would take small groups of students to Blitz certain skills for a couple weeks. She would take these students every day for about 10 minutes. She took students for Phonological Awareness development, Alphabet Knowledge and practicing reading fluently.

7. Describe the kinds of activities children engage in in a blitz. Provide a few examples.

Write it in the Sand: Students write their sight words in sand and say them as they write them. They have to try to write their words as many times as they can before the timer goes. To modify for the alphabet we have students find letters in the sand and match it to the alphabet strip. They say something they know about the letter when they place it on the strip.

Crash! Students flip a card (color coded to match their levels (for example, pink is Primer). If they read the card they roll the dice and move their car that many spaces around the racetrack. If they don't know the word or get a CRASH! card they miss a turn. Another version: have the teacher read the card and the student writes the word in order to move around the racetrack. Inaccurate spelling or drawing a CRASH! Card means they miss a turn. Modification for the Alphabet: students draw an alphabet card. If they know something (name/word/sound) about that card, they roll the dice to move around the racetrack.

Musical Sight Words: Spread the color-coded cards out onto a table. Have students walk around the table to music. When the music stops, each student grabs a card and reads it. If they read it incorrectly, they have to say the word and write it three times on the nearby whiteboard. Once they have finished they bring the word back to the table and continue to play. The modification for the Alphabet: the student flips the alphabet card and must say something (name/word/sound) about that card. If they don't know it they can write on whiteboard and say it with help or have them find something in the classroom starting with that letter.

8. Can you provide hard data that shows blitzing makes a difference (graphs, numbers etc.)?

See the data below for 2015-2016 school year.

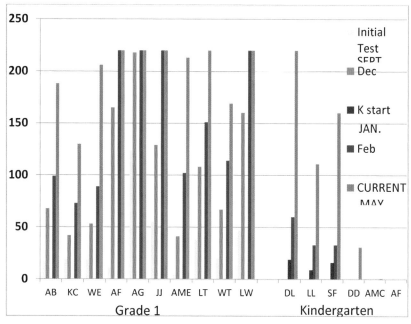

Figure 5

9. What were the biggest speed bumps you faced?

Learning to find stations that were low prep and worked for a variety of levels was challenging. Once we figured out color coding levels it made our lives much easier. Because we are a small rural school with anywhere from 38-45 students, we can't have an adult at each station. We changed schedules to allow for 1 adult at each of 3 stations (which was usually the most we have). We had older students or students who had finished their lists run the other stations. It took time ahead of this to teach these stations to the ones who would be leading them.

We also had to make this time sacred. Students knew they needed to be in on time and were excited for Blitz days. Timing was a bit of a hurdle at first. We quickly figured out which one of us was better as keeping time, while running a station and helping move students around. That person maintained the timekeeping role all year. Another hurdle was changing activities or games. We learned in record speed that it is best to keep all the stations the same until students are well used to the routine of how the Blitz worked. Once they were comfortable with blitzing we could change one or two games at a time.

10. What were your greatest achievements?

Our greatest achievements were seeing the improvement in the students' sight word vocabularies and seeing the engagement and excitement students had for the Blitz. We also took time to celebrate the students' achievements and hard work by having cookies, milk and buddy reading parties.

Below is the Dolch List by Level (with color coding), and the Blitz planners I created (blank and example ones that we used at one point during the year).

Dolch Lists by Level

Level 1	Level 2	Level 3	Level 4	Level 5	Level 6	Level 7
I	at	we	away	jump	three	but
a	can	you	big	little	two	came
me	go	am	blue	look	where	did
my	in	do	come	make	yellow	eat
the	it	he	down	not	all	four
is	see	like	find	one	are	get
	to	and	for	play	ate	good
	up	on	funny	red	be	have
	no	so	help	run	black	into
		an	here	said	brown	must

x25 High Utility Words(1-3)/Pre-Primer (4-6)/Primer(6-10) = 65

Level 8	Level 9	Level 10	Level 11	Level 12	Level 13	Level 14
new	she	well	after	give	let	some
now	soon	went	again	going	live	stop
our	that	what	any	had	may	take
out	there	white	ask	has	of	thank
please	they	who	as	her	old	them
pretty	this	will	by	him	once	then
ran	too	with	could	his	open	think
ride	under	yes	every	how	over	walk
saw	want		fly	just	put	were
say	was		from	know	round	when

Primer(6-10)/Grade 1 (11-14) = 68

Level 15	Level 16	Level 17	Level 18	Level 19	Level 20	Level 21	Level 22	Level 23
always	does	made	tell	why	clean	grow	much	start
around	don't	many	their	wish	cut	hold	myself	ten
because	fast first	off	these	work	done	hot	never	today
been	five	or	those	would	draw	hurt	only	together
before	found	pull	upon	write	drink	if	own	try
best	gave	read	us	yours	eight	keep	pick	warm
both	goes	right	use	about	fall	kind	seven	
buy	green	sing	very	better	far	laugh	shall	
call	its	sit	wash	bring	full	light	six	
cold		sleep	which	carry	got	long	small	

Grade 2 (15-19)/Grade 3 (19-23)

Figure 6

Our Seven Rotating Centers: Sight Words

Figure 7

Our Rough Plan

Figure 8

Teachers' Blitz Stories

7

Rolla Discovery School
SD Peace River South

Donna Chmelyk (K–3 teacher)

"Putting on the Blitz"

What is a Blitz?

A Blitz in our classroom is a focused set of activities, each with an explicit purpose. My objective is to maximize this learning time to make an impact on each and every students' learning need. My goal is to give them exposure and practice in the skills, which are required to keep their learning in literacy solidly moving forward.

Who will Blitz?

All of the children in the class take part in the Blitz. The students are divided into task groups according to their ability level and/or their specific area of need, such as rhyme or blends.

What to Blitz?

We start the year simply learning the routine of the Blitz. Therefore the structure (the use of the timer, the rotation, transitioning quickly, and setting their focus on the task) itself is the Blitz learning activities. I will create games for the students to learn the structure aspects of the Blitz. After they understand the structure and process, we will practice the routine further by doing activities where the tasks are known or at least predictable. By the time I have the testing complete on each student's Alphabet Skills/Phonological Awareness, the Blitz routine is well established and set for learning reading skills.

The learning tasks then become specifically designed to help each student learn the skills they require. The learning tasks may be in Alphabet Identification, Alphabet Sounds, or in the increasing of their working memory. It will also include the sub-skills of Phonological Awareness. These may include: distinguishing words in sentences, distinguishing letters in words, syllables, rhyme, alliteration, onset-rime, isolation of sounds, blending of sounds, segmenting, addition/deletion/substitution of word sounds. For the older students who have strong reading skills, the center focus may be in writing known words, spelling, word wall games, printing skills, etc.

How often?

I set our Blitz in the weekly schedule! I make it as sacred to our routine as the 120 minutes of literacy instruction time. I have heard my Principal say to another person who wanted to schedule some time with her, "No, I can't do it at that time, that's Blitz time."

What makes a Blitz different from regular instruction and practice?

Though I strive to ensure my regular teaching practice is also explicit and focused on individual student need, a Blitz is timed, it has games that are only pulled out for this special time, and with special people coming in to take part such as our Principal, older students and parents. They rotate so they see each adult, the centers are short and exciting. It almost creates a feeling of a party or game show. The students are focused, excited and learning. Our team makes the learning memorable and fun. Each center is specifically designed for the level of learner. Many different skill levels means that each center must have a variety of challenges to the game. The student remembers what they have learned because they are so devoted and 'charmed' if you will, into remembering the specific skill.

I get many suggestions and much support from other teachers in our Primary Literacy Project. The idea of a Blitz came from them and some of the learning games come from the fact that we meet regularly to collaborate and share stories. Our Superintendent, my School Principal and School District 59 have remained strong and steady in supporting the Primary Teachers in this endeavor. My instruction of literacy has become specific and much more effective because of the knowledge that Dr. Mort has brought to me. Thank you, from myself, and my little readers!

Following are examples of the some of the activities/games we use for learning and practicing Alphabet letters, Sight Words and Phonological Awareness in Blitz centers.

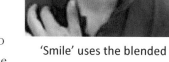

This student with the 'cut out smile' on his mouth is from the activity where we were working on blends. As you can see, "sm" was one of them.

Other times we work with sound boxes on the table using paper Elkonin sound boxes and blocks, and we up the game once they have a good idea of the concept. We tape squares to the wall. The student then uses beanbags to throw at the boxes, saying the sounds as they throw the beanbags.

'Smile' uses the blended 'S' & 'M' letters

This pair of students sitting on the chair with the book were on a word search to find a particular word. When they find it, they report back to me to move a game marker one place. Then they go hurry

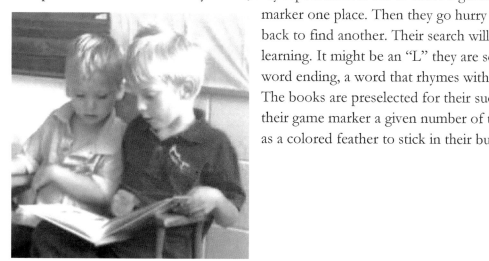

back to find another. Their search will vary depending on their learning. It might be an "L" they are searching for, or a word, a word ending, a word that rhymes with a given word, or a blend. The books are preselected for their success. When they have moved their game marker a given number of times, they get a reward such as a colored feather to stick in their buttonhole.

Finding the letter or word or * to win!

Teachers' Blitz Stories

School District Office
SD 50 Peace River South

Daun Newman (Reading Recovery leader)

Janet's Comments

Daun is a Reading Recovery coordinator and not directly involved in the classroom organization of the Blitzs although she is a frequent participant. What she has reported at the Summits is that the number of children in grade 1 who required reading recovery services based on previous standards no longer qualified due to the rich Joyful Literacy programs in kindergarten.

Janet

My role in Little Prairie School's Blitzes this year has been as a consultant to tweak the centers themselves so that the kids and teachers got the most "bang for their buck" in each center. In addition to adding the writing of words and letters to be learned, gross and fine motor movement has helped consolidate the learning for students as well as simultaneously and mindfully "seeing and saying" so that students internalize that their eyes and ears are allies and must match as a way of teaching them self-monitoring strategies. One other thing that seemed to be a big help was to have teacher-monitored centers where students applied in continuous text the skills they had been working on in the various other centers so that they made the connection to

Readers' Theatre Group K/1.

continuous text and transferred learning to their actual reading and writing in their classroom. Big books, poems on charts and other large print was used to help this process.

I also ran a center where we used this type of material to emphasis concepts about print such as the desired use of punctuation to support expressive, phrased and fluent reading. These types of centers were loud and fun for all especially when the Big Book had been carefully chosen to enhance the skills and involved interesting and repetitive language structures. Although it was not a traditional center, some kids from one class worked on Readers' Theatre based on familiar fairy tales. It worked miracles on their engagement, confidence and expressive, fluent reading.

Jubilee Community School
Meadow Lake, Saskatchewan

Daryl Pearson (principal)
Michelle Hildebrand, Holly MacFarlane, Kim Frey, and Jessica Wolff
  (Jubilee's kindergarten team)

Our Experience with Kindergarten Blitzing

The kindergarten Blitz was a simple yet effective approach to help our students learn the essential literacy skills in kindergarten. Our kindergarten team that coordinated and actualized the Blitz was made up of three kindergarten teachers, Kim Frey, Jessica Wolff and Holly MacFarlane and a student services support teacher, Michelle Hildebrand. Michelle coordinated the assessing, tracking and organization of the learning games for each Blitz. Having a coordinator was essential for the smooth operation of the Blitz and we credit her role in coordinating and planning the process for its success. Unfortunately, Michelle is transferring to a new school but the Blitz will still be an important part of our kindergarten program next year when Holly will take over the role of kindergarten Blitz coordinator. Most of the questions have been answered by Michelle with the concurrence of the kindergarten teachers.

Daryl Pearson, Principal

Michelle: I was a student support services teacher for Jubilee School and had attended a conference in Saskatoon in the fall of last year where I heard Dr. Janet Mort speak on Joyful Literacy. One of my roles for that school year was to support the kindergarten students and improve their Phonological Awareness. The Blitz looked as though it would be a perfect fit.

1. How do you assess and track skills before you begin a Blitz?

We broke down the phonological awareness skills for kindergarten and created a column in a *Circle Chart* for each skill. We (the classroom teacher, myself and another SSST) then used the PAST PAA (Phonological Awareness Assessment) on each student. This was time consuming, but very informative. Our province requires kindergarten teachers to use the EYE assessment, and we used the data from that assessment to guide us.

With all that data we were able to pinpoint certain skills that each student needed to work on. We were then able to choose three or four skills that would fit the needs of all the kindergarten students.

Assessment was ongoing. I was in the classroom daily working on those skills and when the classroom teacher or I saw that a student had mastered the skills, we would mark it off on the *Circle Chart.*

Our Blitz had four focuses when we started (Alphabet name and sound, rhyming, syllables, initial sound). We met as a kindergarten team two or three times through the year to see if we needed to change up the focuses or make any changes to the Blitzes. We did take some away and add in new ones as students mastered these skills.

We also left the freedom of moving students from one skills group to another up to the teacher. So if the student mastered the alphabet skills, then they could go on to whichever skill they needed next.

2. When in the year do you establish blitzing?

We started the Blitz in late fall (as that was when we learned about it). However, we would start blitzing as soon as we felt we had a good grasp on what skills the students needed to work on.

3. Describe how you organize your blitzing.

The classroom teachers and I came up with the four focus skills and then the teachers added their students to whichever skill the student needed to learn. Based on the numbers in each group, I provided games (simple games mostly found on Pinterest) for that skill. I wanted to keep the groups to no more than four or five kids. When we first started, our alphabet group was by far the largest group with about 30 students. So that meant I needed to have at least six games to practice the alphabet.

We blitzed every Friday. When it started, I would go to the classrooms and collect all the "alphabet students" and then divide them up and send them to their first station. Then I would get the "rhyming students," send them to their starting station and so on.

Each game had one adult leader to facilitate. We would stay at the game for about seven minutes and then I would call out when it was time to rotate, and the groups would move to the next game in their skill. Each skill had a minimum of three games because we did three rounds.

4. Who is involved in implementing the Blitz?

I was the one who organized the Blitz, but relied heavily upon teacher support. We used administration, school staff (EA's wellness coordinator, activities coordinator), other SSST teachers, SLPs, OTs, a learning coach,

An expert in each group!

parents, high school work-experience students and any other adult body we had in the school to help us run the games. Late in the year (May), I started using grade 4 students (the oldest students in our school) to run some of the games. This worked, but only because the kindergarten students were already well trained.

5. How many children have been engaged over the past year?

All our kindergarten students were able to experience the Blitz. That would be about 60 students.

6. What skills have your Blitzes focused on?

Alphabet names, alphabet sounds, rhyming words, syllables, initial sounds, final sounds, segmenting words and sentences, sight words.

7. Describe the kinds of activity children engage in, in a Blitz. Provide a few examples.

The games were very simple, ones that I could easily prepare ahead of time.

Kaboom! Write one letter on a Popsicle stick for each letter of the alphabet. Write the word "Kaboom" on a few Popsicle sticks. Place all the Popsicle sticks in a cup, with the words/letters in the cup. Each student pulls out a Popsicle stick and must say the letter and/or sound to keep the stick. The person with the most sticks wins. But if you pull out a Kaboom stick, all your sticks go back in the cup (works for sight words, too).

Fishing Game: Using cut out fish with paperclips, write either letters or words on the fish. Tell the group they are fishing for one specific word or letter. Whoever uses the magnet fishing rod (a skewer with a magnet glued to a string) and "catches" the fish, wins. Play again with a new word/letter.

Rhyming: We read stories with strong rhyming patterns, and let the students predict the rhyme.

Go Fish with sight words.

Memory with sight words or alphabet.

Sorting activities for syllables.

I Spy bottles for initial sound. Who can find an object that start with ____?

"I have ____ who has ____ " worked for alphabet, rhyming, initial sound and sight words.

8. Can you provide hard data that shows blitzing makes a difference (graphs, numbers etc.)?

We have our *Circle Charts*, which are almost completely filled in! Since this was the first year we used *Circle Charts*, we could not compare it to previous years but as a team, we believe that the students going into grade 1 have a stronger skill base than they had in previous years. Again, it is not definitive that it was the Blitz that made the difference, but we believe it was very influential in the difference.

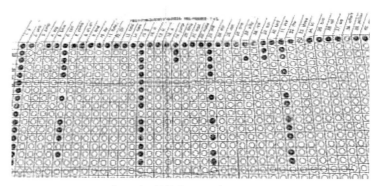

Sample: K Sight Words January

9. What were the biggest speed bumps you faced?

Initially selling the idea to all the teachers. Teachers were hesitant to give up their discovery time or center time to do these 'games.' But within a couple of sessions we were all on board.

Getting the initial assessments done; so time consuming, but so important!

Finding the volunteers to help us. Once someone volunteered, they always agreed to come back again because they enjoyed it. It was just difficult to get people to commit weekly. However, we never were short volunteers and in fact there were weeks we had to turn people away!

10. *What were your greatest achievements?*

Seeing the *Circle Chart* fill up!

Seeing students when they 'get it.' Being able to track our success with data to prove it.

The fact that each child was receiving exactly what they needed while everyone participated at the same time.

Wonderful to see a child move on to another skill.

Seeing how much they enjoyed the games/learning.

Learning Centers: We learn from each other!

Even though the Blitz took time to plan and coordinate, our kindergarten team appreciated the simplicity of the process and the impact it made on the engagement level and literacy skills of our students. We're excited to continue with the Blitz and look forward to making further improvements to help our students learn the essential skills that they need in a joyful learning environment.

Teachers' Blitz Stories

10

**Cache Creek Elementary
SD 74 (Gold Trail)**

Lindsay Stockermans (K teacher)

1. How do you assess and track skills before you begin a Blitz?

I conference with each student and assess their skills using the *Circle Charts* before I begin a Blitz. The Circle Charts make it very easy to see where I need to start with the Blitz.

2. When in the year do you first establish blitzing?

I first started blitzing in October, after attending the mini-summit. I blitzed with phonics and letter recognition until December. I then introduced Sight Words and began blitzing with them.

3. Describe how you organize your blitzing.

My blitzing was organized into three Literacy Stations that I operated daily over the course of a half-hour block. I timed the stations on the Smart Board, and depending on the kids' attention span that day, I went from as little as five minutes to as long as seven minutes per station, then the kids would rotate for a total of three stations.

4. Who is involved in implementing the Blitz?

I was the main person involved in implementing the Blitz. However, my principal, Brooke Haller, provided me with support for my planning and implementing processes, and she helped implement some of the games I created.

5. How many children have been engaged over the past year?

My entire class of eighteen kindergarteners were engaged in the Blitz. I had a grade 7 helper for a couple of months during my blitzing block, and even he was engaged with the kids!

6. What skills have your Blitzes focused on?

My Blitz focused strictly on literacy skills. My class started with phonics, letter recognition and writing from October to December. In January I introduced Sight Words, and we then moved onto blitzing with sight words, reading, writing and recognition.

7. Describe the kinds of activity children engage in, in a Blitz. Provide a few examples.

I had several games designed for the stations.

Activities/Games For Blitz/Lit Stations

Soccer. I took two 8 1/2 x 11 pieces of paper and painted them like soccer fields. I glued plastic cups on one end to act as "goals".

I gave each child one soccer field (sometimes they had to share, as some broke during the year) and a little ball of Play-Doh as a ball.

I would flash them a letter or sight word (depending on the grouping I had), and if they got it right, they got to shoot their soccer ball into the net. They LOVED this game! It was always requested.

Play-Doh. I had laminated sight-word cards (made lovingly by one of the support staff), and I would spread them out on the table and have the kids build the words with Play-Doh. This activity the kids were able to do themselves, so I could work with another group.

Journals. I started with very simple journaling. I would work with a group of kids and they got to write whatever they wanted. I would write what they wanted on a Post-it note and then they would copy it into their journals. I did this for about two months, until the kids became more confident. I then started writing only the words they didn't know (if there were sight words in their sentence, I would make them write it themselves). Then by June, I had some of them writing their journals entirely on their own. It took a lot of encouragement, as they wanted the security of the Post-it note to help them, but once they started realizing they could use their letter sounds to write words, it took off!

Write sight words on white boards.

Whiteboards. Exactly how it sounds! I gave them sight-word cards, a white board and marker and they went to town writing!

Be The Teacher. I used both the Smart Board and easel for this activity. This one had to be teacher-led, due to fights breaking out! The kids would take turns being the teacher. They got to pick whichever sight word they wanted and spell it on the board. The rest of the group was the class and they had to read/guess the word! They also loved this game.

8. Can you provide hard data that shows blitzing makes a difference (graphs, numbers etc.)?

I have my *Circle Charts* to show growth in my students. I loved using the *Circle Charts* to assess!

9. What were the biggest speed bumps you faced?

The biggest speed bumps I faced were support and time! My class was only able to engage in the Blitz activities (my lit stations) for a half an hour per day. I attempted to implement another Blitz with math stations in the afternoon, but it didn't work for my class. We managed to be productive with it some days, but not every day.

10. What were your greatest achievements?

My greatest achievements with my class was 14/17 of my kindergartens were able to recognize/read all 40 of the Pre-Primer Sight Words, and were successfully reading sight word books with little to no assistance by June! I was amazed at the progress they made, and am so proud of them! This was done simply with blitzing for half an hour per day in my literacy stations.

Teachers' Blitz Stories

11

Lauwelnew School
Saanich, British Columbia

Darci Dheensaw (K teacher)

Literacy Blitzing in the Kindergarten Classroom

Blitzing in the kindergarten classroom is the concept of play-based focused learning for vulnerable students. It's put into practice with activities that are straightforward and enjoyable. Vulnerable students are identified at the beginning of the school year using the *Circle Charts* system to assess literacy competence. The *Circle Charts* system, developed by Dr. Janet Mort, is a useful tool for assessing and tracking literacy progress throughout the school year to monitor individual student's strengths and needs. It allows the teacher to use differentiated teaching methods to develop interventions for small group learning. Literacy blitzing can be described in three phases: (1) pre-blitz phase, (2) blitz phase, and (3) post-blitz phase. The goal of blitzing is to focus on the child's needs to achieve literacy success based on their own learning style, their ability to concentrate and the time frame.

At Lauwelnew Tribal School, my kindergarten class has been using the *Circle Charts* system and blitzing concept for the last two years. I have adapted these tools to my personal teaching style and experience in the classroom to make them practical, easy to use and efficient. For example, when using the Alphabet *Circle Chart*, it was easier for me to combine the vowels and consonants on one assessment sheet for quicker assessment and tracking of each child. I also started a mini-blitzing session first thing in the morning for the group of vulnerable children who require extra support to prepare them for the upcoming day and/or to review previous learning sessions. I found great

Lauwelnew Tribal School

success in combining these tools and strategies for all groups of students, but the most vulnerable group has the most to benefit from these focused small group interventions.

The **Pre-Blitz Phase** is an important stage to collect information about students, assess their strengths and needs, connect with parents and develop the monthly teaching schedule. This phase starts at the beginning of the school year and continues throughout the year. In September it is important, therefore, to get a baseline

assessment of the child's literacy competence using the *Circle Charts* system in the following areas: Alphabet Knowledge, Phonological Awareness, Dolch Sight Word knowledge, Writing/Reading knowledge and Oral Language. Throughout the year I reassess the children every Friday. Based on the results of these literacy assessments, I stratify students into three learning cohorts or working groups. Students are grouped together as a cohort based on their skill levels, strengths and needs. Grouping students allows for a quick and easy transition when blitzing activities are conducted.

In my classroom, I have found the following groupings to be useful for learning activities and learning stations. I use a color-coding system to identify the groups when communicating with my EA or volunteer; for example, I might ask my EA to take the yellow group to the reading table. Likewise, the student groupings can be defined using the kindergarten grading system for our school, where Cohort #1 (green group) are typically students who are exceeding skill expectations; Cohort #2 (yellow group) are students who are meeting skill expectations; and Cohort #3 (red group) are students who are not yet meeting expectations for kindergarten literacy skills. I have used this system to identify the most 'vulnerable group' in my classroom, Cohort #3, and have learned from experience that this group often requires extra assistance and time to achieve literacy success for advancement to grade 1. Next, I create blitzing activities to help this vulnerable group.

During the Pre-Blitz Phase, ideally within the first few days of school, I have a **parent orientation** meeting to get to know the family and discuss general kindergarten guidelines and expectations. I strongly believe in a family centered learning approach in which the family plays an integral part in their child's learning at home. I use this meeting to introduce the concept of blitzing and how it can be incorporated at home. I encourage the families to get involved with their child's literacy success, even if it's just for 10 minutes a day. Parent involvement is very important to the success of my literacy program. For example, I had one boy in my class who had an older brother that was constantly getting into trouble at school. I engaged the older brother to help my student at home in reading his letters. This was a win-win situation for everyone involved, as the older brother was excited to be a 'leader' and teach his brother, and the younger brother was excited to learn his letters. Both boys benefited from this collaboration because the older brother had a purpose which kept him out of trouble and the younger brother had an engaging home 'leader' to give him one-on-one time.

Another important task during this phase is for the teacher to organize and **develop a learning schedule** for each month. It should be play-based, yet involve a structured approach to learning. I give the families the monthly outline of the child's literacy learning goals so it becomes an extension of our classroom learning. This gives families more tools to work with their child at home so when I send work home for the child, the family can feel they are working on a common goal. Everyone is on the same page when it comes to learning activities. Every few weeks, I send parents a review of what their child needs to practice at home, based on the weekly *Circle Charts* system and Blitz sessions.

The next phase is the **BLITZ PHASE**. I conduct my **first blitzing activities** as soon as I get a baseline assessment of the children in early September. The initial Blitz typically involves alphabet letters. I like to have two blitzing sessions each day for those students identified as vulnerable. I call these sessions Mini-Blitzes because they are short sessions of 15-30 minutes, depending on the number of children involved and the attention span of the children. Mini-Blitzes occur first thing in the morning during free time or center time. They consist of either a small group of students working with my class EA or a one-on-one session with myself. During the Mini-Blitz we work on previous learning modules or prepare the students for upcoming learning sessions (pre-teaching). In general it's a time to work on items based on the child's needs. Each afternoon at the beginning of the year (the first few months) we have another Mini-Blitz session for the vulnerable group. As before, these children are pulled out of free time to come and work with either the EA or myself. This could be in a small group setting or one-on-one. These sessions provide another opportunity to work on items that the teacher has identified during daily assessment of skill level. In February, the Mini-Blitz sessions shift from the Alphabet to Dolch Pre-Primer Sight Words. Blitzing games and activities integrate Dolch Sight Words that are presented in a fun and creative way.

The number of **people involved in blitzing activities** in my classroom varies depending on who is available that day. Typically, I like to have two or three adults available for blitzing activities including my education assistant (EA), myself (teacher) and another adult (parent helper or another EA). I have sometimes incorporated high school or college students who are interested in volunteering in the school. We welcome any helpers and it requires only a few minutes to train them about the activity. I try to set up the games so the instructions are clear and easy to follow.

The number of **children involved in blitzing activities** depends on the type of blitzing. For the mini-blitzing sessions that involve the vulnerable students, I like to keep the size of the groups to three or four students, unless they are doing one-on-one sessions with me. For the class blitzing sessions, all the children are engaged in the Blitz (approximately seventeen to twenty students). I found when I started class blitzing with only one group at a time, the other children who were not involved in the Blitz got upset if they were not included in playing the captivating games. Therefore I went with the three-station system, so that all the children had an opportunity to experience the blitzing games at the stations.

Mini-blitzing with students.

The literacy **skills I focus on when blitzing** depends on what the children are struggling with. After the weekly assessments I analyze the *Circle Charts* and group the children accordingly, based on skill level. I then choose blitzing activities on the particular literacy skill the children require. For example, if a group of children is having difficulty with the Dolch Pre-Primer words "here, the, away" then I make sure that those three words are in all three stations. The blitzing sessions complement my literacy learning schedule. From September to December I work on alphabet letters, three letters a week. In January and February I typically review the alphabet and include sounds with some introduction of sight words in stories and sentences. By March I have introduced 15-20 sight words. Throughout the year I work on reading literacy.

CLASS BLITZING is a strategy I use for the whole classroom. I use the same concept as the Mini-Blitz but include all three groups of students. At the beginning of the school year I may offer class blitzing once or twice a week in the afternoon. From February onward I incorporate more class blitzing activities as part of the daily class schedule. The activities incorporate play-based learning but involve a degree of structured or focused learning. Every afternoon the class is divided into three play-based literacy stations with designated leaders: the teacher station, EA station or helper station. Students are grouped together based on their predetermined cohort (as described earlier) based on skill level, strengths and needs. Each cohort (green/yellow/red) will work at a certain station with their leader and then move together to the next station. Each center will have one or two blitzing activities based on the lesson plan/module. Each station typically lasts from 15 to 20 minutes. The activities or games are modified according to the cohort skill level. The teacher station often

K students learning and growing!

involves word or letter activities with ongoing instruction and monitoring of the student's ability. The teacher station provides an opportunity to work on guided and shared reading lessons. To keep blitzing activities fresh and exciting, I like to have new stations set up daily to engage the children and have them look forward to the next day's blitzing activities.

The **type of blitzing activity** I use in my kindergarten class varies depending on the intended target: either Mini-Blitzes for the vulnerable students or Class Blitzes for all the students. They may also vary depending on the student's skill level, the literacy teaching module, the number of students involved, or who may be leading the activity. I found it very important to adapt the Blitz as needed for a successful outcome. I try to have a different blitzing activity each day.

I have found that to conduct a **successful Blitz in the classroom**, the games or activities need to be exciting, no matter the age or skill level of the student. The aim is to engage the child in a learning opportunity in which the game is competitive, interesting and educational. I have a passion for creating games that I feel my students will want to play and they don't always realize they are learning an important skill set or acquiring new knowledge along the way. I love seeing the children's excitement when I make a new game for them to play. The biggest factor affecting a successful Blitz is the teacher's passion or belief in this teaching-learning style. I like to have 10-20 games available during the school year to complement various learning modules.

I adapt conventional children's games or choose favorite children's themes when creating games for my classroom; for example, I have adapted **Hopscotch** to learn sight words. I draw the Hopscotch squares on the ground and in each box I write a sight word. The child will toss the beanbag to a designated square and hop from one box to another saying the word in that square. This game requires a variety of skills such as recognition of the sight words, reading and oral language.

I use the game Twister and adapt it to **Twister Sight Words Game** to fit the desired learning activity, such as learning sight words. I put masking tape with sight words on the colored circles on the Twister mat. I make a deck of cards with various sight words. The child picks a card and spins the wheel to indicate if s/he will move their hand or foot to the correct sight word indicated on the card.

A key factor in the success of this phase is to be well organized when implementing the game in order to achieve the desired learning outcome. The teacher needs to determine which resources are needed to construct the activity or game (e.g., cards, laminator, color printing) and will need to set aside a designated time to search the Internet for ideas and for constructing the activity or game. I often do this at home in my own time. Once I have constructed a game, I like to put all the games into large Ziploc bags and in the bag I put the game with the rules and a set of Dolch Sight Words or Alphabet letters. In that way, my EAs or parent helpers can pick

up a game that's ready to go. I change the games daily and I do not use them during my station work in the morning. I want the Blitz time to be fun and exciting for the kids. I typically have three tables set up depending on the number of adult leaders available.

Organizing students' games.

The last phase is the **Post-Blitz Phase**. During this phase I evaluate the games and activities I have used with the children. I modify the games if necessary to improve their effectiveness or adapt to another theme or concept. I also keep data on each child using the *Circle Charts* to analyze how well the children did throughout the year and try and correlate this with the Blitzes they participated in during the month or year. For example, last year there were five students

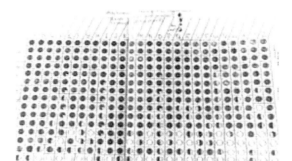

K Alphabet in January of the school year.

K Alphabet beginning of school in September.

identified for the vulnerable group at the beginning of the year. Their initial assessment of Alphabet letter knowledge using the *Circle Charts* system revealed they knew zero letters. Three months later, after daily Mini-Blitz sessions, their alphabet letter knowledge improved to an average of 12 letters; after six months their alphabet knowledge improved to an average of 22 letters. In nine months, four of the vulnerable students had improved their alphabet knowledge to 26 letters. One vulnerable student improved his alphabet knowledge to 22 letters.

I use the phrase **speed bumps** to reflect the challenges I encounter when using the blitzing concepts in my classroom. One of the speed bumps is trying to construct a game that is of high quality. This generally means having access to quality supplies and a laminator. You will need to produce games or activities that last the school year and will engage the children sufficiently to participate in the activities; hence, I always use color and laminate my products. It may cost more, but it is worth it when you see the results. Another challenge is when students enroll in the class later in the year from another school with a different program emphasis or learning philosophy. The biggest speed bump I encounter is the lack of parental involvement. The children who have parents working with them at home appear to struggle less, progress more quickly in skill development and have more confidence in their school performance.

As a teacher, the greatest achievements that blitzing brings to my classroom is seeing the excitement on the children's faces in the morning when they ask me whether I can test them on Alphabet/Sight Words because they have learned them at home the night before. It is so rewarding to know that the commitment and hard work I have put into this learning strategy has inspired my students and brought out the best in them.

 ## Janet's Summary

A Blitz is defined as a "concentrated effort". Our teachers' stories exemplify that. Now you know what a Blitz is: It is a teacher's (or a school's) concentrated effort to group children effectively for concentrated skill instruction to close skill and experiential gaps. Throughout the stories you will have noted common themes:

- The Blitz is a practice mechanism not an instructional mechanism;

- Play is the vehicle for the practice – through games and joyful interactions;

- The Blitz is a temporary mechanism designed for short-term support; children will participate for specific skills for a two- to three-week period;

- Students 'graduate' once mastery has been achieved;

- The Blitz is carefully planned and based on individual assessments to define collective needs;

- A Blitz can be offered daily or weekly depending on need;

- The Blitz is designed and led by a professional, however other adults or senior students can be used, once trained, for the practice activities; and

- The Blitz is presented as a 'treat,' typically children are eager to attend and reluctant to 'graduate.'

A Blitz can be implemented in a classroom or as a school-wide project in a centralized space for efficiency purposes. It is not presented as a Learning Assistance Program or a pull-out program. Celebrations are the norm as we all honor their progress and our own success.

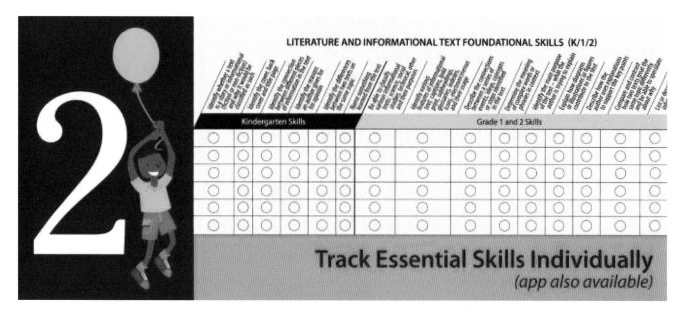

LITERATURE AND INFORMATIONAL TEXT FOUNDATIONAL SKILLS (K/1/2)

Track Essential Skills Individually
(app also available)

 Janet's Introduction

Circle Charts: A Powerful Assessment and Tracking Tool

Why are the 'Circle Charts' so Innovative and Important?

Recent research (2009) has affirmed that without specific foundational skills in kindergarten and grade one, most vulnerable children will struggle throughout their school experience due to a lack of specific skills, confidence and diminished self-concept. Research not only has identified skills essential in kindergarten and grade one but also maintains that 90% of all children should be able to be successful if these skills are mastered in kindergarten, grade one and grade two.

In many jurisdictions fewer than 70% of children enter school ready for literacy expectations, yet the most recent research suggests most 4-year-olds are developmentally ready. The problem is that many young children have not had rich literacy experiences between birth and age five.

The Research Base

These *Circle Charts* provide teachers with a simple tool that will guide the initial assessment at kindergarten entry and track each child's progress on a daily basis. This ongoing assessment will guide daily small group instruction for vulnerable children in a play-based environment enabling many to reach grade two or three achieving at the same level as their more fortunate peers. The charts were developed professionally. The skills identified on the charts are based on the NELP (National Early Learning Panel, 2009) report and the work of major literacy experts who present at the Summits and are well informed about the most recent research.

The most important implementation issue for vulnerable children is that these skills MUST be introduced and embedded seamlessly in a PLAY-BASED environment. This integration of play, literacy and additional explicit instruction for vulnerable children is challenging for teachers – especially those new to the profession.

Essential Research-based Literacy Skills

The Circle Charts assess the following sets of skills:

Reading Essentials

A. The Alphabetic Principle

    1. Phonics and Word Recognition

    2. Phonological Awareness

    3. Word Study

B. Concepts of Print

C. Dolch High Frequency Words

D. Reading Fluency and Comprehension

Writing Essentials

- Emergent Writing
- Development Writing

Oral Language

Literacy Essentials

- Literature and Informational Text Foundational Skills

Circle Chart Template

What do the Circle Charts look like?

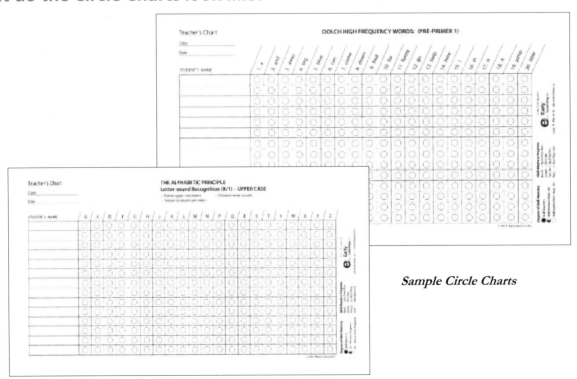

Sample Circle Charts

The Importance of Sight Words

Sight words, which comprise over 60% of all grade 3 level books are the connector words and are one of the fastest ways to encourage reading in young children. All 210 Dolch words are printed on single sheets – ten per page for a specific size of commercial labels – so that teachers can run off labels and paste them onto recipe cards for games, or in sets for individual children. Sight word cards can then be assigned to children, as they are ready, collected on key rings or placed in boxes of personal word collections. This saves hours of work printing, cutting and pasting them and makes it possible to give children their own individual sets.

How do the Circle Charts Work?

- Blank circles indicate the skills that have not yet been mastered by the child;

- Half circles identify skills that require review and re-assessment;

- Filled-in circles indicate skill mastery, and

- The colors indicate in which term the child mastered the skill. In the following chart black was used to indicate progress in the first term; yellow was used to indicate progress in the second term; and red was used to indicate progress in the third term.

Consider the following chart (Figure 9). This is a fictional chart that permits us to examine how the *Circle Charts* can be used to support teacher planning. Let's explore the following trends demonstrated in the charts an how the trends would affect my plans for instruction.

- Andrew had mastered most of the alphabet in the first term while Harry only mastered one alphabet letter. If I were the teacher I would be seeking special assistance for Harry – perhaps a hearing test or special testing by an expert which would depend on my observations of him and the number of intervention efforts I had made. I would certainly be able to make a case for special services based on the comparison with the other children. (One person attending one of the Summits inquired about whether it was possible he had moved in September before the assessments were completed. If this were true I would put a line through his piece of the chart to indicate that.

- Consider Frank's progress. Most of his skill mastery occurred in the second term. Perhaps he responded well to the first Blitz, which may have been held in December.

- Evan is certainly of concern as he has learned only three of the alphabet letters over the course of the year. I would have been seeking external assistance for him well before Christmas.

- In terms of letters I would be blitzing the letters x, y and z after a whole group lesson as so few children have achieved mastery.

- I would design my instructional time with small groups focusing on one letter a time and working only with those who need extra instruction or review on that specific letter leaving others to work in practice centers on other skills.

- I would make note of the half circles and create an alphabet practice center that featured those letters that seem to require more practice through games and hands-on fun activities.

- I may use the *Circle Chart* with parents in the third term (with names removed for privacy purposes) for several reasons: to ask them to support me by playing practice games with their child at home to enhance progress; to celebrate great progress; to express concern about lack of progress compared to others in order to get parental support for testing procedures; to demonstrate to parents that you are doing a GREAT job.

- I would be meeting with my principal weekly with the *Circle Charts* to discuss possibilities for support and more or special resources

Who's ready for small group work? EASY! Who needs special services? EASY! Who needs advanced activities? Easy! Where do I need help? I can prove it now!

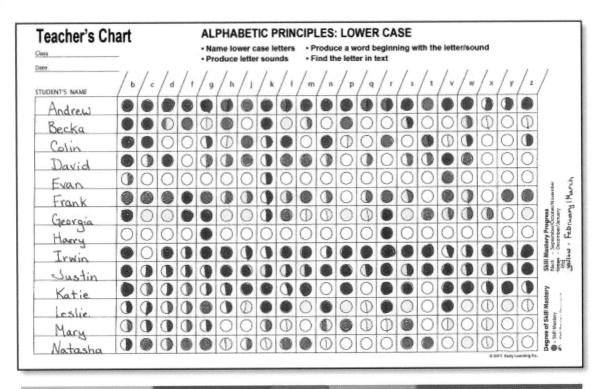

Joyful Literacy Interventions | © Janet N. Mort PhD

Figure 9: Fictional Chart

Skills are taught in a joyful play-based environment in large groups or small groups informed by skill needs or individually as necessary. The goal is skill mastery for tier one and tier two children before the end of grade 2. Blitzing (Chapter One) is an ideal way to close the gaps for children who need extra practice. Tier three children will likely require external support and pullout services. *Circle Charts* should be passed on from kindergarten to grade 1 to avoid unnecessary reassessments.

Results from Blitzing in a Tribal School

Now let's consider the following REAL charts from our local Tribal School. Children's names have been removed for privacy reasons.

A Special Tribal School: Literacy Intervention Results
A Celebration!

Nine Months of Progress: September 2014 - June 2015

FIRST NATIONS SCHOOL: LITERACY INTERVENTION RESULTS (KINDERGARTEN)										
NAME	**ALPHABET (A)** **# OF LETTERS/26**			**SIGHT WORDS (SW)** **%/220 DOLCH**			**PM BENCHMARKS** **BOOK LEVEL**		**PEABODY (Oral Lang.)** **AGE EQUIVALENT**	
	Sept 2014 # letters	**Jan 2015** # letters	**June 2015** # letters	**Sept 2014** Target 18% (40 PrePrimer words)	**Jan 2015**	**June 2015**	**Sept 2014** Target Levels 1/2	**June 2015**	**Sept 2014**	**June 2015**
Child 1	18	26	26	0%	37%	75%	1	14	6.7	6.9
Child 2	11	26	26	0%	3.2%	18%	0	3	4	4.6
Child 3	2	26	26	0%	3.6%	18%	0	3	4.4	4.4
Child 4	6	22	26	0%	2.2%	18%	1	6	6.8	6.8
Child 5	5	22	26	0%	.9%	18%	0	1	6.7	6.8
Child 6	10	25	26	0%	1.8%	18%	1	2	5.11	6.5
Child 7	6	22	26	0%	2.2%	18%	0	1	5.1	5.1
Child 8	0	16	26	0%	2.2%	18%	0	1	3.9	4.5
Child 9	0	10	26	0%	1.4%	18%	0	1	4.3	5.1
Child 10	0	10	26	0%	2.2%	18%	0	1	4.0	4.9
Child 11	0	10	26	0%	1.8%	18%	0	0	3.4	3.7
Child 12	0	11	24	0%	2.2%	17.5%	0	1	5.1	5.11
Child 13	0	1	23	0%	.9%	18%	0	1	3.7	4.4
Child 14	0	12	25	0%	2.2%	18%	0	1	3.8	3.8
Child 15	0	6	24	0%	1.8%	14.4%	0	1	?	5.2
Child 16	0	0	Moved	0%	.5%	Moved	Moved		Moved	
Child 17		New student	24			18%	0	0	3.11	4.11
Child 18		New student	14			14%	0	0	Sp. Ed Designation	

© **Janet Nadine Mort** PhD

PrePrimer 18%   Grade 1 60%
Primer 41%   Grade 2 80%
                 Grade 3 100%

A First Class Beginning:
Early Learning INC.

Figure 10: A REAL K Chart After Blitzing

Many of the children in this school enter kindergarten with little literacy experience. This was their first year in the Joyful Literacy Intervention implementation. The results in this chart come directly from the Circle Chart records for the documentation of mastery in Alphabet and Sight Word progress. Our goal was that all K children master all 26 of the alphabet letters and 18% (40) sight words by the end of the year. If we follow the data from September to June we can see that achieved that goal with over 90% of the children in spite of cultural and experiential literacy gaps for many of them. We can see that only four children knew any letters of the alphabet in September and no children knew any sight words in September.

PM Benchmark testing demonstrates that over 90% of the children were beginning to read before the end of the K year. These results are remarkable for this particular group of children. We can see that in January about half the children were making progress with the alphabet; however, the red numbers in the fifth column show that all but one child were not making good progress with sight words – the key to beginning reading progress.

The Reason? Blitzing!

Darci Dheenshaw, the kindergarten teacher, implemented an in-classroom Blitzing program in January with a focus on both alphabet and sight word mastery. Her program operated four days a week in the early afternoon for an hour. You can read her story in Chapter One for details.

A Special Tribal School: Literacy Intervention Results
A Celebration!

Nine Months of Progress: September 2014 - June 2015

NAME	ALPHABET (A) # OF LETTERS/26			SIGHT WORDS (SW) %/220 DOLCH			PM BENCHMARKS BOOK LEVEL		PEA BODY (Oral Lang.) AGE EQUIVALENT	
	Sept 2014 # letters	Jan 2015 # letters	June 2015 # letters	Sept 2014	Jan 2015 Target 60% (132 Primer words)	June 2015	Sept 2014	June 2015 Target Levels 15/16	Sept 2014	June 2015
Child 1	24	26	26	9%	39.0%	95%	3	17	5	5.7
Child 2	18	26	26	27%	27.0%	40%	1	3	6.3	8
Child 3	15	26	26	3%	28.6%	100%	16	23	4	4.8
Child 4	9	26	26	1.3%	5.0%	69%	Moved		Moved	
Child 5	16	26	Moved	1.3%	5.9%	Moved	Moved	Moved	Moved	Moved
Child 6	19	26	26	1.3%	30.0%	40%	0	4	3.2	4
Child 7	16	26	26	1.3%	12.7%	69%	0	7	4	4.8
Child 8	11	26	26	1.3%	7.7%	94%	5.5	16	5.5	6.4
Child 9	11	20	26	2.3%	2.3%	16%	0	3	4.7	4.1
Child 10	12	26	26	5%	10.5%	84%	0	10	5.11	5.9
Child 11	New student		26			86%	0	10	4.9	5.5
Child 12	New student		26			82%	0	7	4.3	4.9
Child 13	New student		26			39%	0	4		6.2
Child 14			Moved							

PrePrimer 18%   Grade 1 60%
Primer 41%   Grade 2 80%
Grade 3 100%

© **Janet Nadine Mort** PhD

Figure 11: A REAL Grade 1 Chart After Blitzing Began in January

This chart, in September, reflects a class that had not been part of the Joyful Literacy Intervention program in Kindergarten. The results for this class in Alphabet skills and Sight Word knowledge were documented with the use of the *Circle Chart* documentation. We can see that in September only half of the children, even after kindergarten, knew the alphabet and only one child had reached the sight work goal (30% of the sight words) by January. We can see that by June, 100% of the children had mastered the alphabet and almost 90% of the children had mastered the goal of 132 sight words. PM Benchmark scores were still low.

The Reason? Blitzing!

Nancy Eassie, the learning assistance teacher, implemented a cross-classroom grades 1 and 2 Blitzing program in January with a focus on both alphabet and sight word mastery. Her program operated four days a week in the early afternoon for an hour. You can read her story in Chapter One for details.

A Special Tribal School: Literacy Intervention Results
A Celebration!

Nine Months of Progress: September 2014 - June 2015

NAME	ALPHABET (A) # OF LETTERS/26			SIGHT WORDS (SW) %/220 DOLCH			PM BENCHMARKS BOOK LEVEL		PEA BODY (Oral Lang.) AGE EQUIVALENT	
	Sept 2014 # letters	Jan 2015 # letters	June 2015 # letters	Sept 2014	Jan 2015	June 2015	Sept 2014	June 2015	Sept 2014	June 2015
				Target 80% (176 Grade 2 words)			Target Level 22			
Child 1	25	26	26	3%	6%	30%	2	4	5	5.9
Child 2	19	26	26	6.8%	25%	75%	2	14	6.8	8.4
Child 3	21	26	26	17.2%	24%	55%	2	13	5.3	6.2
Child 4	20	26	26	16.3%	30.5%	75%	1	10	5.9	?
Child 5	20	22	26	15.9%	35.5%	98%	9	23	5.11	7
Child 6	19	26	?	3%	5%	10%	1	2	5.7	6.5
Child 7	26	26	26	18.8%	100%	98%	18	24	6.8	7.2
Child 8	21	26	26	18.8%	100%	76%	3	11	7.11	7.6
Child 9	26	26	26	26.8%	77.2%	Moved	Moved	Moved	Moved	Moved
Child 10	23	25	26	18.1%	90.9%	98%	20	22	7.1	7.8
Child 11	17	22	26	29.5%	81.3%	100%	24	30	7.3	8.4
Child 12	25	26	26	32.72%	86.8%	98%	21	21	5.3	6.3
Child 13	26	26	26	0%	19.5%	80%	19	23	6.6	7.11
Child 14	20	26	26	0%	70.5%	80%	15	Moved		
Child 15	25	26	26	0%	31.3%	45%	1	11	5.9	6.1
Child 16	0	25	26	0%	27.2%	84%	1	14	4.9	5.4
Child 17	0	20	26	0%	5.9%	100%	6	14	5.7	6.8
Child 18	0	7	26	0%	3.6%	100%	6	16	5.9	6.11
Child 19	0	24	26	0%	23.1%	98%	6	?	6.3	6.8

FIRST NATIONS SCHOOL: LITERACY INTERVENTION RESULTS (GRADE 2 – CLASS B)

© **Janet Nadine Mort** PhD

PrePrimer 18%   Grade 1 60%
Primer 41%   Grade 2 80%
                  Grade 3 100%

A First Class Beginning:
Early Learning INC.

Figure 12: A REAL Grade 2 Chart After Blitzing Began in January

This chart, in September, reflects a class that had not been part of the Joyful Literacy Intervention program in Kindergarten or in grade 1. We found it shocking that most of the children did not yet know the alphabet in grade two and none had reached an acceptable level of sight word mastery. We decided that the grade two class would be our top priority so Nancy Eassie (the learning assistance teacher) started the blitzing in November. (See her story in Chapter One for details.) If we look at the January results we can see the significant progress that was made due to the blitzing in just two months; however, we can also see what a struggle it was for many children to reach the sight word goals and the PM Benchmarks levels we would have liked them to reach; only half the children were reading at grade level.

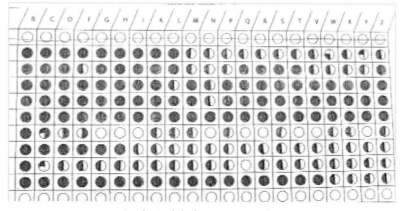

Grade 2 Alphabet in September

The Earlier the Better!

I hope this story and the accompanying three charts bring the point home. For struggling readers, we have to begin as soon as we can. Children at age three are capable of learning about print concepts, alphabet knowledge and can learn these important base skills through joyful shared readings. Those of us who can reach them prior to kindergarten in preschools or daycares have an exceptional and critical opportunity to get vulnerable children primed for literacy success.

The kindergarten chart (in Figure 1 on page 14) is compelling evidence that if we assess and track skills through the *Circle Charts*, then use the charts to plan our instructional strategies on a daily basis we can change the trajectory for many children who, otherwise, have limited choices and opportunities in their lives.

My book, *Joyful Literacy Interventions* (Mort 2015), documents a survey of teacher reactions after a year of implementing the *Circle Charts*. I am pleased to share their comments with you.

Teacher Responses to the Circle Charts.

How Did Teachers Respond to the Use of the Circle Chart in Field Testing?

Over 100 teachers agreed to field-test the Circle Charts in their classrooms in either the pilot sites or in my Kindergarten Intervention Classrooms.

You will find more responses in the Case Study chapter. The pilot sites used the Circle Charts for a full 10 months; the university class used them for three months.

Teachers were asked to consider their experience with the Circle Charts and respond to the following questions:

1. *Has the use of the charts changed your teaching practice? If so, how and in what way? If not, why not?*

2. *Describe how you have used it including frequency, management, sharing of data, or any other description of how it fits into your classroom life.*

3. *If you were to give suggestions to a friend about how to use it what would be your best advice?*

4. *Address the time issues involved. How have you managed to complete the assessments and organize small group instruction?*

5. *How could the charts be improved?*

6. *Include a copy of your circle chart to date with children's names blocked. Shrink to 8.5 x 11 and explain any analysis of the results so far.*

7. *To close, tell a story about a child related to the use of the chart.*

The following excerpts are representative of the university class students' responses, most of whom were experienced teachers.

The *Circle Charts* Provide Clear Learning Outcomes

(Jennifer Schmidt)

The Circle Charts certainly pinpoint the learning outcomes clearly for me as the teacher, as well as for parents and administrators. It is a wonderful tool to show the learning that takes place in a play-based environment! The Circle Charts have made me more aware and "tuned in" to what the children know. I am able to plan lessons around the information in the charts; the charts make it so easy to plan for small-group instruction. At a glance I see which children need more 'doses' of a particular skill. As a result, I include more small-group instruction in my practice. I can check off some things quickly without having to assess each child on each learning outcome (letter names and sounds—it's even easy to assess in a whole-class setting those who have mastered the skills and it frees up time to focus on those who need more 'doses').

I am much more organized and more confident; my teaching is more focused thanks to the Circle Charts. My Circle Charts are on a clipboard that I carry with me always. I use them multiple times each day. I have the children's first names listed alphabetically because I find that easier than last names to scan and find quickly. During large-group instruction, I am able to fill in the obvious ones quickly. I discreetly complete the charts when we are working in small groups. I prefer them not to be a distraction, so I usually keep the clipboard on my lap and complete them while assessing.

Improvements? Looking to the future, if these were to be sold, it would be great if they were available as a digital document that could be adjusted to suit the class. Technologically savvy teachers would probably appreciate being able to complete the charts digitally on their iPads in the classroom with a quick click to fill in circles. (Note from Janet: It's in the works!)

Know Which Students Can Name The Alphabet

(Michelle Fitterer)

*How many of **your** students can name all the letters of the alphabet? Which students can produce letter sounds, but may struggle with recalling letter names? Are there any groups of students having difficulty with segmentation, rhyme production, or deletion? If you had asked me those questions four months ago I wouldn't have been able to answer without having to flip frantically through my assessment binder. Now, after completing the Circle Charts for both the alphabetic principle and phonological awareness, I can answer those questions both quickly and confidently with one glance at my Circle Charts. The use of this assessment tool has helped shape my teaching practice dramatically.*

Alphabet Exchange.

My confidence, as a first-year teacher, has grown since using the Circle Charts. Revisiting them daily has helped me understand which stage my students have reached with their learning and how to prepare small-group instruction to improve their skills. Furthermore, the clear format of the Circle Charts has made it easier to share this formative assessment with my students, their families, and support staff. As a result, the assessment process in my classroom has become transparent. It is common to see my students and me cheering and high-fiving every time we fill in a circle on the chart. Assessment does not have to be an onerous, time-consuming process. My Circle Charts, a colored pencil, and a clipboard are all I need to monitor the progress of my students and plan for further instruction. There is no doubt that I will continue to use this simple and effective assessment tool throughout my teaching career.

In my classroom, everyone knows where our Circle Charts are, what the colored-in circles represent, and why we use them.

- *They hang behind my desk on a clipboard where I can access them quickly for daily use. It is my goal to review them every day so that I can group students more effectively and choose literacy centers based on areas of need.*

- *During our ABC Tub times I can informally assess my students while they play literacy games in a relaxed atmosphere with their peers.*

- *As well, I can hold quick conferences with students during free-play centers to discuss their learning on the charts and set goals for the future.*

- *Sharing the data has been a rewarding process for everyone involved. Students love seeing their line of circles being filled in and they understand what the data means.*

- *I make an effort to involve families in the learning process and often share the Circle Charts with them before or after school. In a matter of moments, a parent and I can share their child's growth and note which alphabet letters or essential literacy skills could be practiced at school and home. In this way, families are receiving more consistent and descriptive feedback on their child's progress rather than receiving three formal report cards in the year.*

Now that I have used the charts I realize just how manageable and quick the process is. For example, to assess my students' knowledge of letter names and sounds I used a combination of whole-group, small-group, and one-on-one instruction to gather my data. Once I fell into a rhythm of filling in the circles on the charts I knew I had found an assessment tool that worked for me.

Improvements? Over the past few months I have made subtle changes to the way I fill in the charts to suit my teaching needs. For example, a student had mastered the letter g (the circle was completely filled in with yellow pencil crayon), but when I revisited this letter a few weeks later she could no longer remember its name or sound. In response, I decided to place a pencil dot beside the colored-in circle to remind me that she required extra practice with this letter, and when she had regained mastery then I would erase the dot.

*Another change I would make for next year is the method I use when filling in half circles. If a student was able to **name** 15 letters of the alphabet I would fill in the left side of the circle; conversely, if a student was able produce the **sounds** for 15 letters I would fill in the right side of the circle. This is an example of how each teacher can make changes to how they use a tool, so that it best suits their teaching practice.*

The most rewarding part of using the Circle Charts as an assessment tool has been sharing the process with my students. Recently, my heart leapt when one of my students pulled a chair up to my desk and said, "Mrs. Cowan, it is my turn next to work on my letters… I have been practicing hard." Just one day earlier, this girl and I had conferred and discovered that she only needed to practice the tricky sounds: q and y. I asked her to think of her favorite words that began with each of those letters, wrote them (queen/yellow) on a sticky note, and then stuck it to her desk for her to practice. I was both surprised and proud that she took the initiative to find me during free center play to show me her learning. She was even more excited when I allowed her to carefully color in the circles herself! Afterwards, we created a secret handshake to celebrate her success and then she happily quizzed me on my letter names and sounds. Assessment is a quick, fun, and shared process in our classroom, thanks to the Circle Charts!

Identify the Students for Specific Instruction

(Shauna Buffie)

The use of Circle Charts has changed my teaching practice. They have made it so much easier to see at a glance which children need skill instruction or skill review on a particular upper- or lower-case letter. I know I do more short pullout small-group instruction sessions simply because I can see on a couple of sheets of paper which students need the same direct teaching or review. Before the use of the Circle Charts I was using small-group instruction strategies but I was probably not targeting all the right children, because I was pulling them based on my memory not at-a-glance data. My instruction prior to the use of the Circle Charts would not have been as individualized or as accurate.

At report card time and parent/teacher/student interview times, it is a useful assessment to share with parents, as it is so easy for them to see what their child has mastered or where they still need some direct instruction or review. As well, using the different colors at different times of the year solidifies when the learning took place and I am able to see and share the progress.

I rely on the Circle Charts for organizing small-group instruction because I have several times built into my day where my students are at activities of choice which lends itself to quickly and easily pulling aside a small group to play a literacy game or work on the alphabet through play-based and hands-on learning opportunities.

Where do My Students Need Support?

(Wendy de Groot)

Using the Circle Charts has helped me to clarify where individual students need support. It lets me know exactly what needs to be focused on and it helps me to "at a glance" organize my students into groups for round-table teaching as well as guide me in large-group teaching. In the past I had a ballpark knowledge of who knew what but now I have precise information at my fingertips.

I began using the Circle Charts in January as part of a university assignment. I had been using various other data management tools but the Circle Charts are much more manageable than the tools I had used previously. You can do the assessments in small chunks of time rather than waiting until you have a larger period of time available; this assists me in getting information quickly.

I used the information for my second-term report cards. For those students that had not yet mastered a significant number of letters/sounds, I set up parent meetings prior to Report Cards going out. I explained and sent home the alphabet binders to give parents who really wanted to support their children at home ideas of how to do so. I then set up a plan to access student support during literacy centers and requested support from our school support staff (through my administrator) to enable myself to work with this small group while my other students were busy doing related activities. Unfortunately I was not given the time because the schedule of support was already set and "it wouldn't be fair" to change it now.

Undeterred, I set up my literacy centers and crossed my fingers that during the teacher-blocked times I would not be interrupted and my students would now be independent enough to move through the schedule with little support. Each week during the first literacy block with my "special guys" I meet with them and we review what we know and choose two letters to focus on for the next couple of days. The letters we started on were letters that were in their name (if those were among the ones not known).

I send a note home to their parents to let them know our focus and I have suggestions to help them support their child at home in addition to the alphabet binder. I do this to give them a little reminder that, yes, this is important and we are working on this at school and hope that you will assist the journey by helping at home. Then for the remainder of the week, during centers, odd freed up times, and other literacy centers blocks, I pull these ones aside and we do some quick review using various tools: Play-Doh, Wikki Stix, our bodies, finger tracing, and reviewing rhymes that help us remember.

I have made each of my students a small set of cards and put them on a ring. When we choose our letters "to really focus on" we write them on one of the cards on the ring. That is kept close at hand and keeps track of the ones we have been working on recently as well, so it works as a quick review. The Circle Charts are also right at my side as we continue to fill in circles for letters/sounds we have mastered and the children are really interested in seeing those circles get shaded in.

Using our bodies to form letters.

To reward success as well as determination, we make a trip down to the office to visit our administrator to share our learning joy! She follows up with a phone call home and I send a "happy gram" in their home folder. I am able to use the Circle Charts to show parents and colleagues the progress and summary of progress of my students. It is a quick visual for all to see.

Advice? I would advise getting started right away. It does not take long to get that first phase completed; from then on it is a working document that is never far away. For kindergarten I have only used it for tracking mastery of letter identification and learning letter sounds but I am going to work with my student teacher to help her use it to track skill mastery in the PE unit she is going to teach next month. (Note from Janet: The Circle Charts can be used as a tracking tool for any set of skills at any grade level – even high school.)

Avaya is a good example of student success in collaboration with parents. She turned five at the end of October. She is the second child (of three) in a very busy house that has recently experienced a family tragedy. She is very social and not really interested in the academics of school. She just likes to play, draw, and do dress-ups. She has a wonderful sense of humor and has recently started to enjoy playing school with her big sister.

After completing my assessment in January/February and noting the big gaps in her letter/sound mastery, I met her parents and showed them her progress (covering up the names of fellow students) and we discussed how we could support Avaya's learning. They already had learning-fun built into their home routines, although they admitted that perhaps they had been neglecting them recently due to the family situation. When I explained how the alphabet binder works they felt it would fit into their existing schedule nicely. I sent the binder home with them and told them that I would be in touch with them again in early April to check on their progress.

Now [after holidays] we are setting up a concentrated six-week schedule of support for my students. I sat down with Avaya to check her progress on the Circle Chart and make our first weekly goal. I was delighted to see that there was significant progress. She happily chatted with me and told me how she practiced at home and with whom. She was tickled-pink to see her circles get completed. She now knows all of her uppercase letters and sounds, and of the ten lowercase letters that she did not previously know, she only has five more to learn! Wow! While working with her I noticed her making funny contorted faces as she identified the letters. I was about to ask her what she was doing but before I could she told me, "I can do this! I just cross my eyes and bump across the alphabet to figure it out." 🙶🙶

(Mort, 2015)

 ## Janet's Summary

Essential to closing the gap for vulnerable children is intimate knowledge about the skill needs of each child – otherwise we are 'shooting in the dark' and hoping to hit something significant that will help children to progress with mastery of hundreds of sequential skills.

It may seem overwhelming at first: All major and important changes in our teaching practice does in the beginning. This time the results make it worthwhile; I can promise. I will, however, make a suggestion that will help. Begin with only one *Circle Chart* – the Alphabet, Sight Words or Print Concepts – and assess only a few children at a time playing, and practicing how to fill in the Circles to your satisfaction until you get comfortable with the process.

Stick with just one *Circle Chart* until you feel comfortable with it. Gradually add other *Circle Charts* in order of your needs. Most of our teachers have only implemented Alphabet Knowledge and Phonological Awareness before Christmas in kindergarten classes, then began Sight Word *Circle Charts* after Christmas.

Remember the *Circle Charts* are just a tool and can be used in any way that is most effective for you – no rules attached! Thousands of teachers now using the *Circle Charts* in a variety of different environments and in a variety of different ways report the following advantages. The *Circle Charts*, implemented in a play- and inquiry-based environment, are a major key to ensuring success for vulnerable children:

- The diligent use of them facilitates explicit instruction in differentiated small groups;
- They inform daily teacher planning and instruction;
- They track individual progress;
- They facilitate reporting to parents;
- They provide compelling evidence for child advocacy to other professionals as children need specialized support; and
- They provide a sense of self-satisfaction and pride for teachers who witness concrete evidence of their own effectiveness as they document student progress with each skill.

•

The *Circle Charts* are in the Appendix and we invite you to reproduce them and enjoy the satisfaction that will come with using them and documenting the progress you are making as well as the children. There is also an online web-based app which is described in the *Joyful Literacy Series*, page xi.

[The little guy in this photo was delighted when he had the opportunity to fill in his circles with the blue pen – instead of me. Try making them part of the process. It's a wonderful experience as we all share the joy of learning as partners, determined to reach our goals together!]

Sincerely,

Janet

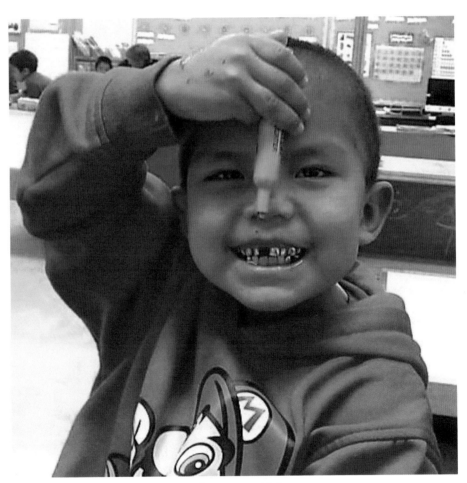

He's unstoppable!

Assess Essential Skills with Ease

Play is Not Enough

Play is NOT enough. The following two quotes from highly credible organizations in the USA and Canada assert:

> "Although the learning in play is powerful, it is often incidental. The child is not necessarily motivated by a need or even a desire to learn principles; learning is a by-product of play, individually unpredictable and not its purpose." - National Learning Panel, 2009

> "The pedagogical value of play does not lie in its use as a way to teach children a specific set of skills through structured activities called play." - Canadian Council on Learning, 2009

These are succinct answers to the question that drove me back to university at age 59 after 40 years in the education system. Why, after witnessing 40 years of innovation and effort by many gifted teachers practicing the latest theories and methods, do I still witness that over 30% of children still do not succeed in school?

Remember that over 30% of the children entering preschools and kindergartens have limited literacy experiences. We provide playful choices for them but even if centers are enriched with literacy activities, vulnerable children are likely to choose the experiences they are most comfortable with—sand, blocks and toys. They are unlikely to choose the alphabet center when they don't even understand what letter symbols mean especially when peers around them do.

$\leq \geq v \infty \surd$ $\mathcal{H} \cong$ ♠: This is what a word or sentence might look like to a child who has had no preschool literacy experience.

Other children who have already learned to print their own names at home will excitedly engage in letter work at the alphabet center experimenting with matching and making new words. So, the "lucky children" (those who entered school with rich literacy experiences) get richer and the "unlucky children" (those who have limited literacy experiences) get poorer—unless they have a teacher who assesses, teaches and tracks sequential literacy skills until mastery is achieved.

Why Did We Fail to Understand the Limitations of Play in Early Learning?

In the last decade there has been considerable attention paid to the role of play in early learning. The importance of play to young children is indisputable but the interpretation placed on it by people who are implementing programs in preschools and schools has not always been beneficial. While the importance of play in preschools typically drives the preschool program, in the kindergarten and primary classrooms play is the theater stage for the increasingly important essential literacy skills.

Unfortunately, some leaders and classroom practitioners have misinterpreted the importance of play in early learning as being the basic function of the kindergarten classroom. There is a reason for this. Many jurisdictions introduced full-day kindergarten in the mid-2000 decade. Unfortunately, this pre-dated the NELP (National Early Literacy Panel) 2008 scientific report on the latest 500 research studies that focus on the impact of essential skills on early learning. Therefore, in some classrooms only play activities are offered, leaving children with little skill instruction and no explicit instruction related to basic literacy skills. Experienced and effective kindergarten teachers understand that the play-based classroom must incorporate skill development so they plan and act accordingly. However, many teachers graduating from university report that they have had no instruction in the basics of literacy skills. They do not know which skills are required for reading achievement, nor do they know how to assess children to determine deficits. While many children may absorb essential skills through play activities, we know that the same is not true for vulnerable children who need repeated explicit teaching.

Similarly, teachers who have been practicing for many years and have experienced limited professional development in the literacy and the early learning field will be using outdated practices in their classrooms: Most of the best research on the science of literacy and brain development has only been published since 2008.

The result is that the 30% of children who enter kindergarten vulnerable in cognitive areas and requiring explicit instruction are arriving in the grade 1 classroom just as vulnerable as they were when they entered kindergarten. This puts excessive pressure on grade 1 teachers, who are expected to be effective literacy instructors and close the experiential gap before the end of grade one—an almost impossible task. Many kindergarten teachers report that their school districts do not provide learning assistance support or other forms of special education for kindergarten classes because senior administrators believe that a play-based environment does not require special education support. This is flawed thinking and is inconsistent with the prevailing literature.

The following are examples from highly respected academic work, in both the United States and Canada that speak to the issue:

- The National Strategy for Early Literacy identifies (as one of the barriers to literacy improvement) "the inability of many Canadian schools to identify and deal effectively with children who already lag behind their peers when they first enter school." The same report identifies as a barrier "the need to improve teacher preparation in the area of reading development and reading instruction... Currently, many children who are well prepared to learn when they enter school, nevertheless fail to acquire strong literacy skills alongside their peers due to the uneven quality of literacy related instruction" (National Strategy for Early Literacy, 2009).

- The same report continues: "It is clear that most literacy challenges can be prevented through an appropriate mix of (a) effective instruction, (b) early learning experience, (c) systematic assessments to identify any children who experience difficulty at an early age, and (d) appropriate intervention" (National Strategy for Early Literacy, 2009).

- A large US database known as the Early Childhood Longitudinal Study program reported "major positive gains for children who participated when these children received between 30 to 60% of additional instructional time in reading and math in a child-centered, play-oriented kindergarten program. Higher child outcomes in both reading and math were well documented in these studies." Results from the Early Childhood Longitudinal Study – Kindergarten Cohort, (ECLS-K) in 1999 showed that "31% of entering kindergarteners were not proficient in recognizing or naming letters."

- "Effective teaching in early childhood education, as in the elementary grades, requires a skillful combination of explicit instruction, sensitive and warm interactions, responsive feedback, and verbal engagement/stimulation intentionally directed to ensure children's learning in a classroom environment that is not overly structured or regimented." This quote comes from School Readiness and the Transition to Kindergarten in an Era of Accountability (Pianta, Cox, & Snow, 2007, p. 8).

How did educators get confused about the role of play in early learning? The answer is simple: We haven't been systematically designing our classrooms to conform to the most recent research (post-2008) that should be informing our practice. We haven't been providing our teachers with the professional experiences that would inform them and enable them to implement best practice. Shame on us!

Worst of all, most governments and school systems have not made vulnerable children a priority. The time is now: Research provides the roadmap. If we interpret the research into an action plan and implement it faithfully, we could change the future for thousands of vulnerable children in our care. Time is of the essence. Every year we delay, thousands remain unlucky—but not just for literacy, now for life.

Research: Assessing, Teaching and Tracking Skills Daily

In order to prepare a broad list of skills developmentally appropriate from pre-k through grade three, I researched many sources including those quoted in this book. Within each skill set are sub-sets that provide a workable basis for early learning teachers. The task of assessment is listed first in the title for good reason: The first task facing the kindergarten teacher is to find out which children have learned the beginning skills (alphabet and phonological awareness) prior to school entry and which children need explicit instruction immediately to close the experiential gap. Ideally, all children will leave kindergarten with similar foundational skills, although it may take vulnerable children up to the end of grade 2 to reach full mastery. These children will simply require more instruction and more practice in applying the skills in classroom environments. The graphic positions this part of the instructional process.

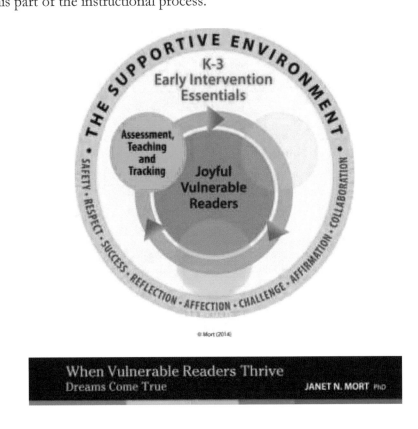

The Problem

1.   So Many Skills

Children must learn over 41 essential skills in their first three years of school. Whether we want to admit it or not, with over 20 children in our classrooms, it is impossible for us to know and remember which children:

- have been taught each skill;

- have mastered each skill;

- need review of a skill;

- need re-instruction of a skill; or

- need support (external to the classroom) for special assessments.

This could amount to over 820 pieces of literacy skill information for one class of twenty children (let alone all the other matters a busy teacher has to remember).

2.   Lack of Working Knowledge

The sciences of literacy and the brain have evolved impressively since 2000; some of the best research, articles, and books have been published only since 2009. Most practicing teachers don't have time to pursue and analyze the multiple documents that might inform and change their practice. Richard Allington (2014) declared in a recent Summit that teachers need a minimum of 60 hours of professional development per year to be prepared for effective classroom implementation. Few school districts offer this opportunity. Since university bureaucracies are often slow to adopt new curricula, many graduating teachers are not well-informed about essential literacy skills. This is an issue I have confronted in my university classes with beginning and experienced teachers. Prior to my last Kindergarten Intervention course, I assessed my class—a mixture of nine new graduates and nine experienced teachers—about the degree of essential skill knowledge they possessed. Highlights of my assessment of those 18 qualified primary teachers are as follows:

- Two experienced teachers could name most of the skills;

- Eight teachers, all experienced and with good district professional development programs, could name fewer than 50% of the skills;

- Seven teachers were able to name fewer than 20% of the skills; and

- One teacher was able to name only 8% of the skills.

This was in spite of the fact that the purpose of my course was to plan classroom intervention strategies. How can teachers intervene when they are not even aware of the essential skills? (At this stage I must declare that my class was an exceptional group of dedicated, enthusiastic and self-motivated professionals; these results, therefore, would have to be considered as the high end of the scale. I shudder to contemplate what the results might have been in a group of randomly selected teachers.)

3.   Meeting Differentiated Needs in a Typical Classroom

Vulnerable children enter pre-k and kindergarten with very few of the essential skills, while some of their classmates have already started to read. The effective teacher's job at these entry levels is challenging to say the least. Teachers need to be highly skilled and knowledgeable about what the skills are, how to assess them, how to teach them and how to track them. Children must be assessed to determine individual skill knowledge and subsequently grouped and re-grouped daily, according to the mastery-level of each skill. The teacher requires a viable tracking system to monitor individual progress on a weekly basis and one that informs instructional planning for daily and weekly instruction. The classroom must be organized to facilitate all of the above.

Organize the classroom to facilitate active learning.

4.   Managing Emotional and Behavioral needs

Approximately 10 % of children enter their first school experiences with social and emotional challenges. These can be disruptive, consume teacher time and energy, and distract from others who enter ready and eager to begin learning. This is complicated by the fact that few schools have ways to identify these needs prior to school entry. The system is simply not ready to meet their needs and frequently does not have the appropriate support systems in place such as external expertise and in-class support. Administrators must make this support system their highest priority especially at the start of the school-entry year.

In my book, *Teaching with the Winning Touch* (Good Apple, 1981), I described the dynamic learning environment we created throughout our kindergarten to grade 7 school. All classrooms were organized with learning centers, projects, inquiries, and choice activities through personal contracts with each child. For its time, the program was a progressive and innovative approach to learning, while desks-in-rows and teacher-led instruction prevailed in other schools.

There was no question that our students were actively engaging in learning, with growing self-esteem and highly-motivated behaviors. The program engendered an atmosphere of love, respect and enthusiasm, with collaboration and respect as the order of the day. We welcomed children from other district schools—vulnerable students thrived in our accepting and inclusive environment.

In retrospect, however, despite higher achievement for all students in the social and emotional domains, I am not certain that academic achievement was adequate for our vulnerable children. Although academically-able students thrived, we were not well-informed about the science of literacy interventions compared to what we know now. Keeping track of who was or was not learning specific skills became a challenging issue. The children were moving from center to center, making tracking of skill mastery and instruction difficult.

Mort, J.N., *Joyful Literacy Interventions: PART ONE Early Classroom Essentials*, 2015

Reading Essential Foundational Skills

A.   Phonics and Word Recognition (K to 2)

1.   The Alphabetic Principle and Letter-sound Recognition (K)

Demonstrate an understanding of the alphabetic principle and letter-sound recognition.

1a. Research and Theory

What is the Alphabetic Principle?

The alphabetic principle is the overarching understanding that there is a correspondence between letters (graphemes) and sounds (phonemes). Children come to realize there is a connection between letters and sounds and the connection is consistent.

What is Letter-sound Recognition?

Letter recognition is the ability to quickly and fluently identify first the names of the letters both upper and lower case, then connect the sound associated with each letter, followed by providing a word that starts with the letter.

Pre-readers' knowledge of letter names, while a good predictor of future reading success, is not enough. Letters need to be identified accurately, but it is the fluency or ease with which they do so that is most important.

Many at-risk children enter kindergarten with little or no knowledge of the alphabet.

By the end of kindergarten, children should be able to identify and form letters of the alphabet and know that letters stand for sounds.

It is also important for children not only to learn the names of the letters, but also a sound or sounds associated with that letter and words that begin with the letter. (Bennett-Armistead, 2007)

Learning letter recognition through Alphabet Bingo.

Why is Letter-sound Recognition so important for the developing literacy learner?

The most powerful predictor of later reading success is the child's knowledge of the alphabet acquired prior to first grade. (Adams, 1990)

Just measuring how many letters a kindergartner is able to name when shown letters in random order appears to be nearly as successful at predicting future reading as is an entire reading readiness test. (Snow et al., 1998)

Alphabet knowledge is currently viewed as one of the most accurate identifiers of a child's later risk of reading difficulties. (Morrow, 2011)

Letter knowledge has been determined to be a precursor to learning letter sounds and that phonological awareness and knowledge of letters are closely linked. Children who demonstrate knowledge about letter names use this information to connect print with speech. (Morrow, 2011)

The ability to name most of the letters automatically will make it easier for students to recognize patterns of letters, which is a key to reading words.

What are the key components of a Letter-sound Recognition intervention?

Joyful Literacy Interventions (Mort, 2014) makes a well-researched case for play as the vehicle for transitioning children from preschools to primary classrooms, yet she also takes the position that play is not enough.

In the last decade there has been considerable attention paid to the role of play in early learning. The importance of play to young children is indisputable but the interpretation placed on it by people who are implementing programs in preschools and schools has not always been beneficial. While the importance of play in preschools typically drives the preschool program, in the kindergarten and primary classrooms play is the theatre stage for the increasingly important (foundational) literacy skills.

Imagination, play and games are an ideal vehicle for emerging letter-sound recognition skills using active strategies such as constructing letters through pipe cleaners, string, play-doh and blocks; action songs using body shapes; sensory experiences using glitter hair gel, shaving cream and Jello powder; environmental print games such as I Spy; and kinaesthetic activities like cutting, pasting and tracing.

Early learners need a learning environment that promotes acceptance and collaboration; practice and privacy; time and patience; experience and engagement; and motivation and movement. (Mort, 2014)

Circle Chart Essential Foundational Skills

The following skills are tracked on the Circle Charts:

Kindergarten Skills

- Discriminate between rhyming and non-rhyming words.
- Produce words that rhyme.
- Isolate initial letters.
- Blend syllables (parts of words).
- Segment (words in sentences).
- Delete compound words.

Grade 1/2 Skills

- Isolate medial letters.
- Isolate final letters.
- Blend phonemes and letters.
- Blend syllables.
- Segment phonemes.
- Segment syllables and compound words.

K literacy play.

1b. Assessment Instructions

Purpose:

To determine which letters and related sounds children can identify.

Achievement Indicators:

- Students will name most of the letters of the alphabet (be fluently familiar with at least 20 letters), upper and lower case, no matter what order they are in.
- Students will say the most common speech sound associated with individual letters and give a word that starts with that sound (demonstrate understanding of the one-to-one correspondence between letter name and a particular sound).
- Students will identify the letter in meaningful text.

Procedure:

- Have one copy of the upper, lowercase and vowel letter pages for use with all students.
- Use a cover sheet and show the student one line at a time. The student should respond unprompted within 2-3 seconds to demonstrate automaticity and fluency.
- If the student is not responding after the first two lines, stop the screening.
- When rescreening, check only the letters that were previously unknown.
- Fill in the result on the Circle Charts.

[School District No. 23 Central Okanagan ELP]

Circle Chart Essential Foundational Skills

Duplicate the following letter worksheets for your assessments:

UPPER CASE LETTERS

M   S   D   F   G

L   J   U   R   W

B   N   O   C   X

E   Z   Q   A   H

T   Y   K   I   V

P

LOWER CASE LETTERS

m	s	d	f	g
l	j	u	r	w
b	n	o	c	x
e	z	q	a	h
t	y	k	i	v
		p		

VOWELS

a	e	i	o	u
A	E	I	O	U

Teacher's Chart

Class _____

Date _____

THE ALPHABETIC PRINCIPLE
Letter-sound Recognition (K/1) – LOWER CASE

- Name lower case letters
- Produce letter sounds
- Produce a word beginning with the letter/sound
- Find the letter in text

EL Early Learning INC.

A First Class Beginning

Janet N. Mort PhD • jnmort@shaw.ca

Skill Mastery Progress

Black – Sept/Oct/Nov
Green – Dec/Jan
Yellow – Jan/Feb/Mar
Red – Apr/May/Jun

Degree of Skill Mastery

● Skill Mastery
◐ Skill Review Required
○ Skill Instruction Required

© 2015 Early Learning Inc.

STUDENT'S NAME	b	c	d	f	g	h	j	k	l	m	n	p	q	r	s	t	v	w	x	y	z
	○	○	○	○	○	○	○	○	○	○	○	○	○	○	○	○	○	○	○	○	○
	○	○	○	○	○	○	○	○	○	○	○	○	○	○	○	○	○	○	○	○	○
	○	○	○	○	○	○	○	○	○	○	○	○	○	○	○	○	○	○	○	○	○
	○	○	○	○	○	○	○	○	○	○	○	○	○	○	○	○	○	○	○	○	○
	○	○	○	○	○	○	○	○	○	○	○	○	○	○	○	○	○	○	○	○	○
	○	○	○	○	○	○	○	○	○	○	○	○	○	○	○	○	○	○	○	○	○
	○	○	○	○	○	○	○	○	○	○	○	○	○	○	○	○	○	○	○	○	○
	○	○	○	○	○	○	○	○	○	○	○	○	○	○	○	○	○	○	○	○	○
	○	○	○	○	○	○	○	○	○	○	○	○	○	○	○	○	○	○	○	○	○
	○	○	○	○	○	○	○	○	○	○	○	○	○	○	○	○	○	○	○	○	○
	○	○	○	○	○	○	○	○	○	○	○	○	○	○	○	○	○	○	○	○	○
	○	○	○	○	○	○	○	○	○	○	○	○	○	○	○	○	○	○	○	○	○
	○	○	○	○	○	○	○	○	○	○	○	○	○	○	○	○	○	○	○	○	○
	○	○	○	○	○	○	○	○	○	○	○	○	○	○	○	○	○	○	○	○	○

THE ALPHABETIC PRINCIPLE
Letter-sound Recognition (K/1) – UPPER CASE

- Name upper case letters
- Sequence uppercase letters
- Produce letter sounds

Degree of Skill Mastery

● Skill Mastery
◐ Skill Review Required
○ Skill Instruction Required

Skill Mastery Progress

Black – Sept/Oct/Nov
Green – Dec/Jan
Yellow – Jan/Feb/Mar
Red – Apr/May/Jun

E. Early Learning INC.
A First Class Beginning

Janet N. Mort PhD • jnmort@shaw.ca

© 2015 Early Learning Inc.

Teacher's Chart

Class _____

Date _____

STUDENT'S NAME	B	C	D	F	G	H	J	K	L	M	N	P	Q	R	S	T	V	W	X	Y	Z
	○	○	○	○	○	○	○	○	○	○	○	○	○	○	○	○	○	○	○	○	○
	○	○	○	○	○	○	○	○	○	○	○	○	○	○	○	○	○	○	○	○	○
	○	○	○	○	○	○	○	○	○	○	○	○	○	○	○	○	○	○	○	○	○
	○	○	○	○	○	○	○	○	○	○	○	○	○	○	○	○	○	○	○	○	○
	○	○	○	○	○	○	○	○	○	○	○	○	○	○	○	○	○	○	○	○	○
	○	○	○	○	○	○	○	○	○	○	○	○	○	○	○	○	○	○	○	○	○
	○	○	○	○	○	○	○	○	○	○	○	○	○	○	○	○	○	○	○	○	○
	○	○	○	○	○	○	○	○	○	○	○	○	○	○	○	○	○	○	○	○	○
	○	○	○	○	○	○	○	○	○	○	○	○	○	○	○	○	○	○	○	○	○
	○	○	○	○	○	○	○	○	○	○	○	○	○	○	○	○	○	○	○	○	○
	○	○	○	○	○	○	○	○	○	○	○	○	○	○	○	○	○	○	○	○	○
	○	○	○	○	○	○	○	○	○	○	○	○	○	○	○	○	○	○	○	○	○
	○	○	○	○	○	○	○	○	○	○	○	○	○	○	○	○	○	○	○	○	○
	○	○	○	○	○	○	○	○	○	○	○	○	○	○	○	○	○	○	○	○	○

THE ALPHABETIC PRINCIPLE
Letter-sound Recognition (K/1) – VOWELS

Teacher's Chart

Class _____

Date _____

STUDENT'S NAME

| a | e | i | o | u | A | E | I | O | U |

Degree of Skill Mastery
- ● Skill Mastery
- ◑ Skill Review Required
- ○ Skill Instruction Required

Skill Mastery Progress
Black – Sept/Oct/Nov
Green – Dec/Jan
Yellow – Jan/Feb/Mar
Red – Apr/May/Jun

E. Early Learning INC.
A First Class Beginning

Janet N. Mort PhD • jnmort@shaw.ca

© 2015 Early Learning Inc.

2.   Phonological Awareness

Demonstrate understanding of spoken words, syllables, and sounds.

2a.   *Research and Theory*

What is Phonological Awareness?

Phonological Awareness is the ability to hear, recognize and play with the sounds in our oral language. It is a hearing/listening skill. Phonological Awareness is an umbrella term that involves the ability to work with the sounds of language at the word, syllable and phoneme level. It includes rhyming, alliteration, sentence and syllable blending and segmenting.

What is Phonemic Awareness?

Phonemic Awareness is the most complex phonological awareness skill. It is the understanding that spoken words consist of a sequence of speech sounds and an awareness of the individual sounds or phonemes. It is the ability to attend to the sounds of language as being separate from the meaning of language.

Phonemic Awareness is the ability to segment words into sounds, blend them back together and manipulate the sounds to make new words.

What is Phonics?

Phonics is the ability to apply letter-sound knowledge when translating print into speech. Phonics provides readers with a tool to unlock or decode the pronunciation of written words. Phonemic Awareness skills precede phonics skills because children must first develop an understanding of how spoken language maps to written language. Phonemic Awareness bridges the spoken word (oral) to the written word (print).

Why are Phonological Awareness, Phonemic Awareness and Phonics so important to the developing literacy learner?

- Approximately 20% of children will have difficulty with phonological awareness upon entering school and will eventually struggle with figuring out how sounds work in print (phonics, decoding, spelling).

- Without phonemic awareness, a child may be able to learn letter-sound relationships by rote, but will not be able to use and coordinate letter-sound knowledge to read or spell new words.

- Phonemic awareness plays a critical role in the development of skills required in the manipulation of phonemes and the application of phonics to reading and spelling.

- Current research suggests that the greatest impact on phonemic awareness development is achieved when there is a combination of interaction with print and explicit attention to the sound structure in spoken words. Teachers making the underlying sound structure explicit when at the same time referring to the print. (Cunningham et al., 1998)

[Adapted from Vacca & Vacca et al, 2012]

What are the key components of a Phonological Awareness Intervention?

Teach Phonological Awareness with Joyful Interventions

The new science of neural understanding can be translated into exciting and practical classroom strategies and many promising implications for vulnerable children. Vulnerable children do not need "skill and drill." They need joyful interventions, plenty of laughter, friendship, and promise: the promise of a joyful and literate future – forever. Struggling children need to believe they can "do it." Intriguing play centers embedded with skills in a game environment work for all children.

Games work! Tim Rasinski, renowned literacy researcher, emphasizes the importance of using a game approach to skill development.

> I have found that word identification instruction seems to be most engaging, authentic and effective when it feels like a game for students and teachers. Think of all the games we play as teachers in one form or another – Scrabble, Boggle, Scrabble Slam, Crossword Puzzles, Wheel of Fortune, Taboo [and so on]. If adults love games that involve words, why wouldn't students? Indeed, that is what we have found. Making words, word ladders, word sorts, word bingo, word walls all have the feel of a game that makes the students want to engage. (Vacca & Vacca, 2012)

For maximum impact, Phonological Awareness skills are introduced and taught in whole-class sessions. Games and playful activities such as word sorts are introduced there, then placed in practice centers where children can explore ways to apply the skills in meaningful literacy contexts while teachers work with small groups of children who have been assessed as requiring additional instruction.

[Adapted from Vacca & Vacca et al, 2012]

Joyful Literacy Interventions (Mort, 2014) describes how many teachers have used assessment procedures in joyful early learning classrooms that integrate skill assessment and tracking. The following quote is from a teacher describing how she uses the Circle Charts to implement skill development interventions:

In my classroom, everyone knows where our Circle Charts are, what the colored circles represent, and why we use them.

- They hang behind my desk on a clipboard where I can access them quickly for daily use. It is my goal to review them every day so that I can group students more effectively and choose literacy centers based on areas of need.

- During our ABC Tub times I can informally assess my students while they play literacy games in a relaxed atmosphere with their peers.

- As well, I can hold quick conferences with students during free-play centers to discuss their learning on the charts and set goals for the future.

- Sharing the data has been a rewarding process for everyone involved. Students love seeing their line of circles being filled in and they understand what the data means.

- I make an effort to involve families in the learning process and often share the Circle Charts with them before or after school. In a matter of moments, a parent and I can share their child's growth and note which alphabet letters or essential (foundational) literacy skills could be practiced at school and home. In this way, families are receiving more consistent and descriptive feedback on their child's progress rather than receiving three formal report cards in the year. (Mort, 2014)

Smiling students enjoying "Hop and Pop" games.

Janet's Comments

We appreciate the collaboration of School District No. 23 Central Okanagan as this section (pages 93-98) originated in their district and is reproduced with the permission of the Superintendent of Schools.

2b. Assessment Instructions

Purposes:

- To determine if a student can both discriminate and produce rhymes.
- To determine if a student can identify initial sounds in common words.
- To determine if a student can blend together syllables to form a word.
- To determine if a student can segment a sentence of one-syllable words, segment words into syllables and segment words into phonemes.
- To determine if a student can delete one word from a compound word.

Achievement Indicators:

- Use rhyming to identify whether words rhyme and produce a word that rhymes with another.
- Use sound discrimination to tell the difference between single speech sounds.
- Use blending to orally blend syllables into a whole word.
- Use segmentation to clap the words in a 3 to 6 word single-syllable word sentence.
- Identify 2 words in a compound word.
- Identify the first sound and ending sound in a one-syllable word.

Procedure:

1. Before using the phonological awareness section with individual students, demonstrate the process with the whole class first.

2. Practice rhyming, isolating, blending, segmenting and deleting together.

3. Demonstrate isolating phonemes using 3 *unifix* or wooden cubes. (2 of the same color, 1 different - ☐ ■ ■) This will help make an abstract concept more concrete.

4. Expose students to the process and language of the phonological awareness section prior to screening. This will save time and may even be enough to solidify the concept for some students.

5. Screen students individually in a quiet setting because these are auditory tasks. Prepare an area free of noise and have the *unifix* blocks available.

6. Rescreen students at a later date for only the sections where a student has received 3 or less. (A score of 4/5 is considered mastery and would warrant a full circle. A score of 2/5 or 3/5 score would warrant a half circle and a need for further review or practice. Less than 2/5 would indicate a need for re-teaching.)

7. Fill in the result on the Circle Charts.

Kindergarten Skills Assessment Instructions

Discriminate between rhyming and non-rhyming words

Directions: "I'm going to say two words and ask you if they rhyme. Listen carefully."
Demonstration item: "Fan rhymes with man. Do fan and boy rhyme?"
Additional demonstration items: *mitt/fit, mitt/bit, mitt/hen*

Stimulus	Response	
1. look/took		
2. fun/sun		
3. farm/car		
4. hop/sand		
5. dad/sad		
Total		/5

Note: nonsense words are acceptable.

Produce words that rhyme

Directions: "I'm going to say a word and I want you to tell me a word that rhymes with it. Listen carefully."

Demonstration item: "Tell me a word that rhymes with bat."

Stimulus	Response	
1. rap		
2. win		
3. same		
4. trouble		
5. flower		
Total		/5

Isolate initial letters

Materials: 3 blocks – 2 of the same color.

Place the blocks in a row with different colored block at the beginning of the row:

Directions: "I'm going to say a word and ask you to tell me the beginning or first sound of the word. Listen carefully."

Demonstration item: Say "cat." Then ask, "What's the beginning sound in the word cat?" or "What sound does the word cat start with?" Point to the first block.

Popcorn wands for word practice.

Stimulus	Response	
1. bug		
2. sick		
3. pan		
4. duck		
5. fudge		
Total		/5

Blend syllables

Directions: "I will say the parts of a word and you are to tell me what the word is."
ta-ble, ba-na-na

Stimulus	Response	
1. ba – by		
2. win – dow		
3. tel – e – phone		
4. pop – si – cle		
5. lem – on – ade		
Total		/5

Segment (words in sentences)

Directions: "I will say a sentence and I want you to tap one time for each word that I say. My house is big."

Tester should demonstrate by tapping on table once for each word in the sentence.

Stimulus	Response	
1. Tom can jump.	3 taps/	
2. My dog is black.	4 taps/	
3. Some boys can skip.	4 taps/	
4. I have six blue books.	5 taps/	
5. The kite is up high.	5 taps/	
Total		/5

Delete Parts of Compound Words

Directions: "Listen – I will say a word to you and say it again without one of its parts. "Cowboy" – Now I'll say it again but I won't say "boy." The answer is "cow." Now I want you to try. Say "football." Now say it again but don't say "foot." (Answer: "ball.")

Stimulus	Response	Correct Response	
1. Say mailbag	Say it again, but don't say bag.	mail	
2. Say sunlight	Say it again, but don't say sun.	light	
3. Say backpack	Say it again, but don't say pack	back	
4. Say shoelace	Say it again, but don't say lace	shoe	
5. Say driveway	Say it again, but don't say drive.	way	
Total			/5

K to 2 Skills Assessment Instructions

(Continue to teach and practice K skills as necessary. By grade 2 most skills should be mastered; if not re-teaching will be required).

Isolate medial letters

Materials: 3 blocks – 2 of the same color.

Place blocks in a row with different colored block in the middle of the row: ■ □ ■

Directions: "I'm going to say a word and ask you to tell me the middle sound in the word. Listen carefully."

Demonstration item: Say "*cat.*" Then ask, "*What's the middle sound in the word cat?*" Point to the middle block.

Additional demonstration items: *dog, mouse*

Stimulus	Response	
1. bug		
2. sick		
3. pan		
4. duck		
5. fudge		
Total		/5

Isolate final letters

Materials: 3 blocks – 2 of the same color.

Place blocks in a row with a different colored block at the end of the row: ■ ■ □

Directions: "I'm going to say a word and ask you to tell me the end or last sound of the word. Listen carefully."

Demonstration item: Say "cat." Then ask, "What's the end sound in the word cat?" or "What sound does the word cat end with?" Point to the last block. (Additional demonstration items: *dog, mouse.*)

Stimulus	Response	
1. bug		
2. sick		
3. pan		
4. duck		
5. fudge		
Total		/5

Blend phonemes/letters

Directions: "I will say parts of a word and you tell me the word."
"c-a-t / d-o-g / b-l-ue"

Stimulus	Response	
1. b-oy		
2. m-a-n		
3. c-l-ea-n		
4. w-i-n-d-ow		
5. b-a-b-y		
Total		/5

Segment phonemes

Directions: "I will say a word and I want you to clap for each sound in the word."
"*Cat.*" Tester will demonstrate by clapping for each phoneme. (c-a-t - 3 claps)

Stimulus	Response	
1. on	2 claps/ o - n	
2. clap	4 claps/ c – l – a – p	
3. seashell	5 claps/ s – ea – sh – e - ll	
4. plant	5 claps/ p – l – a – n – t	
5. slip	4 claps/ s – l – i– p	
Total		/5

Segment syllables/compound words

Directions: "I will say a word and I want you to tap one time for each part of the word."
"*Ba-na-na.*" Tester should demonstrate by tapping on an arm for each part of the word.

Stimulus	Response	
1. cowboy	2 taps/ cow - boy	
2. baseball	2 taps/ base - ball	
3. computer	3 taps/ com – pu - ter	
4. watermelon	4 taps/ wa – ter – me - lon	
5. refrigerator	5 taps/ re – frig – er – a - tor	
Total		/5

PHONOLOGICAL AWARENESS (K/1)

Teacher's Chart

Class _____

Date _____

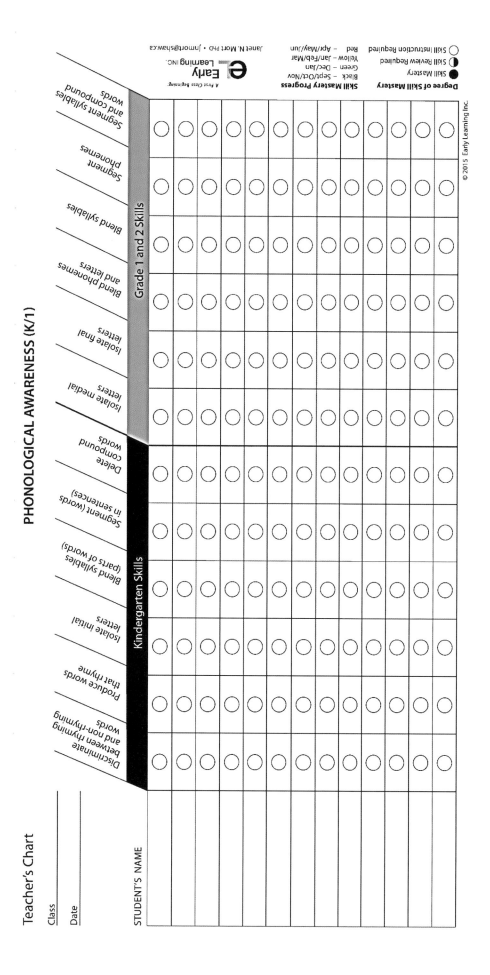

Skill Mastery Progress
A First Class Beginning

Black – Sept/Oct/Nov
Green – Dec/Jan
Yellow – Jan/Feb/Mar
Red – Apr/May/Jun

Degree of Skill Mastery

● Skill Mastery
◐ Skill Review Required
○ Skill Instruction Required

Early Learning INC.
Janet N. Mort PhD • jnmort@shaw.ca

© 2015 Early Learning Inc.

STUDENT'S NAME

Grade 1 and 2 Skills:
- Segment syllables and compound words
- Segment phonemes
- Blend syllables
- Blend phonemes and letters
- Isolate final letters
- Isolate medial letters

Kindergarten Skills:
- Delete compound words
- Segment (words in sentences)
- Blend syllables (parts of words)
- Isolate initial letters
- Produce words that rhyme
- Discriminate between rhyming and non-rhyming words

3.   Word Study (K to 2)

Know and use word attack, word analysis and decoding skills to analyze letter-sound relationships.

3a.   *Research and Theory*

What is Word Study?

Word Study is an all-encompassing term that refers to word attack, analysis and decoding which, in turn, refers to the act of analyzing letter-sound relationships or using the knowledge of phonics to segment the visual components of a word and blend them back together into a recognizable word.

Phonics provides the reader with a tool to "attack" the pronunciation of a word that is not immediately recognized. Word attack, word analysis, decoding or phonics is, therefore, mediated word identification because readers must slow down to devote conscious attention to figuring out the unknown word. (Vacca & Vacca, 2012)

Why is Word Study so important for the developing literacy learner?

Through word study children learn how words work. The term encompasses word identification, phonics, spelling and vocabulary instruction.

The work requires students' active involvement and thinking skills. Even the youngest children can be "theory builders and hypothesis testers" of how words work.

When we engage children in word play, games and similar activities to consider and conjecture about the way words are alike and different, we also promote motivation if we accomplish this in a playful way. When we relieve tension we increase the mind's ability to concentrate.

Word study readiness will be different for different children. We teach to the zone of "proximal development" (Vygotsky, 1978) relying on word features that are already understood and therefore do not need to be taught, matching the level of instruction to each student.

Making a conscious effort to talk through small group activities, partner discussions, collaborative activities and one-to-one teacher conversations can result in higher motivation, better knowledge of student readiness, and effective planning for next steps.

Word studies must be purposeful, pre-planned and build on what students already know. Teachers inform their instruction by assessing students' understanding and grouping children accordingly. Teaching the word study skill or process in a whole group setting before assessing individual children simplifies the assessment process and is recommended.

Grades 1 and 2 Circle Chart Essential Foundational Skills

The following skills are tracked on the Circle Charts:

Consonant Study

- Decode and spell initial consonant blends.
- Decode and spell final consonant blends.
- Decode and spell initial consonant digraphs.
- Decode and spell final consonant digraphs.
- Decode and spell complex consonant patterns.

Vowel Study

- Decode regularly spelled one-syllable words.
- Decode words with the final (magic) -e and state that the final (magic) -e determines the vowel sound.
- Recognize and propose same-vowel word families.
- Decode and sort words based on long and short vowels in regularly spelled one-syllable words.
- Decode R-controlled vowels.
- Decode and spell vowel digraphs (teams).
- Decode other vowel patterns.
- Recognize the connection between the use of vowels and the number of syllables in words.
- Decode regularly spelled two-syllable words.

Prefix and Suffix Study

- Decode and spell words with simple inflectional endings.
- Decode words that have a prefix or suffix.

Contractions

- Decode contractions.
- Create contractions from two words.

Literacy station word play.

3b.   Assessment Instructions

Note: Reference books such as *Words Their Way* (Bear et al., 2012) and *Word Sorts* (Ganske, 2006) provide excellent word lists of word families and detailed sub-skill analyses. The skill lists and samples provided here are intended only as teacher guides and examples of core word study skills that are foundational in the early years.

Purpose:

To determine the children's ability to analyze letter sound-relationships or use their knowledge of phonics to segment the visual components of a word and blend them back together into recognizable words.

Achievement Indicators:

Children will be able to demonstrate proficiency in the skills over time. While the skills are generally designated by grade level, it is expected that children will progress through the skills at different rates based on their background experience and instructional readiness.

Procedure:

For each skill, if the child scores half or more of the selected items correctly then fill in half of the circle; if the child scores all selected items correctly then fill in the whole circle; if the child scores only a few items then leave the circle blank.

Consonant Study

- Students will orally decode blends, digraphs, and complex consonant patterns that have been selected by the teacher (suggested presentation is as lists or on word cards).

- Students will spell the letters contained in blends, digraphs and complex consonant patterns, selected by the teacher, either orally or on paper.

Sample Consonants Skills

Decode and spell initial consonant blends such as:
bl, br, cl, cr, dr, fl, fr, gl, gr, pl, pr, sc, sk, sl, sm, sn, sp, st, sw, tr

Decode and spell final consonant blends such as:
ld, lf, lt, mp, nd, nt, sk, st

Decode and spell initial consonant digraphs such as:
sh, ch, gh, ph, qu, th, wh

Decode and spell final consonant digraphs such as:
ch, ck, ff, ll, mb, ng, nk, ph, sh, ss, th, tch, zz

Decode and spell complex consonant patterns such as:
gn, kn, wr, hard and soft c, hard and soft g

Vowel Study

- Students will orally decode one-syllable words and words with the final (magic) -e (suggested presentation is as lists or on word cards) as selected by the teacher.

- Students will be able to state that the final (magic) -e determines the vowel sound.

- Using the words from the above two skills, students will propose other words that share the same vowel word family.

- Students will decode and then sort regularly spelled one-syllable words into short vowel words and long vowel words (suggested presentation is words on cards).

- Students will orally decode a list of R-controlled vowel words selected by the teacher.

- Students will orally decode a list of words containing vowel digraphs (teams) selected by the teacher.

- Students will spell words containing vowel digraphs (teams) selected by the teacher either orally or on paper.

- Students will orally decode a list of words containing other vowel patterns as selected by the teacher.

- Students will state the connection between the use of vowels and the number of syllables in words by clapping the number of syllables in a word that has been provided by the teacher and identifying the vowels that correlate with the number of syllables.

- Students will orally decode two-syllable words selected by the teacher (suggested presentation is as a list or on word cards).

Sample Vowel Skills

Decode regularly spelled one-syllable words such as:
-ab, -ack, -ag, -all, -all, -an, -ap, -ar, -arm, -arn, -art, -ash, -at, -ay, -eck, -ed, -ell, -est, et, -ew, ick, -ig, -ild, -in, -ind, -ing, -ink, -ip-, it, -ob, -ock, -og, -ood, -op, -ork, -orn, -ot, -ox, -ub, -uck, -uff, -ug, -ump, -un, -unk, -ut

Decode words with the final (magic) -e and state that the final (magic) -e determines the vowel sound such as:
-ace, -age, -ake, -ame, -ane, -ape, -ate, -ide, -ile, -ine, -ire, -ite, -ode, oke, -ome, -one, -ope, -ube, -ume, -use, -ute

Recognize and propose same-vowel word families using words decoded from the previous 2 skills

Decode and sort words based on long and short vowels in regularly spelled one-syllable words such as:
cap, cape, fin, fine, hop, hope, hug, huge, green, paint, boat

Decode R-controlled vowels such as: ar, er, ir, or, ur

Decode and spell vowel digraphs (teams) such as:
-ai as in rain, -ea as in team, -ee as in been, -ey as in money, -ie as in piece, -oa as in boat, -oe as in goes, -ow as in grow, -ue as in blue, -ui as in fruit

Decode other vowel patterns such as: ay, ei, ew, igh, oi, ou, ow, y as in 'my', y as in pretty

Recognize the connection between the use of vowels and the number of syllables in words such as:
tip (1), set (1), ball (1), helmet (2), dragon (2), crayon (2), banana (3), animal (3), forever (3)

Decode regularly spelled two-syllable words with long vowels such as:
mon-key, rep-tile, pa-per, ho-tel, la-dy, ti-ger, mu-sic, pre-tend, fo-cus, spi-der

Learning and practicing skills together.

Prefix and Suffix Study

- Students will orally decode words with simple inflectional endings selected by the teacher (suggested presentation is as a list or on word cards).

- Students will spell words with simple inflectional endings selected by the teacher either orally or on paper.

- Students will orally decode words that include a prefix or suffix that have been selected by the teacher (suggested presentation is as a list or on word cards).

Sample Prefix and Suffix Skills

Decode and spell words with simple inflectional endings such as:
-ed, -er, -est, -ing, -s

Decode words that have a prefix or a suffix such as:
common prefixes: un- as in undo, re- as in reread, dis- as in disagree

common suffixes: -ed as in walked, -ful as in playful, -ly as in lovely, -ness as in happiness, -less as in helpless

---

Contraction Study

- Students will orally decode contractions that have been selected by the teacher (suggested presentation is as a list or on word cards).

- Students will state the contraction that is made from the two words given by the teacher.

Sample Contraction Skills

Decode contractions such as:
we'll, that's, aren't, you've, doesn't, she's, don't, who's, he'll, there's, weren't, what's

Create contractions from two words such as:
were not, let us, should have, would not, they will, you will, where is, here is, could have

---

WORD STUDY (1/2)

Teacher's Chart

Class _____

Date _____

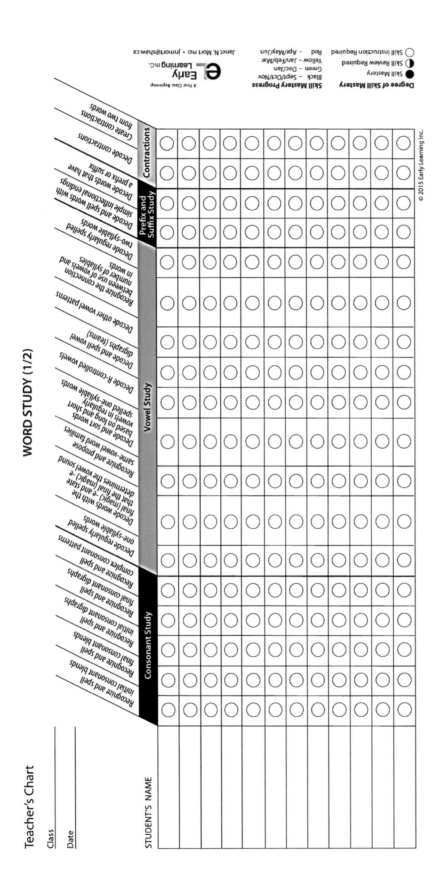

B.   Concepts of Print (K/1)

Demonstrate understanding of the organization and basic features of print.

a.   *Research and Theory*

What are the Concepts of Print?

Concepts of print refer to all the knowledge related to how print is organized and used.

Children need to know that:

- Words are read and pictures are viewed.

- Words appear and are read in English from left to right across the page.

- Letters are placed next to each other to form words.

- Letters each have a large and small version and can be printed in various forms. (Nevills & Wolfe, 2009)

Marie Clay calls concepts about print "the rules of the road," and writes, "Teachers must teach so that all children become knowledgeable about these foundational concepts so they open doors to literacy." She explains that teachers who have an understanding of what aspects of print their students are attending to can introduce them to print conventions through rich experiences with reading and writing and can be accomplished through focused instruction in the first six months of kindergarten. (Clay, 2000, pp. 24-25)

The development of concepts of print depends upon children's exposure and the meaningful interaction they have with print.

It takes over 1,000 hours of being read to for young children to become proficient at understanding how books and print works and how to read for themselves. (Bennett-Armistead, 2007)

Why are learning the Concepts of Print so important for the developing literacy learner?

Studies have shown that word and print awareness serve as key predictors of later reading achievement and comprise important elements of the foundation of emergent literacy knowledge. (Justice & Ezell, 2001)

Concepts of Print knowledge represent experience with handling, manipulating, and interacting with books, and are key skills necessary for possessing literacy awareness.

An assessment of each child's level of understanding (and sometimes misunderstanding) of the concepts of print helps teachers know what their students are attending to in print and what still needs to be learned. This knowledge enables teachers to design and focus teaching points in literacy mini-lessons and other classroom literacy experiences that encourage children in their understanding of how print works.

What are the key components of a Concepts of Print Intervention?

The NELP (*National Early Learning Panel*) Report identifies Shared Reading (and Writing) as one of the seven greatest contributors to future literacy success. Through shared reading and writing experiences several times a day, teachers can engage children in rich literacy learning. Through Big Books, poems, posters, rhymes, and projected print children experience all literacy skills and concepts in meaningful context including:

- The joy of reading.

- Explicit instruction about print including the concepts of print in action.

- Phonics and phonological awareness.

- Word study skills.

In *Joyful Literacy Interventions* (Mort, 2014) teacher Kathleen describes how she uses shared reading to teach concepts of print:

> Shared reading sessions help me teach about text features, concepts of print, phonemic awareness, sight-words and punctuation. Frequent shared reading sessions build a feeling of community and cohesiveness in the class as the children join in the reading and become inspired by each other's abilities to "read" along. Through multiple readings of a shared book, they build their own personal reading skills in the comfort and safety of a situation where everyone is invited to join in if they are ready, yet those who just want to watch and listen are allowed that freedom.

Circle Chart Essential Foundational Skills

The following skills are tracked on the Circle Charts:

Concepts of Print

Book Concepts
- Front cover
- Title
- Print carries message (not only illustrations)

Directionality
- Beginning of text
- Left to right sequence
- Return sweep

Word Concepts
- One word
- First word
- Last word
- Spaces between words

Letter Concepts

- First letter in word
- Last letter in word
- Period
- Capital letter

Punctuation Marks

- Question mark
- Exclamation mark

Shared reading invites participation of all students.

b.   Assessment Instructions

Note: Ideally, these skills will be mastered in kindergarten; many children will enter kindergarten with these understandings. Review the skills in shared readings with the entire class and with children in small groups. The assessment can be conducted individually or in small groups.

Purpose:

To evaluate the child's knowledge of how print works.

Achievement Indicators:

Children will be able to:

- Demonstrate the directionality of print and where it starts on the page.

- Identify the title, author and illustrator.

- Track with their fingers during oral reading by the teacher or their own reading to show an understanding of the concept of words.

- Recognize simple common punctuation and point to examples in the context of shared reading or shared writing.

Procedure:

1. Choose a simple picture book (preferably a Big Book or projected book so that all the children can see it) with one or two sentences per page and read it to your class.

2. Model the achievement indicators using the book with your whole class before the first screening with individuals.

3. Screen your students individually.

4. When rescreening, review only the items that were previously unknown.

Hand the child the closed book and ask:

- ❑ Can you show me the cover of the book and the title?

- ❑ Show me your favorite picture. How do pictures help us?

- ❑ Can you show me where we should start reading the story?

- ❑ If we start here, which way should we go next?

Check for knowledge of directionality. Follow the print with your finger as you read to the child. When you reach the right side of the page ask:

- ❑ Where should I go now?

Check for return sweep. Ask the child to follow the print with her/his finger as you read. Was the child able to track as you read?

After reading a few pages present the child with the following tasks:

☐ Point to a word you know on the page or one you wonder about. Point to the first word on the page. Now point to the last word on the page.

☐ Choose any word now; point to the first letter in the word and the last letter in the word.

☐ Point to a space between words. Why do you think we have spaces?

Point to a period and ask: "*What is this for?*" Do the same with a capital, a question mark, and an exclamation mark.

If the child can read, ask him to read the story to you. Does the child's reading closely match the text?

Read the story to the child asking him/her to follow the words as you read.

Ask the child to reread the story, tracking as s/he reads. Does the child's reading closely match the text?

Ask the child what the story is about. Does the child understand that print conveys meaning?

[School District No. 23 Central Okanagan ELP]

Involve parents in shared reading time.

CONCEPTS OF PRINT (K/1)

Class _____

Date _____

(INSTRUCTIONS: Use a predictable book of about 8 pages where pictures support text, with periods and question marks. Hand the book to the child closed with the spine facing the child. Begin. Read the book a page or two at a time pausing to ask the next few questions in the list as appropriate to the text.)

Degree of Skill Mastery
● Skill Mastery
◑ Skill Review Required
○ Skill Instruction Required

Skill Mastery Progress
Black – Sept/Oct/Nov
Green – Dec/Jan
Yellow – Jan/Feb/Mar
Red – Apr/May/Jun

E.L. Early Learning inc.
A First Class Beginning.
Janet N. Mort PhD • jnmort@shaw.ca

© 2015 Early Learning inc.

Categories and skills (column headers):

Punctuation Marks: Exclamation mark, Question mark

Letter Concepts: Capital letter, Period, Last letter in word, First letter in word

Word Concepts: Spaces between words, Last word, First word, One word

Directionality: Return sweep, Left to right sequence, Beginning of text

Book Concepts: Print carries the message (not the illustrations), Title, Front cover

STUDENT'S NAME

C.   Dolch High Frequency Words (Sight Words K to 2)

Recognize, spell and print as many high frequency words as possible, as early as possible by sight.

a.   *Research and Theory*

What are High Frequency Words?

Wikipedia (2014) is the source of the following definition and lists of sight words by grade level. There are a number of commonly used lists; one of the most frequently referenced is the Dolch list.

What is the Dolch list?

The Dolch word list is a list of frequently used English words compiled by Edward William Dolch, a major proponent of the "whole-word" method of beginning reading instruction. The list was prepared in 1936 and was originally published in his book *Problems in Reading* in 1948.

Dolch compiled the list based on children's books of his era. The list contains 220 "service words" that have to be easily recognized in order to achieve reading fluency in the English language. Even today, between 50% and 75% of all words used on the Internet, in schoolbooks, library books, newspapers, and magazines are included in the Dolch basic sight word vocabulary.

Although some of the 220 Dolch words are phonetic, children should be encouraged to learn these words by sight to enhance fluency; hence the alternative term "sight word."

Some teachers use the term "glue words" because sight words glue the child's organic words together to make sentences (*I can dance*) and therefore facilitate reading and writing processes. (*I* and *can* are sight words; the word *dance* originates in the child's experience.) Other teachers call them "popcorn words" because they "pop up" frequently in text.

The list is divided according to the grades in which Dolch intended that children would memorize the words. Grade designations are assigned to words based on the degree of difficulty. It should be noted, however, that since Dolch developed the word lists our society has become increasingly literate through technology and environmental text so it is reasonable to expect progress can be extended.

The Dolch List

Pre-primer: a, and, away, big, blue, can, come, down, find, for, funny, go, help, here, I, in, is, it, jump, little, look, make, me, my, not, one, play, red, run, said, see, the, three, to, two, up, we, where, yellow, you

Primer: all, am, are, at, ate, be, black, brown, but, came, did, do, eat, four, get, good, have, he, into, like, must, new, no, now, on, our, out, please, pretty, ran, ride, saw, say, she, so, soon, that, there, they, this, too, under, want, was, well, went, what, white, who, will, with, yes

1st Grade: after, again, an, any, as, ask, by, could, every, fly, from, give, giving, had, has, her, him, his, how, just, know, let, live, may, of, old, once, open, over, put, round, some, stop, take, thank, them, then, think, walk, were, when

2nd Grade: always, around, because, been, before, best, both, buy, call, cold, does, don't, fast, first, five, found, gave, goes, green, its, made, many, off, or, pull, read, right, sing, sit, sleep, tell, their, these, those, upon, us, use, very, wash, which, why, wish, work, would, write, your

3rd Grade: about, better, bring, carry, clean, cut, done, draw, drink, eight, fall, far, full, got, grow, hold, hot, hurt, if, keep, kind, laugh, light, long, much, myself, never, only, own, pick, seven, shall, show, six, small, start, ten, today, together, try, warm

Why is the mastery of High Frequency Words so important for the developing literacy learner? Numerous recent researchers have addressed this question:

Toward a Theory of Automatic Information Processing in Reading (LaBerge & Samuels, 1974). Decades ago, LaBerge and Samuels alerted us to the significance of high-frequency words. Their research revealed that 90% of all the words that people read are made up of only 5,000 words.

Beginning to Read: Thinking and Learning About Print (Adams, 1990). Adams makes the first step obvious! He reports that the following 13 words are 25% of the words children find in early literacy experiences. These words should be first on the list to learn: a, and, for, see, she, in, it, is, of, that, the, to, was and you.

Early Intervention for Reading Difficulties: The Interactive Strategies Approach (Scanlon, Anderson, & Sweeney, 2010) Scanlon et al. challenge us to stretch our expectations of children instead of relying on dated and limiting curriculum guidelines:

> Because knowledge of high-frequency words provides children with so much access to reading materials and allows them to be strategic in learning new words, setting higher expectations for sight word knowledge is probably in the children's best interests. (p. 228)

Reading and Learning to Read (8th ed.) (Vacca & Vacca, 2012)
Vacca and Vacca provide us with a technical definition for rapid word recognition and emphasize that learning by "sight" is only one of the important ways that children recognize words and caution us about limiting sight word instruction to flash cards: Children typically use many different cues in word solving:

> Word recognition suggests a process that involves immediate identification. Immediately recognized words are retrieved rapidly from lexical memory. Word recognition is sometimes referred to as sight word recognition or sight vocabulary. These terms suggest a reader's ability to recognize words rapidly and automatically. In this chapter we use immediate word recognition to describe rapid recognition. Keep in mind, however, that the process of immediate word recognition is far more complicated than merely recognizing words on flash cards. When a word is retrieved rapidly from memory, the process is often triggered by the application of letter-sound knowledge. Learning to read words rapidly involves making associations between particular spellings, pronunciations, and meaning by applying knowledge of letter/sound relationships.

Skilled readers use the strategy of immediate word recognition on 99% of the printed words that they encounter…. Immediate identification of words is the result of experience with reading, seeing, discussion, using, and writing words. (p. 224)

The implication is clear: Teaching phonics, phonological awareness, sight words, print awareness, word study and other literacy skills will be best accomplished when taught simultaneously in an integrated, contextual way.

What are the key components of a High Frequency Words intervention?

In *Joyful Literacy Interventions*, Dr. Janet Mort describes the power of sight words in her implementation pilot sites:

Since I started this journey, determined to find the path to literacy success for vulnerable children, I have become increasingly aware of the need for educators to respond to compelling research, and therefore I have become intolerant of some teachers' resistance to assessing, teaching, and tracking sight word mastery. In the face of scientific evidence, as well as "on the ground" success there are no excuses left. Consider the following: Our pilot sites (Chapter 9) have been working with hundreds of vulnerable primary children on developing sight-word capacity. We taught these children the first 10 sight words and began to create stories from their own memories and experiences. We added sight words in clusters of ten as they achieved mastery and their stories became more sophisticated.

Consider the following example of the power of sight words:

1. One child's organic words (from his/her own experience) were: monster, closet, screamed, babysitter.

2. The complete story was subsequently dictated by the child and written by the teacher:

3. There was a monster in my closet. I screamed. My babysitter chased it away.

4. We counted the sight words (underlined): Nine

5. We counted the organic words: Four

Without the sight words there would have been no story! With a combination of sight words and the child's organic words, we have a reader and a writer.

Over 90% of kindergartners are developmentally capable of learning two words (*I* and *can*) by memory, remembering jump, play, sit and hop with clues from their drawings; then creating their own books: "I can _____ (jump, play, sit, hop)!" These are their first experiences with reading and writing, which they can proudly share with proud moms and dads. This is a FIRST moment in the never-ending cycle of success that they will never forget: They have joined the world of literacy.

Circle Chart Essential Foundational Skills

The following 220 sight words are tracked on the Circle Charts. Dolch assigned these grade levels in 1945; however, we have found that many grade 2 children are capable of mastering all of them before the end of grade two. Times have changed: Children have many more experiences with common words through environmental literacy, software games and other multi-media programs.

Complete Dolch Word List Divided by Level

Pre-primer	Primer		Grade One	Grade Two		Grade Three
a	all	under	after	always	why	about
and	am	want	again	around	wish	better
away	are	was	an	because	work	bring
big	at	well	any	been	would	carry
blue	ate	went	ask	before	write	clean
can	be	what	as	best	your	cut
come	black	white	by	both		done
down	brown	who	could	buy		draw
find	but	will	every	call		drink
for	came	with	fly	cold		eight
funny	did	yes	from	does		fall
go	do		give	don't		far
help	eat		going	fast		full
here	four		had	first		got
I	get		has	five		grow
in	good		her	found		hold
is	have		him	gave		hot
it	he		his	goes		hurt
jump	into		how	green		if
little	like		just	its		keep
look	must		know	made		kind
make	new		let	many		laugh
me	no		live	off		light
my	now		may	or		long
not	on		of	pull		much
one	our		old	read		myself
play	out		once	right		never
red	please		open	sing		only
run	pretty		over	sit		own
said	ran		put	sleep		pick
see	ride		round	tell		seven
the	saw		some	their		shall*
three	say		stop	these		show
to	she		take	those		six
two	so		thank	upon		small
up	soon		them	us		start
we	that		then	use		ten
where	there		think	very		today
yellow	they		walk	wash		together
you	this		were	which		try
	too		when			warm

* 'shall' has dropped out of use

DOLCH HIGH FREQUENCY WORDS: (PRE-PRIMER 1)

Degree of Skill Mastery
- ● Skill Mastery
- ◐ Skill Review Required
- ○ Skill Instruction Required

Skill Mastery Progress
Black – Sept/Oct/Nov
Green – Dec/Jan
Yellow – Jan/Feb/Mar
Red – Apr/May/Jun

EL Early Learning INC.
A First Class Beginning
Janet N. Mort PhD • Jnmort@shaw.ca

© 2015 Early Learning Inc.

Teacher's Chart

Class _____

Date _____

STUDENT'S NAME

STUDENT'S NAME	1. a	2. and	3. away	4. big	5. blue	6. can	7. come	8. down	9. find	10. for	11. funny	12. go	13. help	14. here	15. I	16. in	17. is	18. it	19. jump	20. little
	○	○	○	○	○	○	○	○	○	○	○	○	○	○	○	○	○	○	○	○
	○	○	○	○	○	○	○	○	○	○	○	○	○	○	○	○	○	○	○	○
	○	○	○	○	○	○	○	○	○	○	○	○	○	○	○	○	○	○	○	○
	○	○	○	○	○	○	○	○	○	○	○	○	○	○	○	○	○	○	○	○
	○	○	○	○	○	○	○	○	○	○	○	○	○	○	○	○	○	○	○	○
	○	○	○	○	○	○	○	○	○	○	○	○	○	○	○	○	○	○	○	○
	○	○	○	○	○	○	○	○	○	○	○	○	○	○	○	○	○	○	○	○
	○	○	○	○	○	○	○	○	○	○	○	○	○	○	○	○	○	○	○	○
	○	○	○	○	○	○	○	○	○	○	○	○	○	○	○	○	○	○	○	○
	○	○	○	○	○	○	○	○	○	○	○	○	○	○	○	○	○	○	○	○
	○	○	○	○	○	○	○	○	○	○	○	○	○	○	○	○	○	○	○	○
	○	○	○	○	○	○	○	○	○	○	○	○	○	○	○	○	○	○	○	○
	○	○	○	○	○	○	○	○	○	○	○	○	○	○	○	○	○	○	○	○
	○	○	○	○	○	○	○	○	○	○	○	○	○	○	○	○	○	○	○	○

Teacher's Chart

Class _____

Date _____

DOLCH HIGH FREQUENCY WORDS (PRE-PRIMER 2)

STUDENT'S NAME

Word list:
- 21. look
- 22. make
- 23. me
- 24. my
- 25. not
- 26. one
- 27. play
- 28. red
- 29. run
- 30. said
- 31. see
- 32. the
- 33. three
- 34. to
- 35. two
- 36. up
- 37. we
- 38. where
- 39. yellow
- 40. you

Degree of Skill Mastery

● Skill Mastery
◑ Skill Review Required
○ Skill Instruction Required

Skill Mastery Progress

Black – Sep/Oct/Nov
Green – Dec/Jan
Yellow – Jan/Feb/Mar
Red – Apr/May/Jun

Early Learning Inc.
A First Class Beginning.

Janet N. Mort PhD • Jnmort@shaw.ca

© 2015 Early Learning Inc.

DOLCH HIGH FREQUENCY WORDS: (PRIMER 1)

Teacher's Chart

Class _____

Date _____

STUDENT'S NAME

| 41. all | 42. am | 43. are | 44. at | 45. ate | 46. be | 47. black | 48. brown | 49. but | 50. came | 51. did | 52. do | 53. eat | 54. four | 55. get | 56. good | 57. have | 58. he | 59. into | 60. like |

Degree of Skill Mastery

○ Skill Instruction Required
◑ Skill Review Required
● Skill Mastery

Skill Mastery Progress

Black – Sept/Oct/Nov
Green – Dec/Jan
Yellow – Jan/Feb/Mar
Red – Apr/May/Jun

A First Class Beginning

Ⴒ Early
Learning INC.

Janet N. Mort PhD • jnmort@shaw.ca

© 2015 Early Learning Inc.

DOLCH HIGH FREQUENCY WORDS: (PRIMER 2)

Teacher's Chart

Class _____

Date _____

Skill Mastery Progress
Black – Sept/Oct/Nov
Green – Dec/Jan
Yellow – Jan/Feb/Mar
Red – Apr/May/Jun

Early Learning INC.
A First Class Beginning.

Janet N. Mort PhD • jnmort@shaw.ca

Degree of Skill Mastery
● Skill Mastery
◖ Skill Review Required
○ Skill Instruction Required

© 2015 Early Learning Inc.

STUDENT'S NAME	61. must	62. new	63. no	64. now	65. on	66. our	67. out	68. please	69. pretty	70. ran	71. ride	72. saw	73. say	74. she	75. so	76. soon	77. that	78. there	79. they	80. this
	○	○	○	○	○	○	○	○	○	○	○	○	○	○	○	○	○	○	○	○
	○	○	○	○	○	○	○	○	○	○	○	○	○	○	○	○	○	○	○	○
	○	○	○	○	○	○	○	○	○	○	○	○	○	○	○	○	○	○	○	○
	○	○	○	○	○	○	○	○	○	○	○	○	○	○	○	○	○	○	○	○
	○	○	○	○	○	○	○	○	○	○	○	○	○	○	○	○	○	○	○	○
	○	○	○	○	○	○	○	○	○	○	○	○	○	○	○	○	○	○	○	○
	○	○	○	○	○	○	○	○	○	○	○	○	○	○	○	○	○	○	○	○
	○	○	○	○	○	○	○	○	○	○	○	○	○	○	○	○	○	○	○	○
	○	○	○	○	○	○	○	○	○	○	○	○	○	○	○	○	○	○	○	○
	○	○	○	○	○	○	○	○	○	○	○	○	○	○	○	○	○	○	○	○
	○	○	○	○	○	○	○	○	○	○	○	○	○	○	○	○	○	○	○	○
	○	○	○	○	○	○	○	○	○	○	○	○	○	○	○	○	○	○	○	○
	○	○	○	○	○	○	○	○	○	○	○	○	○	○	○	○	○	○	○	○

Teacher's Chart

Class

Date

DOLCH HIGH FREQUENCY WORDS: (PRIMER 3)

Degree of Skill Mastery
- ● Skill Mastery
- ◑ Skill Review Required
- ○ Skill Instruction Required

Skill Mastery Progress
- Black – Sept/Oct/Nov
- Green – Dec/Jan
- Yellow – Jan/Feb/Mar
- Red – Apr/May/Jun

Early Learning INC.
A First Class Beginning
Janet N. Mort PhD • jnmort@shaw.ca

© 2015 Early Learning Inc.

STUDENT'S NAME	81. too	82. new	83. under	84. want	85. was	86. well	87. went	88. what	89. white	90. who	91. with	92. yes								
	○	○	○	○	○	○	○	○	○	○	○	○	○	○	○	○	○	○	○	○
	○	○	○	○	○	○	○	○	○	○	○	○	○	○	○	○	○	○	○	○
	○	○	○	○	○	○	○	○	○	○	○	○	○	○	○	○	○	○	○	○
	○	○	○	○	○	○	○	○	○	○	○	○	○	○	○	○	○	○	○	○
	○	○	○	○	○	○	○	○	○	○	○	○	○	○	○	○	○	○	○	○
	○	○	○	○	○	○	○	○	○	○	○	○	○	○	○	○	○	○	○	○
	○	○	○	○	○	○	○	○	○	○	○	○	○	○	○	○	○	○	○	○
	○	○	○	○	○	○	○	○	○	○	○	○	○	○	○	○	○	○	○	○
	○	○	○	○	○	○	○	○	○	○	○	○	○	○	○	○	○	○	○	○
	○	○	○	○	○	○	○	○	○	○	○	○	○	○	○	○	○	○	○	○
	○	○	○	○	○	○	○	○	○	○	○	○	○	○	○	○	○	○	○	○
	○	○	○	○	○	○	○	○	○	○	○	○	○	○	○	○	○	○	○	○
	○	○	○	○	○	○	○	○	○	○	○	○	○	○	○	○	○	○	○	○
	○	○	○	○	○	○	○	○	○	○	○	○	○	○	○	○	○	○	○	○

DOLCH HIGH FREQUENCY WORDS: (GRADE ONE 1)

Teacher's Chart

Class _____

Date _____

STUDENT'S NAME

Degree of Skill Mastery
● Skill Mastery
◐ Skill Review Required
○ Skill Instruction Required

Skill Mastery Progress
Black – Sept/Oct/Nov
Green – Dec/Jan
Yellow – Jan/Feb/Mar
Red – Apr/May/Jun

EL Early Learning Inc.
A First Class Beginning.
Janet N. Mort PhD • jnmort@shaw.ca

© 2015 Early Learning Inc.

Word list (columns):
93. after
94. again
95. an
96. any
97. ask
98. as
99. by
100. could
101. every
102. fly
103. from
104. give
105. going
106. has
107. had
108. her
109. him
110. his
111. how
112. just

DOLCH HIGH FREQUENCY WORDS: (GRADE ONE 2)

Teacher's Chart

Class

Date

Early Learning Inc.
A First Class Beginning

Janet N. Mort PhD • Jnmort@shaw.ca

Skill Mastery Progress
Black – Sept/Oct/Nov
Green – Dec/Jan
Yellow – Jan/Feb/Mar
Red – Apr/May/Jun

Degree of Skill Mastery
● Skill Mastery
◗ Skill Review Required
○ Skill Instruction Required

© 2015 Early Learning Inc.

STUDENT'S NAME	113. know	114. let	115. live	116. may	117. of	118. old	119. once	120. open	121. over	122. put	123. round	124. some	125. stop	126. take	127. thank	128. them	129. then	130. think	131. walk	132. were

DOLCH HIGH FREQUENCY WORDS: (GRADE TWO 1)

Teacher's Chart

Class _____

Date _____

STUDENT'S NAME

Column headers (words):
133. always
134. around
135. because
136. been
137. before
138. best
139. both
140. buy
141. call
142. cold
143. does
144. don't
145. fast
146. first
147. five
148. found
149. gave
150. goes
151. green
152. its

Degree of Skill Mastery

● Skill Mastery

◑ Skill Review Required

○ Skill Instruction Required

Skill Mastery Progress

Black – Sept/Oct/Nov
Green – Dec/Jan
Yellow – Jan/Feb/Mar
Red – Apr/May/Jun

EL Early Learning Inc.

A First Class Beginning

Janet N. Mort PhD • Jnmort@shaw.ca

© 2015 Early Learning Inc.

DOLCH HIGH FREQUENCY WORDS: (GRADE TWO 2)

Degree of Skill Mastery

● Skill Mastery
◑ Skill Review Required
○ Skill Instruction Required

Skill Mastery Progress

Black – Sept/Oct/Nov
Green – Dec/Jan
Yellow – Jan/Feb/Mar
Red – Apr/May/Jun

EL Early Learning INC.
A First Class Beginning

Janet N. Mort PhD • jnmort@shaw.ca

© 2015 Early Learning Inc.

Teacher's Chart

Class

Date

STUDENT'S NAME

153. made
154. many
155. off
156. or
157. pull
158. read
159. right
160. sing
161. sit
162. sleep
163. tell
164. their
165. these
166. those
167. upon
168. us
169. use
170. very
171. wash
172. why

DOLCH HIGH FREQUENCY WORDS: (GRADE TWO 3)

Teacher's Chart

Class _____

Date _____

STUDENT'S NAME

173. which
174. wish
175. work
176. would
177. write
178. your

Degree of Skill Mastery

○ Skill Mastery

◑ Skill Review Required

○ Skill Instruction Required

Skill Mastery Progress

Black – Sept/Oct/Nov
Green – Dec/Jan
Yellow – Jan/Feb/Mar
Red – Apr/May/Jun

A first Class Beginning:

EL Early Learning INC.

Janet N. Mort PhD • Jnmort@shaw.ca

© 2015 Early Learning Inc.

DOLCH HIGH FREQUENCY WORDS: (GRADE THREE 1)

Teacher's Chart

Class _____

Date _____

Degree of Skill Mastery

● Skill Mastery
◑ Skill Review Required
○ Skill Instruction Required

Skill Mastery Progress

Black – Sept/Oct/Nov
Green – Dec/Jan
Yellow – Jan/Feb/Mar
Red – Apr/May/Jun

Early Learning Inc.
A First Class Beginning!
Janet N. Mort PhD • Jnmort@shaw.ca

© 2015 Early Learning Inc.

STUDENT'S NAME	179. about	180. better	181. bring	182. carry	183. clean	184. cut	185. done	186. draw	187. drink	188. eight	189. fall	190. far	191. full	192. got	193. grow	194. hold	195. hot	196. hurt	197. if	198. keep
	○	○	○	○	○	○	○	○	○	○	○	○	○	○	○	○	○	○	○	○
	○	○	○	○	○	○	○	○	○	○	○	○	○	○	○	○	○	○	○	○
	○	○	○	○	○	○	○	○	○	○	○	○	○	○	○	○	○	○	○	○
	○	○	○	○	○	○	○	○	○	○	○	○	○	○	○	○	○	○	○	○
	○	○	○	○	○	○	○	○	○	○	○	○	○	○	○	○	○	○	○	○
	○	○	○	○	○	○	○	○	○	○	○	○	○	○	○	○	○	○	○	○
	○	○	○	○	○	○	○	○	○	○	○	○	○	○	○	○	○	○	○	○
	○	○	○	○	○	○	○	○	○	○	○	○	○	○	○	○	○	○	○	○
	○	○	○	○	○	○	○	○	○	○	○	○	○	○	○	○	○	○	○	○
	○	○	○	○	○	○	○	○	○	○	○	○	○	○	○	○	○	○	○	○
	○	○	○	○	○	○	○	○	○	○	○	○	○	○	○	○	○	○	○	○
	○	○	○	○	○	○	○	○	○	○	○	○	○	○	○	○	○	○	○	○
	○	○	○	○	○	○	○	○	○	○	○	○	○	○	○	○	○	○	○	○
	○	○	○	○	○	○	○	○	○	○	○	○	○	○	○	○	○	○	○	○

DOLCH HIGH FREQUENCY WORDS: (GRADE THREE 2)

Skill Mastery Progress

Black – Sept/Oct/Nov
Green – Dec/Jan
Yellow – Jan/Feb/Mar
Red – Apr/May/Jun

Degree of Skill Mastery

● Skill Mastery
◑ Skill Review Required
○ Skill Instruction Required

El Early Learning INC.

A First Class Beginning

Janet N. Mort PhD • jnmort@shaw.ca

© 2015 Early Learning Inc.

Teacher's Chart

Class _____

Date _____

STUDENT'S NAME

199. kind
200. laugh
201. light
202. long
203. much
204. myself
205. never
206. only
207. own
208. pick
209. seven
210. show
211. six
212. small
213. start
214. ten
215. today
216. together
217. try
218. warm

Sight word concentration.

b.   *Assessment Instructions*

Note: While it makes sense to work through the sight words in the order indicated, students should be encouraged to learn as many words as possible as quickly as possible, since a child's ability to read with increasing degrees of difficulty and fluency is directly connected to sight word mastery (as well as the other factors such as decoding ability).

Purpose:

To evaluate the child's knowledge of sight words in order to establish a systematic instructional plan for learning sight words for each child.

Achievement Indicators:

Children will be able to:

- Identify an increasing number of sight words spontaneously without attempting to "sound the words out."
- Find the words in the environment and in text.
- Use the sight words in a complete sentence.
- Print sentences using the sight words.

Procedure:

A Strategy for Monitoring Sight Word Assessments - Using Key Word Rings

Materials:
Label sheets 5163 or 8163 for printing sight words; recipe cards; rings that will hold 10 cards (shower curtain rings work fine); sight word envelopes divided into sets of 10; and stickers (optional).

Type sight words on the label template to print one sight word per label. This standard label size is designed to fit recipe cards which can then be repeatedly used in other games and activities as well as on the Key Word Rings.

Process:

1. Assess children to determine where they start in the progression of sight-word mastery.

2. Put their 10 cards from the envelope onto key word rings with the child's name on it on a colored card. (Get children to decorate the card with their names.) Have a place to hang the cards.

3. Set up sight word games that can use each child's sight words (snap, practice activities between peers. Children practice their 10 sight words daily. As children master each word put a sticker on the card or sign it. Remember that children need to be able to use the word in a sentence and find it in a book as well. Create an evolving list of sight words on a word wall for class reference, games and practice.

4. Once each set of 10 cards is mastered, the cards get sent home for practice with parents.

5. Mastery is noted on the Circle Charts.

6. The next set of cards is loaded on the ring (et cetera).

Read it, write it, stamp it! Working with support staff.

D.   Reading Fluency and Comprehension (K to 2)

Read and comprehend emergent-reader texts with purpose and understanding.

a.   Research and Theory

What is Reading Fluency?

Reading fluency is defined as the ability to read expressively, accurately and meaningfully with understanding and at an appropriate speed. Fluency combines accuracy, automaticity, and oral reading prosody which, when taken together, facilitate comprehension. (Vacca et al., 2012)

1. Accuracy of decoding is a result of the reader's sight-word vocabulary and use of decoding strategies. Accuracy is assessed using a running record. The number of errors or miscues a student makes while reading a passage orally determines accuracy.

2. Automaticity of word recognition is the ability to recognize words quickly with little cognitive effort or attention. Automaticity or reading rate is assessed as the words correct per minute (WCPM).

3. Prosody of oral text reading is the ability to read with proper phrasing and expression. Prosody is typically assessed based on a four-point rubric which is a more holistic view of fluency's three components.

Why is Reading Fluency and Comprehension so important to the developing literacy learner?

It is commonly recognized that reading fluency is more than just the ability to read quickly (reading rate); it includes an understanding of the message being conveyed by the text.

- It is important to note that prosody is most accurately defined as the expression with which one reads a given text. Because prosody is made up of intonation, timing, stress, and focus, the level of comprehension is often visible in this oral expression of reading.

- Prosody is a sign that indicates the reader is constructing the meaning of the passage while the words are being identified and pronounced.

- While automatic word recognition ensures that fluent readers can accurately and effortlessly decode text, it does not account for their ability to make oral reading sound like spoken language.

- If young readers are not able to read a given text with a certain amount of prosody, then it is highly probable that their lack of fluency is an indicator of not comprehending the text. Prosody is the oral interpretation of written text using the elements of oral speech.

(Stahl & Kuhn, 2002; Rasinski, 2004; Morrow, Kuhn, & Schwanenflugel, 2006; Meisinger, Bradley, Schwanenflugel & Kuhn, 2009).

What are the key components of a Fluency and Comprehension intervention?

Vacca and Vacca et al. negate the use of round-robin reading as a dated practice, which focuses on accuracy instead of automaticity and comprehension.

The authors describe how to develop fluency and comprehension in both whole group settings and with individual students. They point out that "to really improve fluency students need explicit instruction focused on word accuracy, automatic reading, prosody, and how to self-monitor in order to improve their own fluency" (2012, pp. 276-289). They propose a number of key strategies that will support fluency and comprehension:

Strategies for Groups of Students

- Choral reading – Struggling students need to listen to mature readers read with expression and interpret and practice different ways of orally reading selections. Through the use of choral reading techniques, students use prosodic cues such as pitch, loudness, stress and pauses. It provides practice in a non-threatening environment.

- Echo reading – This is a modeling oral reading strategy in which the teacher reads a line of the story and students echo by reading the line back. It provides support and scaffolding.

- Reader's theater – This is an oral presentation of drama by two or more readers who read a text rich in dialogue. The emphasis is on what the audience hears and not what it sees. It motivates children to repeatedly read the same material to increase fluency and therefore comprehension.

Strategies for Pairs and Individual Students

- Repeated readings – The National Reading Panel (2000) is an important strategy for improving reading fluency ensuring that the student is actually reading and not just skimming or scanning. Students read the same passage silently several times until they believe they can read it fluently and emphasize prosody (the way athletes practice a skill). Poetry is especially effective.

- Paired repeated reading – Students select their own passages, select different passages, read silently first, read to each other three times seeking help as necessary, then self-evaluate and discuss the experience with their partners.

- Peer tutoring and cross-age reading – Students are paired with a student with a different level of proficiency so that the tutee is supported through the text and the tutor is stimulated by providing guidance through discussion and questioning.

- Automated reading – This strategy involves the child listening while reading a text employing simultaneous listening and reading along with a tape of an adult.

- Oral recitation – The first component involves direct instruction including comprehension, practice and then performance. The second component, indirect instruction, involves practicing until mastery is achieved.

- Involving parents – Teachers can support home-reading programs by holding after-school method workshops for parents, sending home leveled books and expecting parents to read with their children daily.

Enhanced fluency results in improved comprehension!

[School District No. 23 Central Okanagan ELP]

Circle Chart Essential (Foundational) Skills

The following skills are tracked on the Circle Charts.

Fluency

- Reads text with accuracy and fluency
- Reads text with expression and volume
- Reads text with phrasing
- Reads text with pace

Comprehension

- Engages in stories independently
- Engages in story reading in groups
- Responds to stories with questions or comments
- Retells stories including setting, theme, plot and conclusion
- Summarizes the reading
- Participates in extension activities post-reading
- Recognizes text features such as table of contents, author's notes/biography and introduction

Shared reading time.

b.   Assessment Instructions

Purpose:

To read and comprehend emergent-reader texts with purpose and understanding.

Achievement Indicators:

- Read "grade-appropriate" literary and information texts independently and collectively, with accuracy, fluency and comprehension including expression and a sense of phrasing (3 or more words at a time in meaningful phrases).

- Change voice inflection in response to written cues, punctuation marks or words that evoke emotion.

- Read "just-right texts" aloud with fluency, expression and comprehension.

Procedure:

- Listen to the child orally read a chosen passage estimated to be at his/her instructional level. The same passage should be used for accuracy, comprehension and fluency.

- Use the rubric to determine expression and volume, phrasing, smoothness and pace of the oral reading.

- Code the fluency rubric according to the student's instructional level.

[School District No. 23 Central Okanagan ELP]

Reading Fluency and Comprehension Scale (K to 2)

Use the following scales to consider reader fluency on the dimensions of expression and volume, phrasing, smoothness, and pace.

Dimension	1 Not Yet Meeting Expectations	2 Approaching Expectations	3 Meeting Expectations	4 Exceeding Expectations
A. Accuracy and Fluency	Frequent extended pauses, hesitations, false starts, sound-outs, repetitions, and/or multiple attempts.	Several "rough spots" in text where extended pauses and hesitations are more frequent and disruptive.	Occasional breaks in smoothness caused by difficulties with specific words and/or structures but some efforts are made to self-correct using context.	Generally smooth reading with some breaks, but word and structure difficulties are resolved quickly, usually through self-correction.
B. Expression and Volume	Reads with little expression or enthusiasm in voice. Reads words as if simply to get them out. Little sense of trying to make text sounds like natural language. Tends to read in a quiet voice.	Some expression. Begins to use voice to make text sound like natural language in some areas of the text, but not others. Focus remains largely on saying the words. Still reads in a quiet voice.	Sounds like natural language through the better part of the passage. Occasionally slips into expressionless reading. Voice volume is generally appropriate throughout the text.	Reads with good expression and enthusiasm throughout the text. Sounds like natural language. The reader is able to vary expression and volume to match his/her interpretation of the passage.

Dimension	1 Not Yet Meeting Expectations	2 Approaching Expectations	3 Meeting Expectations	4 Exceeding Expectations
C. Phrasing	Monotonic with little sense of phrase boundaries, frequent word-by-word reading.	Frequent 2 or 3 word phrases giving the impression of choppy reading; improper stress and intonation that fail to mark ends of sentences and clauses.	Mixture of run-ons, mid-sentence pauses for breath, and possibly some choppiness; reasonable stress/intonation.	Generally well phrased, mostly in clause and sentence units, with adequate attention to expression.
D. Pace (during focused readings with minimal disruption)	Slow and laborious.	Moderately slow.	Uneven mixture of fast and slow reading.	Consistently conversational.
E. Comprehension	Lack of interest in stories in general and inability to respond to questions about the reading or use context (illustrations) to draw conclusions about the text.	Some confusion about the flow of the story; sporadic interpretation of the story. Cannot retell the entire story. Interested in stories independently and in groups.	While sometimes hesitant, can retell parts of the story, reads with indications of enthusiasm when fluent, can discuss the context and parts of stories.	Can discuss all aspects of the story, generating comments and questions, predicting throughout, discussing the context of the story/book and enthusiastic about extending the ideas in the story.

Source: Assessing Reading Fluency (2004), Timothy Rasinski, Pacific Resources

Discovering whole new worlds through reading.

READING FLUENCY AND COMPREHENSION (K/1/2)

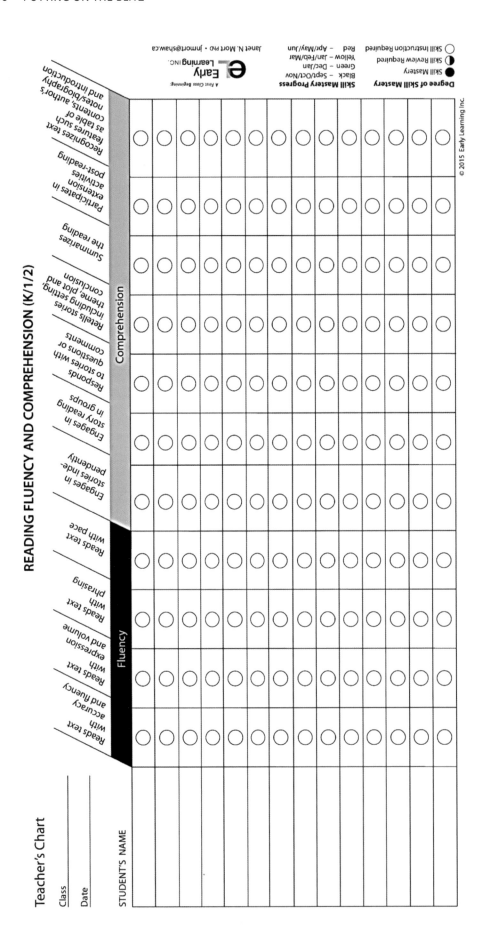

Teacher's Chart

Class _____

Date _____

Degree of Skill Mastery

● Skill Mastery

◑ Skill Review Required

○ Skill Instruction Required

Skill Mastery Progress

Black – Sep/Oct/Nov

Green – Dec/Jan

Yellow – Jan/Feb/Mar

Red – Apr/May/Jun

EL Early Learning INC.

A first Class Beginning!

Janet N. Mort PhD • Jnmort@shaw.ca

© 2015 Early Learning Inc.

Early Writing
Essential Foundational Skills (K to 2)

Janet's Comments

We appreciate the collaboration of School District No. 23 Central Okanagan as this section (page 137-146) originated in their district and is reproduced with the permission of the Superintendent of Schools.

Emergent Writing Development

a.   *Research and Theory*

Use a combination of drawing, dictating, and writing to express opinions about ideas and/or books, to provide information, and to tell a story or series of events.

What is Emergent Writing Development at the (K to 2) level?

Children learn the uses of written language before they learn the forms and their writing develops through constant invention and reinvention of the forms of written language. (Morrow, 2009)

Drawing and writing are both ways of representing thinking and children use both to communicate their ideas.

With drawing, ideas are represented through objects and through writing, ideas are represented through symbols that represent words.

Regardless of where children are at on the continuum of writing development, they have intentions about their representations. It is important to acknowledge their representations to reinforce their attempts at writing as meaning something. (Trehearne, 2011)

Children who have had little experience with "pretend writing" may be reluctant to make marks on paper in Kindergarten because they are comparing themselves to their peers who seem to be making more conventional-like marks when they write. It is important to foster a safe learning environment where all attempts at early writing are celebrated, encouraged and valued.

Sometimes children will not write unless the conventional spelling is provided for them. To help maintain their interest in writing, they should be helped as a way of encouraging and supporting their engagement in the act of representing their ideas. (Morrow, 2009)

Why is Emergent Writing Development so important for the young literacy learner?

The single most important thing you can do to help young children become writers is to provide them with time to write, materials with which to write, and to demonstrate the process and importance of writing to them in social situations. (Cunningham & Allington, 1994)

- Literacy learning starts with drawing, then writing, and finally reading. Children's main resource for literacy learning is their knowledge of the ways to symbolize experience and to use those symbols for communicating. (Morrow, 2009)

- Young children typically take more pleasure in the process of writing than in its final product. The act of writing is their center of interest and over time become more interested in the products. They may not initially be concerned if others can read their writing, but over time the purpose and audience of their writing becomes more relevant to them. (Morrow, 2009)

- When young children begin to engage in early writing they are beginning to make sense of their world and represent their thinking in a more permanent and concrete way. Oral language development is foundational to children's ability to represent their thinking in writing. Children cannot write what they cannot first think or say.

Early writing can:

- Enhance early reading including word identification, decoding and comprehension,

- Support the development of phonological awareness and the alphabetic principle, and

- Begin to bridge phonemic awareness to phonics because the more children write, the better they become at segmenting sounds and blending them into words.

When young children begin to write, they:

- Need to first understand and secondly apply the concepts of print including directionality,

- Have something important enough to record,

- Possess the background knowledge and oral language vocabulary to express themselves, and

- Have the necessary fine motor skills and knowledge of letter formation. (Trehearne, 2011)

The Emergent Writing Development Continuum

Early writing development is characterized by children's moving from playfully making marks on paper to communicating messages on paper, to creating texts. For most children the process for writing occurs as a continuum.

There are definite stages of writing development along the continuum; however, they are not exact and sequential. Children will move back and forth through the stages as they write and represent for different purposes and audiences.

Phase 1:
Birth to 3 years – Scribbling

| Younger children typically take more pleasure in the *process of writing* than in its *final* product. The act of writing is their center of interest – using an instrument to make marks that are not representative of anything meaningful. |  Age: 3.0 |

Phase 2:
Ages 3 to 6 Scribbling to Conventional Writing

| **Emergent Writers:** **Drawing as Writing**

 The child sees drawing as a form of communication and can "read" their drawings as if there is writing on them. The child is beginning to understand there is a purpose and audience for their writing. |  Age 3.8 |

Emergent Writers:
Scribbling as Writing

The child scribbles with intent to represent meaningful communication. Often the scribbles are from left to right and the movement of the pencil is adult-like. The child is making connections between the scribbles and the drawing and can tell about what is represented.

Age: 4.2

Emergent Writers:
Letter-Like Forms

The child's scribbles begin to resemble letter-forms, but are not always representative of actual letters. Children begin to represent the symbols they see in environmental print and in exposure to books and begin to mimic them without meaningful connections.

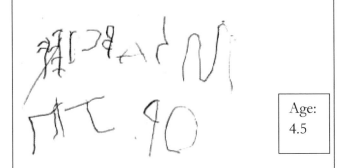

Age: 4.5

Emergent Writers:
Random & Non-Phonetic Letter Strings

The child is reproducing actual letters in a left to right sequence in random order that represents meaningful messages. The letter sequences may be learned from environmental print or her own name. The order of the letters are often changed or written repetitively in long strings. The writing may also be produced from copying.

Age: 5.0

Early Writers:
Invented Spelling

The child is creating spellings of words based on their phonemic awareness skills of isolating and segmenting sounds and their increasing knowledge of the letters that represent those sounds. One letter may represent an entire word, the initial and final consonants may be represented and words sometimes run together without spaces. Invented spelling typically can be interpreted by the adult reader.

Age: 5.9

.I A m PLNThsO
"I am playing in the snow,

Developing Writers:
Conventional Writing

The child is writing with increasing understanding of concepts of print including word spacing, directionality, capitalization and punctuation. The spellings of words are becoming progressively more accurate and reflective of phonetic patterns and rules as well as oddities. The form of the writing looks conventional with complete sentences and some attention to presentation.

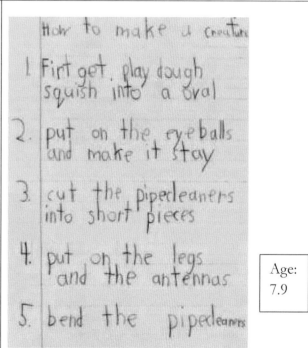

Age: 7.9

By the end of Kindergarten, children should be located within the "Early Writer" section of the developmental continuum using invented spelling with complete thoughts in phrases and sentences. To reach this level requires many opportunities to write with mini-lessons to scaffold their learning. (Morrow, 2009 & Trehearne, 2011)

What are the key components of an Emergent Writing intervention?

A Literate Learning Environment

(Vacca & Vacca et al, 2012)

Children should be free to ask questions and take risks because errors are expected and accepted. Plan the environment so that children are engaged in using and interpreting print in meaningful ways.

Early Writing Opportunities

Many children will experience their first opportunity to write in the kindergarten environment. The writing area should be well stocked with a variety of paper and tools as well as activities that encourage the use of print. Samples of print are readily available: alphabet books, the alphabet, children's names, and labeled artifacts. Teachers interact with children by responding to questions, extending knowledge, modeling use of print, and encouraging attempts to write.

Literacy 'practice and play centers' provide a natural context where young children can play with print, literacy; practice centers and props could include:

- The Kitchen Center
  Telephone books, cookbooks, blank recipe cards, food coupons, grocery ads, play money, empty product containers, message boards, notepads, pens/pencils, markers

- The Office Center
  Calendars, appointment books, message pads, signs, pamphlets, magazines, racks for filing, in/out trays, business cards, forms, blank checks, clipboards, writing tools

- The Post Office Center
  Envelopes, stationery, stamps and stamp pads, mailbox, mail tote bag, address labels, calendars, trays, posters about mail, computer, mailman uniform, writing tools

- The Library Center
  Book return cards, stamps for books, many books, bookmarks, paper, writing tools, ABC index cards, telephone posters for books, file folders, computer, sign-in/sign-out sheets

Children in Grade 1 and 2 will evolve to more complex centers once they begin to become more independent readers and writers:

- Independent Writing Centers might include writing activities like: lists, letters, stories, book-creation, descriptions, research, practicing letter formation, use of reference materials, author studies, and computer work

- Support materials might include: labels, photos, magazines, word walls, name charts, varieties of paper, envelopes and tools, alphabet resources like books, strips, dictionaries, samples of high-quality writing, blank books, help charts, and real objects for motivation

"Children have a strong desire to express themselves through drawing, scribbling, copying, and producing their own written language. Exploring written language with paper and pencil helps children form the expectation that print is meaningful." (Vacca & Vacca, 2012)

b.   *Emergent Writing (K) Assessment Instructions*

Purpose:

To observe and collect information on student's alphabet and word writing fluency.

Achievement Indicators:

- Begin to hear and record sounds in words, relying heavily on the most obvious sound(s) in a word.

- Show an understanding that the sequence of letters in a written word represents the sequence of sounds or phonemes in a spoken word through the alphabetic principle.

- Print their own names and the names of some family members or friends.

- Usually print from left to right and from top to bottom.

- Print most letters recognizably (some letters may be poorly formed and or reversed; may use upper and lowercase letters indiscriminately).

- Spell some short familiar words conventionally like me, you, I.

- Print using invented spelling and orally describe to others what has been written.

- Show an understanding that the same arrangements of letters always construct the same word.

Procedure:

Collect Emergent Writing Samples.

Directions to students:

1. I want to see how many letters of the alphabet you can print. Print as many letters as you can.
    Stop task when child indicates he/she is finished.

2. I want to see how many words you can write.
    Can you write your first name? Can you write your last name?
    If the child does not respond, ask if he or she knows any single letter or two letter words.

3. Do you know how to write 'is' (pause), 'to' (pause), 'I' and then suggest other words like 'a', 'in', 'am', 'see', 'we', 'at', 'go', 'me', 'on', 'up'.
    If the child continues to struggle, use the following questions as guidelines:

4. Do you know how to write any children's or family names?
    Do you know how to write things you do?
    Do you know how to write about things in your house?
    Do you know the names of things you ride?
    Do you know how to write about things you eat?

Give the child up to 10 minutes to write the words he or she knows.
When writing has stopped or when excessive prompting is needed, stop the task.

Assessment Worksheet 1

Alphabet Knowledge

Name: _____   Date: _____

Print the alphabet:

Time limit: 10 minutes

Assessment Worksheet 2

Vocabulary Knowledge

Name: _____   Date: _____

Write your name:

Write as many words as you can:

Time limit: 10 minutes

Assessment Worksheet 3

Rubric for Emergent Writing Development (K)

Collect samples of your student's personal writing from journals, writing center activities or writer's workshops. Use the following rubric to determine what the writing samples depict. Use the information to guide instruction, develop mini-lessons and report on student progress.

b.   *Developmental Writing (1/2) Assessment*

Purpose:

To determine what students know about using writing to communicate and where their writing falls along the developmental continuum.

Achievement Indicators:

Grade 1

Students will create straightforward personal writing and representations that express simple ideas, feelings, likes and dislikes featuring:

- Ideas represented through words, sentences, and images that connect to a topic,
- Sentence fluency using simple sentences that relate to each other,
- Word choice attempting to use descriptive words and interesting details,
- Voice showing some evidence of individuality, and
- Organization that follows a form or text presented or modelled by the teacher, such as a list, card, or letter.

Students will use some features and conventions of language to express meaning in their writing and representing, including:

- Complete simple sentences,
- Use "s" to form plural of familiar words,
- Capital letters at the beginning of people's names and of sentences, can capitalize the pronoun "I",
- A period to mark the end of a sentence,
- Words from oral language vocabulary as well as less familiar words from class-displayed lists,
- Knowledge of consonant and short vowels sounds to spell phonically regular one-syllable words,
- Spelling irregular high-frequency words from memory,
- Spelling unknown words through phonic knowledge and skills and visual memory,
- Legible printing from left to right of all uppercase and lowercase letters, and
- Appropriate spacing between letters and words.

Grade 2

Students will create straightforward personal writing and representations that express connections to personal experiences, ideas, likes and dislikes, featuring:

- Ideas developed through the use of relevant details that connect to a topic,
- Sentence fluency using some variety in sentence length and pattern,

- Word choice using some varied and descriptive language,

- Voice showing some evidence of individuality; and

- A logical organization of ideas.

Students will use some features and conventions of language to express meaning in their writing and representing, including:

- Complete simple sentences, and begin to use compound sentences,

- Some paragraph divisions,

- Noun-pronoun and subject-verb agreement,

- Past and present tenses,

- Capital letters at the beginning of proper nouns and sentences,

- Periods, question marks, or exclamation marks at the end of sentences,

- Commas to separate items in a series,

- Words from their oral vocabulary, personal word list, and class lists,

- Spelling words of more than one syllable, high frequency irregular words, and regular plurals by applying phonic knowledge and skills and visual memory,

- Spell unfamiliar words by applying phonic knowledge and skills and visual memory,

- Conventional spelling of common words, and

  Letters printed legibly, consistent in shape and size, with appropriate spacing between letters and words.

Procedure:

Have students create personal writing and representations like free writes, reading response, journal entries, story descriptions, personal letters, and impromptu writing.

1. Collect a writing sample to evaluate after students have produced several pieces of impromptu writing over time.

2. Use the Grade 1 and 2 Writing Rubrics throughout the year to gauge progress. Use different color highlighters to code each writing sample.

3. When evaluating student writing, weight the elements as follows:

   - Meaning is foremost;
   - Style and form are secondary and strengthen the meaning, and
   - Conventions are weighted the least and function to clarify communication

[School District No. 23 Central Okanagan ELP]

Group writing activities.

Circle Chart Essential Foundational Skills

The following skills are tracked on the Circle Charts.

Emergent Writing (K)

- Begin to hear and record sounds in words,
- Show an understanding that the sequence of letters in a written word represents the sequence of sounds or phonemes in a spoken word,
- Print their own names and the names of some family members or friends,
- Usually print from left to right and from top to bottom,
- Print most letters recognizably,
- Spell some High Frequency Words conventionally,
- Print using invented spelling and orally describe what has been written, and
- Show an understanding that the same arrangements of letters construct the same word.

Developmental Writing (1)

Personal Writing

- Represent ideas through words, sentences, and images that connect to a topic,
- Develop sentence fluency by using simple sentences that relate to each other,
- Develop word choice by attempting to use descriptive words and interesting details, and
- Develop voice by showing some evidence of individuality.

Conventions of Language

- Complete simple sentences,
- Use "s" to form plural of familiar words,
- Uses capital letters for names and beginning of sentences,
- Uses a period for the end of a sentence,
- Uses words from their oral language vocabulary and class-displayed lists,
- Uses consonants and short vowels sounds to spell one-syllable words,
- Spells phonically irregular high-frequency words from memory,
- Attempts to spell unknown words,
- Prints legibly from left to using uppercase and lowercase letters, and
- Uses spacing between letters and words.

Developmental Writing (2)

Personal Writing

- Develop ideas through the use of relevant details that connect to a topic,
- Uses variety in sentence length and pattern,
- Uses some varied and descriptive language,
- Shows some evidence of individuality,
- Puts ideas in a logical organization,
- Completes simple sentences, beginning to use compound sentences,
- Uses some paragraph divisions,
- Corrects noun-pronoun and subject-verb agreement, and
- Uses past and present tenses.

Conventions of Language

- Uses capital letters at the beginning of proper nouns and sentences,
- Uses periods, question marks, or exclamation marks at the end of sentences,
- Uses commas to separate items in a series,
- Uses words from their oral vocabulary, personal word list, and class lists,
- Spells words of more than one syllable, high frequency words, and plurals,

Practicing and helping together.

- Attempts to spell unfamiliar words,
- Uses conventional spelling of common words,
- Prints legibly, consistent in shape and size, and
- Uses appropriate spacing between letters and words.

EMERGENT WRITING (K)

Teacher's Chart

Class

Date

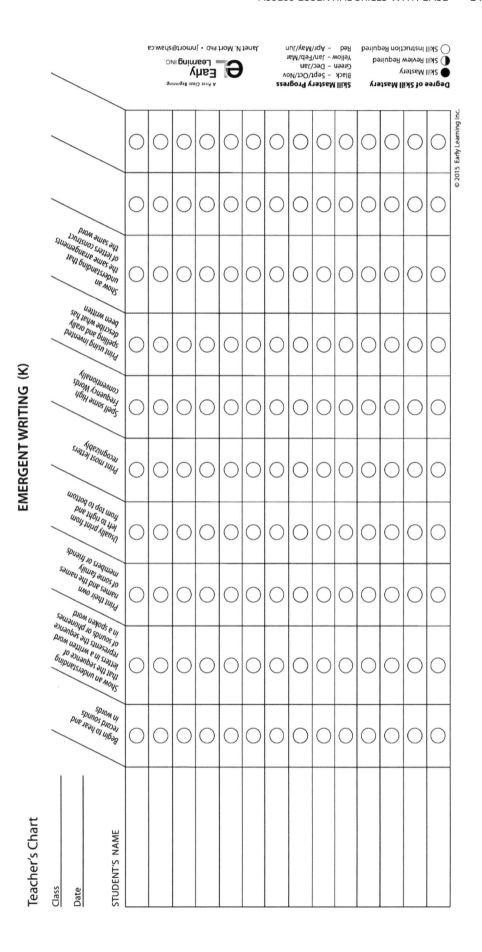

EL Early Learning INC.
A First Class Beginning!

Janet N. Mort PhD • jnmort@shaw.ca

Skill Mastery Progress
Black – Sept/Oct/Nov
Green – Dec/Jan
Yellow – Jan/Feb/Mar
Red – Apr/May/Jun

Degree of Skill Mastery
● Skill Mastery
◐ Skill Review Required
○ Skill Instruction Required

© 2015 Early Learning Inc.

STUDENT'S NAME

Begin to hear and record sounds in words

Show an understanding that the sequence of letters in a written word represents the sequence of sounds or phonemes in a spoken word

Print their own names and the names of some family members or friends

Usually print from left to right and from top to bottom

Print most letters recognizably

Spell some High Frequency Words conventionally

Print using invented spelling and orally describe what has been written

Show an understanding that the same arrangements of letters construct the same word

DEVELOPMENTAL WRITING (GRADE 1)

Teacher's Chart

Class _____

Date _____

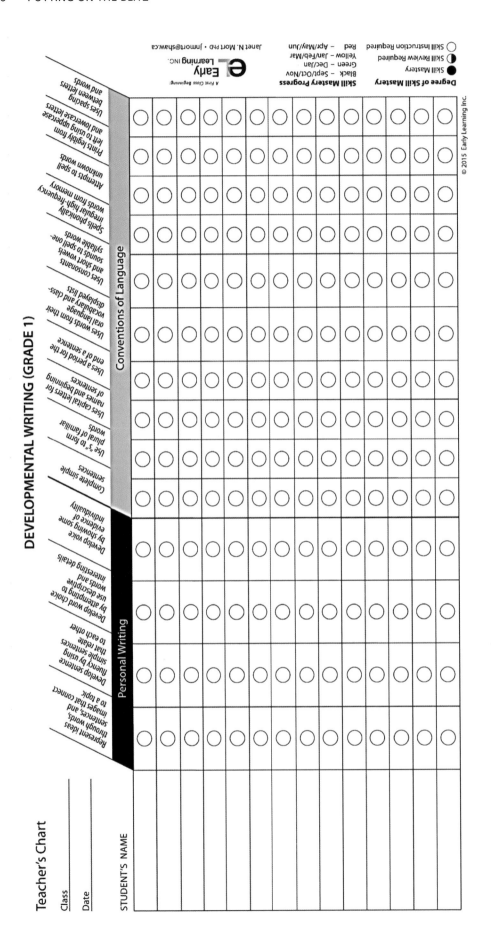

Degree of Skill Mastery

- ● Skill Mastery
- ◑ Skill Review Required
- ○ Skill Instruction Required

Skill Mastery Progress

A First Class Beginning

- Black – Sept/Oct/Nov
- Green – Dec/Jan
- Yellow – Jan/Feb/Mar
- Red – Apr/May/Jun

EL Early Learning INC.

Janet N. Mort PhD • Jnmort@shaw.ca

© 2015 Early Learning Inc.

STUDENT'S NAME

Conventions of Language
- Uses spacing between letters and words
- Uses uppercase and lowercase letters
- Prints legibly from left to right
- Attempts to spell unknown words
- Spells phonetically irregular high-frequency words from memory
- Uses consonants and short vowels sounds to spell one-syllable words
- Uses words from their oral language vocabulary and class-displayed lists
- Uses a period for the end of a sentence
- Uses capital letters for names and beginning of sentences
- Use "s" to form plural of familiar words
- Complete simple sentences

Personal Writing
- Develop voice by showing some evidence of individuality
- Develop word choice by attempting to use descriptive words and interesting details
- Develop sentence fluency by using simple sentences that relate to each other
- Represent ideas through words, sentences, and images that connect to a topic

DEVELOPMENTAL WRITING (GRADE 2)

Teacher's Chart

Class _____

Date _____

STUDENT'S NAME

Conventions of Language

- Uses appropriate spacing between letters and words
- Prints legibly, consistent in shape and size
- Uses conventional spelling of common words
- Attempts to spell unfamiliar words
- Spells words of more than one syllable, high frequency words, and plurals
- Uses words from their oral vocabulary, personal word list, and class lists
- Uses commas to separate items in a series
- Uses periods, question marks or exclamation marks at the end of sentences
- Uses capital letters at the beginning of proper nouns and sentences

Personal Writing

- Uses past and present tenses
- Corrects noun-pronoun and subject-verb agreement
- Uses some paragraph divisions
- Completes simple sentences, beginning to use compound sentences
- Puts ideas in a logical organization
- Shows some evidence of individuality
- Uses some varied and descriptive language
- Uses variety in sentence length and pattern
- Uses relevant details that connect to a topic
- Develops ideas throughout use of

Skill Mastery Progress

Black – Sept/Oct/Nov
Green – Dec/Jan
Yellow – Jan/Feb/Mar
Red – Apr/May/Jun

Degree of Skill Mastery

● Skill Mastery
◐ Skill Review Required
○ Skill Instruction Required

e. Early Learning INC.
A First Class Beginning:
Janet N. Mort PhD • Jnmort@shaw.ca

© 2015 Early Learning Inc.

Oral Language
Essential Foundational Skills (K to 2)

Janet's Comments

We appreciate the collaboration of School District No. 23 Central Okanagan as section (page 152-158) originated in their district and is reproduced with the permission of the Superintendent of Schools.

Oral Language: Speaking and Listening

a.   Research and Theory

What is Language?

Language is made up of socially shared rules that include the following:

- What words mean ("star" can refer to a bright object in the night sky or a celebrity).

- How to make new words (friend, friendly, unfriendly).

- How to put words together ("Peg walked to the new store," rather than "Peg walked store new.").

- What word combinations are best in what situations ("Would you mind moving your foot?" could change to "Get off my foot, please!" if the first request did not produce results).

A language is an arbitrary code of symbols and rules designed for the purposes of communication. Every language is invented by a group of people who want to agree on how to arrange their thoughts, what to call things, and how to use this code in social and other communication situations. Here are a few examples from the English language.

- When you ask a question, you reverse the noun and verb and your voice goes up at the end of the sentence. ("You are going to the store." vs. "Are you going to the store?")

- The object that you drive has been labeled a car, truck, or van.

- When you answer the phone, you typically start with a short greeting "Hello…," to which you expect a brief response like, "Hi. This is _____." before you continue with the topic of the call.

The Parts of Language

Language can be divided into three main parts, as described above:

- Form is how thoughts are arranged in sounds, words, and sentences.
- Content is how meaning is conveyed through language.
- Use is how language is shared among people and rules for communication.

You also may hear different terms related to each part of language:

- **Form** – syntax (word order/grammar), morphology (meaning units/building blocks), phonology (the sound system).

- **Content** – semantics (words and their meanings).

- **Use** – pragmatics (social rules of language in context).

Understanding and Expressing Language

For each part of language described above, there also two foundational skills children must master: *to understand language* and *to express language*.

- Understanding means both listening and comprehending language, whether spoken or written. You may hear the term language or auditory comprehension, which also is a combination of listening and understanding skills.

- Expressing includes formulating thoughts into language and then speaking or writing. You may hear the term language production, which also means the same thing.

Writing, speaking and hearing the morning message.

As an example, a child may understand what a parent means when he or she is told, "Please close the door and come here," but the child may not yet be able to express that complex sentence form independently. Understanding and expressing skills may develop at different rates in some children.

Three Main Language Categories in the Classroom

Three main language categories are often described as receptive language, expressive language, and social language.

Receptive Language: "I understand what is said" which demonstrates comprehension of spoken language, following simple commands. Children with receptive language can follow simple commands, point to objects, and respond to simple who, what and where questions. Children develop receptive language before they develop expressive language.

Expressive Language: "You understand what I say" which demonstrate articulation and use of conventional language. Children with expressive language use complex sentence structures and appropriate grammar while others are speaking with incorrect usage, simple phases, or unintelligible speech, often a developmental delay due to lack of experience.

Social Language: "I hear empathically and respond appropriately" which demonstrates appropriate use of language during stressful times, provides acceptable outlets for anger and frustration, and uses respectful ways to disagree with someone.

Building Language Skills

There are two other very critical "big picture" pieces that help language skills develop. One is cognition, or thinking skills. The other is hearing ability. It is important to consider teaching thinking and language skills together, but also to make sure your child is hearing well, too.

What is Speech?

Speech is the verbal means of communication. Speech consists of the following:

- Articulation: How speech sounds are made (children must learn how to produce the "r" sound in order to say "rabbit" instead of "wabbit").

- Voice: Use of the vocal folds and breathing to produce sound (the voice can be abused from overuse or misuse and can lead to hoarseness or loss of voice).

- Fluency: The rhythm of speech (e.g. hesitations or stuttering can affect fluency. When a person has trouble understanding others (receptive language), or sharing thoughts, ideas, and feelings completely (expressive language), then he or she may have a language disorder.

When a person is unable to produce speech sounds correctly or fluently, or has problems with his or her voice, then he or she may have a speech disorder.

Language and speech disorders can exist together or by themselves. The problem can be mild or severe. In any case, a comprehensive evaluation by a certified speech-language pathologist (SLP) would be important.

Why Is Oral Language Development so critical for young literacy learners?

Oral language is the foundation of all eventual literacy learning. You have to be able to speak and understand before you can read and write. Children who have a strong base of oral language when they enter school are already on their way to literacy success. Therefore, for those who don't have a strong language base it is critical that activities in the classroom are designed to close the gap.

By age three children from richly literate homes have heard 30 million more words than children from underprivileged homes. Children are generally much like their parents when it comes to language acquisition and communication styles. 3-year-old measures of accomplishment in language predicted third-grade school achievement [without interventions]. (Hart & Risley, 2003)

Children at the kindergarten age need to be able to do the following:

- Produce the sounds needed for speech,

- Demonstrate comprehension of spoken language,

- Listen for short periods of time with focused attention,

- Demonstrate phonemic awareness,

- Rhyme, identify initial phonemes, and manipulate sounds,

- Follow two- and three-step directions,

- Verbalize daily experiences and personal needs,

- Incorporate new vocabulary into daily speech,

- Answer simple questions about a read-aloud or story,

- Ask meaningful questions,

- Re-tell events in sequence,

- Hear and respond to patterns in sounds and language,

- Hear and use conventions of speech,

- Engage in conversations with peers and adults,

- Use age-appropriate social language for manners and conflict resolution,

- Demonstrate auditory memory, and

- Use pitch and inflexion to convey meaning.

In this circumstance there is no time to wait. While phonics, decoding, and comprehension are foundational elements in the literacy process and we rush to provide interventions – and appropriately so – communication skills, which are what oral language is, are a prerequisite to early reading. Research has established that phonemic awareness is dependent upon oral language. The more competent the child is in phonemic awareness; the more the child engages in oral language; the more capable the child will be in ensuing reading and writing language.

What are the key components of an Oral Language Intervention?

Many researchers recommend that 40 – 60% of class time be spent on oral language development in the primary years. This can be accomplished by orchestrating independent practice centers where children interact in carefully planned activities that generate collaborative conversations among children. Peers are 'conversational torchbearers:' How will you create an environment, rich in peer dialogue, where those who are language challenged can be enriched by the children around them in a natural and playful way?

The linkages between oral language skills and phonemic awareness skills both can be accomplished together through a wealth of oral language that emphasizes phrasing, rhyme, and rhythm through word play, games and song. In whole group activities children accomplish the same through finger plays, nursery rhymes, raps, and chanting. This fun with language needs to be carefully planned to be effective. In small group center practice, drama and puppet centers, retelling centers, listening centers, phonemic awareness game centers, word play and cooperative construction centers all encourage language interplay.

Storytelling, class discussions on topical subjects, shared reading and writing, class dramatizations, and choral reading all provide the teacher with opportunities to model and encourage expanded language opportunities and experiences. Integrating social studies and science subjects into the literacy program is an enriching way to expand language knowledge and usage.

Language plays a pivotal role in self-regulation and conflict resolution. Children become self-regulated when they can use language tools – the words to say and how to say them – as well as the practice in using them. Teachers achieve this by integrating the language of conflict into class discussions; intervening and modeling language and behavior in real-class conflicts; and dramatizing pretend-scenarios that may practically occur in classroom experiences.

Class drama explores expressive language!

Oral language is the bridge that connects developmental readiness to academic expectations….make strong oral language and integral part of every lesson: a natural tool for transitions, for informal conversations, and for planned instruction. That careful attention to oral language serves both as interventions for language-deprived children and as reinforcement for language-fluent children. Oral language: so simple, so natural, and yet so powerful in its effect on self-confidence, the ability to understand one's world, and the potential for learning success….the first truly human skill a child develops: oral language. (Middendorf, p. 125, 2009).

Circle Chart Essential Foundational Skills (K to 2)

The following skills are tracked on the Circle Charts:

Receptive

- Understands classroom language and follows classroom routines.
- Understands vocabulary specific to subject and situation.
- Follows oral direction.

Expressive

- Shares personal experiences and feelings related to classroom topics and book discussions.
- Speaks fluently and with expression (prosody).
- Asks appropriate questions.
- Can retell aspects of a story and give information about a topic.
- Uses language to explain, inquire and compare.
- Uses speech that is understandable; produces speech sounds correctly (e.g. articulation).
- Uses appropriate sentence structure (e.g. grammar).
- Uses appropriate vocabulary for subject and situation.

Social

- Is an active participant in classroom language activities.
- Understands and uses appropriate social conventions for conversations when listening and speaking.
- Ignores distractions and stays focused during listening activities.

b.   Assessment Instructions

Purpose:

To determine if students are in need of additional oral language support to develop their expressive, receptive and social language skills.

Achievement Indicators:

- Use speaking and listening to interact with others for the purposes of: contributing to a class goal, exchanging ideas on a topic, making connections, and engaging in play.
- Use speaking to explore, express, and present ideas, information, and feelings by generally staying on topic, using descriptive words about people, places, things and events, telling and retelling stories and experiences in logical sequence, and sharing connections made.

- Listen for a variety of purposes and demonstrate comprehension by retelling or restating, following two step instructions, asking questions for clarification and understanding, and sharing connections made.

- Use strategies when interacting with others, including sharing and making connections, asking questions for clarification and understanding, taking turns as a speaker and listener.

- Use strategies when expressing and presenting ideas, information, and feelings including accessing prior knowledge, organizing thinking by following a simple framework, predicting some things the audience needs to know.

- Use strategies when listening to make and clarify meaning, including preparing for listening, focusing on the speaker, asking questions, and recalling ideas.

- Demonstrate enhanced vocabulary knowledge and usage.

Procedure:

Teachers should assess student's oral language through observation in multiple situations where they are able to demonstrate their language knowledge in a variety of contexts. Observe student interactions with peers:

- Listening to the language students use in responding to open-ended questions or reflecting on their learning during sharing time,

- Reviewing the products students develop (stories, role-plays, news telling, self-evaluations),

- Listening to the student's responses to books, and

- Observing the student's use of language structures to support reading and writing.

(Trehearne, 2004, p. 32)

1. Refer to the Oral Language Checklist and the Social Responsibility Quick Scale and use them as guidelines for observation of oral language on a daily basis.

2. When enough information has been gathered, complete the checklist for each student. (Timeline – January).

3. If a student appears to be at-risk in any of the items, pay closer attention to the student's oral language skills in that item over a concentrated period of time (one week).

4. Use the results of the checklists to inform instructional practice and guided learning activities for your students.

5. Document your findings on the *Circle Chart*.

Oral Language Checklist (Kindergarten to Grade 1)

Student Name: _____   Teacher: _____

School: _____

Date:	K - Jan		K - Jun		Gr. 1 - Jan		Gr. 1 - Jun	
	concern		concern		concern		concern	
Receptive	no	yes	no	yes	no	yes	no	yes
Understands classroom language and follows classroom routines								
Understands vocabulary specific to subject and situation								
Follows oral directions								
Expressive								
Shares personal experiences and feelings related to classroom topics and book discussions								
Speaks fluently and with expression (prosody)								
Asks appropriate questions								
Can retell aspects of a story and give information about a topic								
Uses language to explain, inquire and compare								
Uses speech that is understandable-produces speech sounds correctly (e.g. articulation)								
Uses appropriate sentence structure (e.g. grammar)								
Uses appropriate vocabulary for subject and situation								
Social								
Is an active participant in classroom language activities								
Understands and uses appropriate social conventions for conversations when listening and speaking								
Ignores distractions and stays focused during listening activities								

*   Key: also refer to the "Teacher's Guide to Interpreting the Oral Language Checklist

** Note: Any "yes" that has been identified should be carefully considered. You may wish to consult your S/L Pathologist for further information.

Tier 1 Student	1-2 concerns	No, not a concern in language. Teach to areas of concern.
Tier 2 Student	3 concerns	Yes, a concern in language. *Refer to Interpretation Guide.
Tier 3 Student	>3 concerns	Yes, a concern in language. *Refer to Interpretation Guide.

See Page 76 for Interpretation guide

[Source Unknown]

Oral Language Checklist (Grade 2 to Grade 3)

Student Name: _____   Teacher: _____

School: _____

Date:	Gr. 2 - Jan		Gr. 2 - Jun		Gr. 3 - Jan		Gr. 3 - Jun	
	concern		concern		concern		concern	
Receptive	no	yes	no	yes	no	yes	no	yes
Understands classroom language and follows classroom routines								
Understands vocabulary specific to subject and situation								
Follows oral directions								
Expressive								
Shares personal experiences and feelings related to classroom topics and book discussions								
Speaks fluently and with expression (prosody)								
Asks appropriate questions								
Can retell aspects of a story and give information about a topic								
Uses language to explain, inquire and compare								
Uses speech that is understandable-produces speech sounds correctly (e.g. articulation)								
Uses appropriate sentence structure (e.g. grammar)								
Uses appropriate vocabulary for subject and situation								
Social								
Is an active participant in classroom language activities								
Understands and uses appropriate social conventions for conversations when listening and speaking								
Ignores distractions and stays focused during listening activities								

*   Key: also refer to the "Teacher's Guide to Interpreting the Oral Language Checklist

** Note: Any "yes" that has been identified should be carefully considered. You may wish to consult your S/L Pathologist for further information.

Tier 1 Student	1-2 concerns	No, not a concern in language. Teach to areas of concern.
Tier 2 Student	3 concerns	Yes, a concern in language. *Refer to Interpretation Guide.
Tier 3 Student	>3 concerns	Yes, a concern in language. *Refer to Interpretation Guide.

See Page 76 for Interpretation guide

[Source Unknown]

Teacher's Guide to Interpreting the Oral Language Checklist:

Tier 1 Student: 1-2 concerns on the entire oral language checklist.

1. Not considered to be at-risk yet.

2. Pay closer attention to the student's oral language skills over a concentrated period of time (e.g. one week).

3. Use the results of the checklists to inform instructional practice and guide learning activities for your students.

Tier 2 Student: 3 concerns on the entire oral language checklist.

1. Considered to be at-risk in oral language development.

2. Will require supplemental intervention in oral language development specific to the identified item on the oral language checklist.

3. Use the results of the checklists to inform instructional practice and guide learning activities for your students.

Tier 3 Student: More than 3 concerns on the entire oral language checklist.

1. Considered to be at-risk in oral language development.

2. Students will most likely require supplemental intervention by a specialist.

3. Consult with the school-based team about your concerns regarding the oral language development of the student.

Specific Social Language Concern:

1. If a student has no areas of concern in receptive and expressive language, but at least 1 area of concern in social language, this is a possible indication of a behavior-based concern.

2. Refer to the next page for the Social Responsibility Performance Standard Quick Scale to confirm your evaluation.

3. If additional support is required in the area of social language consult with the school-based team about your concerns.

[Source Unknown]

ORAL LANGUAGE: SPEAKING AND LISTENING (K/1/2)

Teacher's Chart

Class _____

Date _____

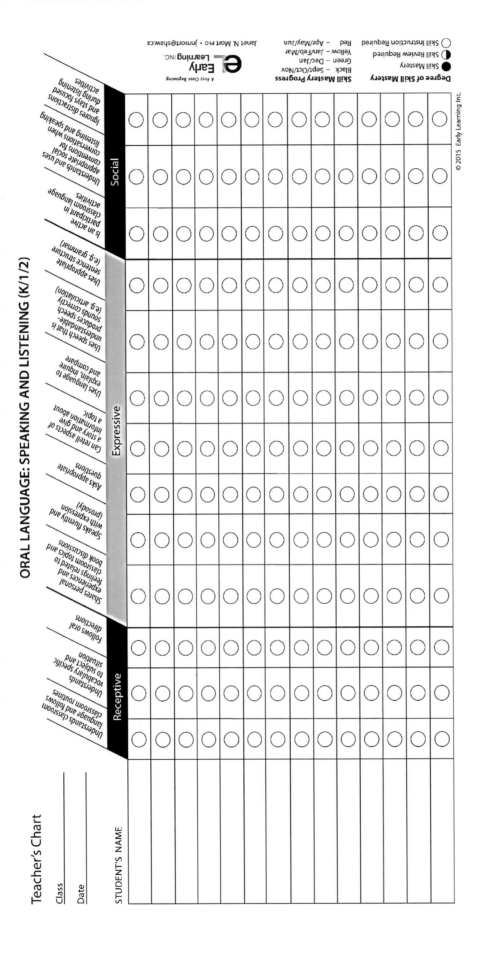

Degree of Skill Mastery

● Skill Mastery
◗ Skill Review Required
○ Skill Instruction Required

Skill Mastery Progress

Black – Sept/Oct/Nov
Green – Dec/Jan
Yellow – Jan/Feb/Mar
Red – Apr/May/Jun

A First Class Beginning

EL Early Learning INC.

Janet N. Mort PhD • jnmort@shaw.ca

© 2015 Early Learning Inc.

STUDENT'S NAME

Receptive
- Understands classroom language and follows classroom routines
- Understands vocabulary specific to subject and situation
- Follows oral directions

Expressive
- Shares personal experiences and feelings related to classroom topics and book discussions
- Speaks fluently and with expression (prosody)
- Asks appropriate questions
- Can retell aspects of a story and give information about a topic
- Uses language to explain, inquire and compare
- Uses speech that is understandable- produces speech sounds correctly (e.g. articulation)
- Uses appropriate sentence structure (e.g. grammar)

Social
- Is an active participant in classroom language activities
- Understands and uses appropriate social conventions for conversations when listening and speaking
- Ignores distractions and stays focused during listening activities

Literacy Essentials

Literature and Informational Text Foundational Skills (K to 2)

Demonstrate an understanding of and ability to use both literature and informational text for a variety of purposes.

Exposure to and Use of Literature and Informational Text

a.   Research and Theory

What is the difference between Literature and Information Texts?

The term *children's literature* generally refers to fictional stories written at various ability levels and targeted to young children in developmental stages of reading. Many teachers use a literature-based approach to reading instruction, thereby accommodating individual student differences in abilities. Children are often encouraged to select their own books focusing on meaning, interest and enjoyment. Literature is used as a springboard for writing. Through literature children learn naturally about story structures, characters, life situations, and opportunities for inquiry.

Informational texts are generally non-fiction trade books often used in content areas to explore specific ideas and concepts in breadth and depth. There are three types:

Narrative informational texts: The author tells a fictional story that conveys factual information. They are typically read from beginning to end.

Expository informational texts: These texts do not tell a story but rather contain information that follows specific text structures such as description, sequence, cause and effect, comparison and contrast, and problem solving. They do not have to be read from beginning to end.

Mixed-text informational text: These texts include narrative stories and contain factual information in the surrounding text.

Why is understanding the difference between Literature and Informational Text so important?

(Adapted from Vacca & Vacca et al., 2012)

There are many benefits of using both types of text across the curriculum. They can provide children with intense involvement in a topic from a variety of perspectives especially when using a thematic approach. Informational texts can be used to teach concepts and facts while literature selections bring an emotional understanding to the topic.

Intense involvement in a subject generates background knowledge that makes concepts easier to grasp. The combination of the two types of texts helps to prepare and motivate students to read a variety of genres. Without a specific introduction to non-fiction texts many children may not experience the pleasure of both. Most families focus on fiction exclusively for family reading experiences.

What are the key components of a Literature and Information Text Intervention?

Shared Reading in large-group classroom settings is an ideal way to introduce both types of texts. In *Joyful Literacy Interventions,* Janet Mort cites the NELP (*National Early Literacy Panel*) Report, which identified Shared Reading as one of the most effective strategies for future reading success in young children. (NELP, 2009)

Kletzien and Dreher (2004) recommend that teachers use informational texts as read-alouds as well as fiction, displaying charts of mixed books for children to sort into categories as either fictional or informational.

Because informational texts are usually more difficult than leveled fiction texts, other authors suggest using strategies such as:

- Pairing students of different abilities,
- Audio-recording informational texts for children,
- Kaleidoscope reading (children read different selections and share what they learned),
- Adapting literature circles to encourage talk,
- Implementing book clubs with a small group of children reading followed by whole-class activities,
- Giving students sticky pad notes so children can mark places where they experienced connections with their own background or had questions arise,
- Brainstorming similar issues from personal experience that match with the text before reading it,
- Modeling how to recognize structures in text with diagrams,

- Establishing literature response journals,

- Using the arts to express understandings from the text – dramatizing, quilting, and writing poetry and song writing about the main ideas.

Electronic texts can be used as well with key pal projects (partners in different locations)

- Global classrooms (partners in different cultures),

- Electronic appearances (special guests visit by long distance),

- Information searches parallel problem solving on similar issues, and social action projects.

"In essence, when fictional and nonfiction trade books are integrated into content area instruction, students have opportunities to become intensely involved with the subject matter, build their background knowledge by using meaningful text, tap their interest and abilities, and learn new and often difficult vocabulary." (Vacca & Vacca et al., 2012)

Main Reference Source for Section 4: Literature and Informational Text Adapted from *Reading and Learning to Read* by Vacca and Vacca et al. (2012)

Circle Chart Essential Foundational Skills

The following skills are tracked on the Circle Charts:

Literature (K to 2)

Kindergarten Skills

- Recognize common types of texts (stories, poems, information).

- Name authors, illustrators and their role in the story.

- Describe the relationship between illustrations and the story.

- Identify characters, settings and major events in the story.

- Compare the adventures of characters in the story.

Grade 1/2 Skills

- Describe the overall structure of a story, including how the beginning begins the story and the ending concludes it.

- Acknowledge differences in points of view of characters using different voices for dialogue.

- Use information gleaned from illustrations to embellish understanding of the text.

- Compare and contrast different versions of the same story.

Informational Text (K to 2)

Kindergarten Skills

- Identify whether a text is a story or informational (fiction or non-fiction) and why it would be classified as such.

- Identify the cover, back cover and title page.

- Identify the connection between different pieces of information in the text.

- Identify the reasons an author gives for his opinion.

- Identify the differences between two texts on the same topic.

- Name something learned from the text.

Grade 1/2 Skills

- Be able to classify various informational texts: science, social studies, technical, other and their purposes.

- Identify various features of informational text: captions, bold print, subheadings, glossaries, indexes, icons, electronic menus and their usage.

- Describe the connections between a series of events, ideas, concepts or steps identified in the text.

- Determine the meaning of complex words or phrases in context.

- Identify the main purpose of the text – what the author is trying to explain.

- Explain how diagrams or illustrations or figures contribute to the text.

- Describe how the author uses explanations to support the key points.

- Compare and contrast how two texts treat the same topic differently and be able to speculate about why?

- List or describe information learned from the text.

Discovering the world of books.

b.   *Assessment Instructions*

Purposes:

To determine whether students can effectively use both informational text and fictional text to enhance their learning.

Achievement Indicators:

Students will:

- Understand the difference between informational text and fictional text,

- Be able to identify and sort different types of text,

- Know which type of text serves which purposes best,

- Understands that both types of text can be used in an integrated way,

- Can describe their understanding of what they have read – persons, places, concepts and events.

Procedure:

The most meaningful assessments for use of literature and informational texts will be authentic assessments. The teacher documents the students' growth in using texts through:

1. Real-life classroom tasks and assignments,

2. Observations of behaviors in the whole group, small groups and of individuals,

3. Anecdotal records, checklists, interviews and criteria-referenced lists,

4. Student self-assessments and reflection,

5. Portfolios and collections or other products,

6. Analysis of student products.

Some formal assessments may be desirable to determine learning progression, knowing what the reader knows, and knowledge of new literacies.

Teacher's Chart

Class _____

Date _____

LITERATURE AND INFORMATIONAL TEXT FOUNDATIONAL SKILLS (K/2)

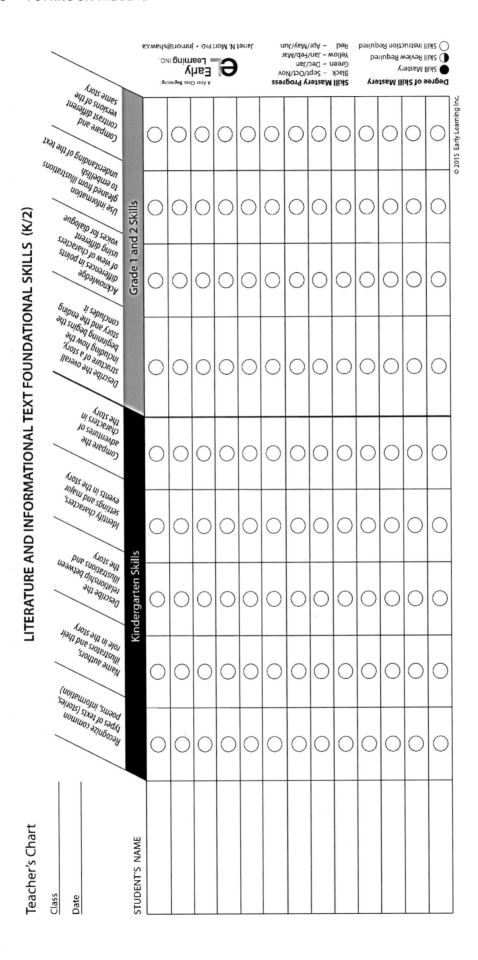

Degree of Skill Mastery
- ● Skill Mastery
- ◑ Skill Review Required
- ○ Skill Instruction Required

Skill Mastery Progress
- Black – Sept/Oct/Nov
- Green – Dec/Jan
- Yellow – Jan/Feb/Mar
- Red – Apr/May/Jun

Early Learning INC.
A First Class Beginning

Janet N. Mort PhD • Jnmort@shaw.ca

© 2015 Early Learning Inc.

Grade 1 and 2 Skills
- Compare and contrast different versions of the same story
- Use information gleaned from illustrations to embellish understanding of the text
- Acknowledge differences in points of view of characters using different voices for dialogue
- Describe the overall structure of a story, including how the beginning begins the story and the ending concludes it

Kindergarten Skills
- Compare the adventures of characters in the story
- Identify characters, settings and major events in the story
- Describe the relationship between illustrations and the story
- Name authors, illustrators and their role in the story
- Recognize common types of texts (stories, poems, information)

STUDENT'S NAME

Teacher's Chart

LITERATURE AND INFORMATIONAL TEXT FOUNDATIONAL SKILLS (K/1/2)

Class _____

Date _____

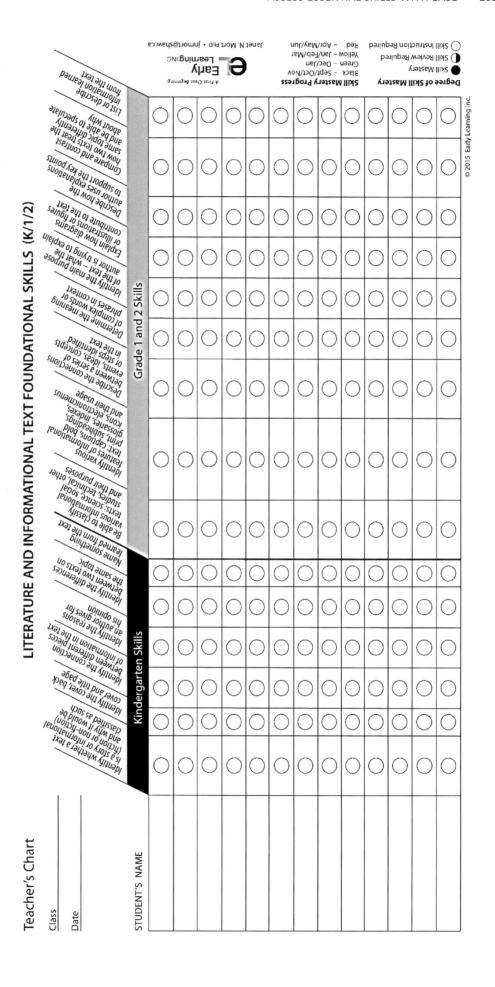

Janet N. Mort PhD • jnmort@shaw.ca

E. Early Learning INC.

A First Class Beginning

Skill Mastery Progress

Black – Sept/Oct/Nov
Green – Dec/Jan
Yellow – Jan/Feb/Mar
Red – Apr/May/Jun

Degree of Skill Mastery

● Skill Mastery
◐ Skill Review Required
○ Skill Instruction Required

Grade 1 and 2 Skills

Kindergarten Skills

STUDENT'S NAME

Janet's Summary

As you will have noted, the skills for K to 3 are laid out in a sequential order based on the importance of the skill to the process of beginning to read. While many of these skills can overlap during instruction (alphabet, sight words, print concepts and phonological awareness during the first year in kindergarten, these skills must be mastered before children can proceed with more formal literacy instruction such as word families and guided reading.

Enjoy the photo below of a proud kindergarten graduate and his mom and dad. I used to respond with cynicism to these kindergarten graduation ceremonies but now I know better.

Proud K 'graduate' and his parents.
Childtime Learning Center, Katy, Texas

The most profound fact I have learned in this past three years of academic and practical data-gathering research at the classroom level is that if children don't learn the basic essentials (the alphabet, phonological awareness, at least 40 sight words and print concepts) in playful game-like concepts, and wallow daily in a joyful environment of rich language, reading, writing and creative activities, they will likely have begun the slide into limited school success in the future unless they have extraordinary instructional and practice support at home.

When we have to teach these essential skills in grades one and two we begin to run out of time and the children quickly begin to identify that they have some kind of learning problem. Once self-concepts begin to be bruised it is very difficult to turn those worrisome feelings around – even in grades two and three.

We also know from the research that if children are experiencing difficulties in the intermediate grades, we need to retrace our steps and go right back to these beginning skills and begin a gain to close the gaps. It makes incredible sense, therefore, to ensure the kindergarten startup is strong and each child reaches mastery for each skill right from the get-go!

Sincerely,

Janet

Hit a Home Run with ALL Early Learners through Games and Play

 Janet's Introduction

Vulnerable Children Need Explicit Skill Instruction

Teaching essential skills joyfully requires a lot more than a focus on games. Language skills like phonemic awareness are embedded in everyday oral language as well as writing and print experiences. There is a significant link between the use of language and cognitive growth. Self-confidence and emotion are directly connected to a child's openness and willingness to learn. Skills cannot be learned without context and meaningful connections.

Games are the major focus of Chapter Four. We wanted to provide you with some exceptional games that you can use in your Blitzing or even your practice centers. The point we want to make is that in order for games to be effective they must be highly structured and organized with attentions to: targeted skill, anticipated outcome, resources required, clear instructions to children, and an assessment strategy. While many of the games are targeted to grades K to 2, simple variations will make them useful for other grades and other skills.

We have provided you with over 30 games – enough in our experience to implement a Blitz over the course of a full year.

- Contrary to recent decades of practice, it is now clear that explicit instruction must begin in kindergarten especially for vulnerable children.
- Oral language is the vehicle for phonemic awareness learning; therefore, creating environments that are rich in talk are essential for phonemic awareness.
- 'Lucky' children have five times the number of working words in their vocabulary. Does your classroom structure encourage 'talk' between the 'haves' and 'have-not' children?

- Print, as context, is also a vehicle for phonemic awareness learning. Frequent reading and writing experiences enhance phonemic awareness skills.

- At the same time, vulnerable children need explicit instruction in small groups. The classroom organization must make room for both invisibly.

- Peers are 'conversational torchbearers.' How will you create an environment, rich in peer dialogue, where those who are language challenged can wallow in the experiences of the 'lucky ones.'

- Emotions allow or block learning. Is your classroom happy, busy, interactive and safe?

- Do you and your children laugh and play with language?

A classroom with a well-balanced mix of rich language experiences, creative play opportunities, targeted skill instruction, an efficient assessment and tracking system, and a plethora of joyful games as the delivery mechanism for skill practice will be the perfect early learning experience when planned and implemented by a loving and nurturing teacher.

Janet's Comments

Dear Reader:

I am proud to introduce you to my colleague **Shauna Lothrop**, kindergarten teacher from Quesnel, British Columbia. Shauna has been part of the research strategy of the Joyful Literacy Implementation program for the past three years and has been a regular speaker at our ongoing Summits. Working individually in her school she has been using the blitz concept in her kindergarten classroom with literacy games as the children's main practice strategy. She is pleased to provide you with some of her most popular games!

Janet

Shauna Lothrop

These games have been developed to be used with the grade(s) level indicated; however, each game could be adapted for use at any primary grade level depending on the skill or skill level being targeted.

Alphabet Games

Name of Game: **GRAB BAG**

Author: Shauna Lothrop

Targeted Skill: Letter Naming

Anticipated Outcome: Students will be able to correctly name the alphabet letters pulled from a bag and then identify the letter again on a recording sheet.

Grade Level: Kindergarten, Grade 1

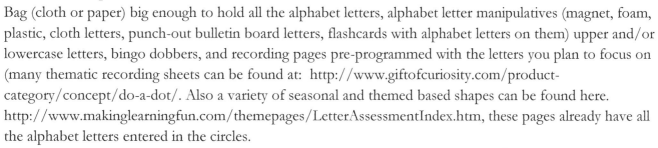

Resources Required:

Bag (cloth or paper) big enough to hold all the alphabet letters, alphabet letter manipulatives (magnet, foam, plastic, cloth letters, punch-out bulletin board letters, flashcards with alphabet letters on them) upper and/or lowercase letters, bingo dobbers, and recording pages pre-programmed with the letters you plan to focus on (many thematic recording sheets can be found at: http://www.giftofcuriosity.com/product-category/concept/do-a-dot/. Also a variety of seasonal and themed based shapes can be found here. http://www.makinglearningfun.com/themepages/LetterAssessmentIndex.htm, these pages already have all the alphabet letters entered in the circles.

Explanation to Teacher (game construction):

Print out the recording page you plan to use. Print a target letter in each of the circles. Photocopy enough recording pages for your group. Gather the bag and the alphabet manipulatives you plan to use. Put all the alphabet manipulatives in the bag.

Explanation to Teacher (how game works):

One student reaches in the bag and pulls out one letter. They name the letter (or ask for help from their friends if they do not know the name) and find it on their recording page, then all the students use their bingo dobbers to dob over that letter on their recording sheets. The student passes the bag of letters to the child sitting next to them and the game continues until all letters on the recording page are covered.

Directions to Children:

Pull one letter out of the bag, tell us the name of that letter, find it on your page, then you get to put a dob on it. Pass the bag to the friend sitting beside you so they can have a turn.

Assessment Strategy:

Teacher observes to see which letters are difficult for the students to name. Once complete, the teacher can ask individual students to name a few letters on their recording page.

Variations of the Game:

Use only uppercase letters or only lowercase letters in the bag and on the recording sheet. Mix upper and lowercase letters in the bag and on the recording sheet. If working on identifying certain letters put only those letters in the bag and program the recording sheet with only those letters. When students are ready, ask them to name the letter and give its sound before dobbing it on the recording sheet. Ask students to name the letter and identify something that starts with that letter.

Name of Game:	**WHAT'S THE MISSING LETTER?**
Author:	Shauna Lothrop
Targeted Skill:	Letter Naming, Letter Order
Anticipated Outcome:	Students will be able to order and name the letters of the alphabet. Students will be able to identify the missing letter of the alphabet.
Grade Level:	Kindergarten, Grade 1

Resources Required:
Set of alphabet manipulatives (magnets, foam, plastic, cloth letters, punch-out bulletin board letters, flashcards with alphabet letters on them), basket/bucket/bag to hold the letters; floor or table space.

Explanation to Teacher (game construction):
Gather a complete set of alphabet manipulatives and place them in the basket/bucket/bag.

Explanation to Teacher (how game works):
Students can work in pairs or small groups. One student (the hider) will secretly remove a letter of the alphabet from the basket/bucket/bag. You can designate a special spot to place the removed letter. The other student(s) must then take the remaining alphabet manipulatives and put them in order from A-Z. Along the way they will encounter a missing letter. Encourage the students to complete putting the whole alphabet in order, to ensure that they are correct about which letter is missing. When the alphabet is all in order they can question the hider about which letter they think is missing. The hider can go and retrieve the missing letter and place it in the correct position. Then the students can all sing the alphabet song from A-Z.

Directions to Children:
One of you is going to be the hider. You will pick one letter out of the bucket/basket/bag to hide over here (designated hiding spot). Then your friend(s) will take the rest of the letters and try to build that alphabet. When they are done they will ask you if you hid the letter '___'? If they are right you can go and get that letter and put it in the alphabet where it belongs. Then you can all sing and point to all the letters of the alphabet.

Assessment Strategy:
The teacher can ask the hider to see if he/she can whisper the name of the letter they have chosen to hide. The teacher can observe the rest of the group as they put the alphabet in order.

Variations of the Game:
The hider can hide two or more letters each time. The hider can hide three or four letters that spell a sight word or an easy "cvc" word. The group needs not only to identify the missing letters but also figure out which word those letters can spell.

Name of Game:	**HUFF & PUFF**
Author:	Shauna Lothrop
Targeted Skill:	Letter Name, Letter Sounds, Sound Fluency
Anticipated Outcome:	Students will be able to name and produce the correct sound(s) for letters. Students will increase their oral fluency when producing letter sounds.
Grade Level:	Kindergarten, Grade 1

Resources Required:
Lightweight blocks or cubes that have alphabet letters printed on the faces (check out Dollar Stores for packages of small foam blocks), basket/bucket/bag to hold the blocks.

Explanation to Teacher (game construction):
Print letters of the alphabet on each side of every block. You may want to have the same letter printed on all six sides of the block or you may choose to put different letters on the six sides. If you are targeting specific letters/sounds it is likely more beneficial to have the same letter printed on each side of the block.

Explanation to Teacher (how game works):
Students take turns pulling a block from the bucket/basket/bag and placing it in front of them. They name the letter on the block and say its sound. If they correctly name the letter and say its sound, they get to start building a tower with the blocks they pull. If a student is not able to name the letter or correctly say the sound the teacher gets to Huff & Puff and blow the tower down and the students begin to build their tower again. In order to build in fluency practice, ask the students to say all the sounds of the letters in their tower on each turn.

Directions to Children:
You are going to get a chance to build a tower with blocks. You will pull a block from this bucket/basket/bag and if you can tell me the name of the letter and its sound you can use it to build a tower. Each time you add a new block to your tower you have to tell me the sounds of all of the other letters in your tower. If you can't remember a letter or its sound I get to Huff & Puff and blow your tower down!

Assessment Strategy:
The teacher will observe each child's ability to name letters and produce their sound.

Variations of the Game:
If you are focusing on particular letters/sounds just have available blocks with those letters/sounds on them for the students to use in building their towers. Add blends or consonant digraphs to sides of the blocks ('st,' 'br,' 'th,' etc.). Have the students say the sound of the blend or consonant digraph and name something that starts with it.

Name of Game:	**DIG AND FIND**

Author:	Shauna Lothrop

Targeted Skill:	Alphabet identification, Letter/Sound Association

Anticipated Outcome: Students will be able to accurately name letters of the alphabet. OR Students will be able to accurately produce the sound associated with a letter

Grade Level:	Kindergarten, Grade 1

Resources Required:
Tub, filler material (rice, shredded paper, beans, gems, etc.), a set of alphabet letters (magnetic, foam, beads, etc.). Optional: cookie sheet with alphabet listed on it.

Explanation to Teacher (game construction):
Find a tub and fill it 1/2 full with your choice of filler material. Put the alphabet letters in and mix them around so that some are hidden within the filler material.

Explanation to Teacher (how game works):
Students will reach into the tub, find an alphabet letter, pull it out, say its name or sound. If using cookie sheets, the students can then match the letter to the letter on the cookie sheet. OR the students can begin to arrange the letters in alphabetical order on a table top or on the floor before then reach in for another letter.

Directions to Children:
You are going to get the chance to reach into this tub with your hand and find an alphabet letter. When you pull it out you will tell us what letter you found (and say its sound). Then you will match it to the letter on the cookie sheet. OR Then you will start arranging the letters on the table/floor.

Assessment Strategy:
The teacher will observe the ease with which the students can name and/or produce the sound of the letters chosen. The teacher can also observe the ease with which the students match or organize the letters into the alphabet.

Variations of the Game:
This game allows for a lot of variation and differentiation. Students can pull letters and name the letter, produce the sound, produce a word that starts with that letter. If small cards with sight words are hidden in the tub the students can pull a card and read the sight word. Students could pull a sight word card, read it, then orally say a sentence with that sight word in it.

Phonological Awareness Games

Name of Game: ## FILL A BUCKET

Author: Shauna Lothrop

Targeted Skill: Segmenting a Sentence into Words

Anticipated Outcome: Students will be able to segment a simple sentence and state how many words are in the sentence.

Grade Level: Kindergarten

Resources Required:
Sentence strips with simple three- to six-word sentences printed on them, a little bucket/container for each student, small manipulatives to use as counters.

Explanation to Teacher (game construction):
Prepare several (10 to 15) sentence strips with easy three- to six-word sentences (e.g., I can jump, or We like red crayons); gather small counters (i.e., macaroni, beads) and buckets/containers.

Explanation to Teacher (how game works):
Give each student a bucket/container and a pile of small counters. Show the students one of the sentence strips. Model putting one counter under each word; count up how many counters were used in that sentence. Tell the students that that sentence has 'x' number of words in it. Ask them to put x counters in their bucket. Repeat having the students listen to you read the sentence and then one at a time they put a counter under each word in the sentence, count how many words (counters), and then put the counters in their bucket.

Directions to Children:
We are going to try to fill our little buckets with _____ (counters) as we listen and then count the words in sentences. I will read you a sentence then we will take turns putting a _____ (counter) under each word in the sentence. We will count how many words are in each sentence and then put that many counters in our buckets. We will keep going until our buckets are full.

Assessment Strategy:
The teacher will observe as each student repeats the sentence and puts a counter under each word.

Variations of the Game:
Once familiar with the concept, the students can suggest sentences that the teacher can record on sentence strips. The teacher may encourage the students to use sight words in the sentences and the students can help to print those sight words in the sentences.

Name of Game:	**RING AROUND THE ROSIE**
Adapted From:	Purposeful Play for Early Childhood Phonological Awareness by H. Yopp and R. Yopp.
Targeted Skill:	Onset and Rime (Rhyme) Blending
Anticipated Outcome:	Students will be able to blend the onset and rime of an action word in order to determine and perform the action.
Grade Level:	Kindergarten

Resources Required:

List of action words (i.e., jump, hop, swim, crawl, sleep, etc.).

Explanation to Teacher (game construction):

Write out a list of action words.

Explanation to Teacher (how game works):

Students form a circle and practice singing Ring Around the Rosie as they walk around the circle. Students will sing the first two lines (Ring around the rosie, a pocketful of posies); next the teacher will say an action word broken into onset and rime (e.g., 'cr' 'awl'). Then the students will sing "We all will crawl!" and they will begin crawling around.

Directions to Children:

We are going to sing some of the song Ring Around the Rosie but instead of Hush-a, hush-a, I'm going to say an action word slowly. You have to put the parts of the word together to figure out which word I'm trying to say. Then we'll finish off the song "We all will _____" (fill in with action word).

Assessment Strategy:

The teacher will observe and monitor whether the students are able to blend the onset and rime together correctly and perform the desired action.

Variations of the Game:

Ask the students to suggest some action words and even lead the group with their action word separated into onset and rime. As students become good at blending onset and rime, start to say the phonemes in the words to see whether the students can blend all the letter sounds.

Name of Game:	WHERE'S THAT SOUND?

Author: Shauna Lothrop

Targeted Skill: Phoneme Identification: Identifying where a specific sound is in a word.

Anticipated Outcome: Students will be able to identify whether a sound is heard at the beginning, middle, or end of a word.

Grade Level: Kindergarten, Grade 1

Resources Required:
List of CVC words

Explanation to Teacher (game construction):
Prepare a list of CVC words, prepare train graphic (or other three-part graphic of your choosing).

Explanation to Teacher (how game works):
Decide with the students how they will identify where the targeted sound is in a word: Physically (touch head = beginning sound; touch waist = middle sound; touch feet = ending sound) or on a graphic of a train with three parts (engine = beginning sound; passenger car = middle sound; caboose = end sound). Teacher says a CVC word out loud then asks the students to identify on their body or on the graphic where the targeted letter is in the word.

Directions to Children:
I'm going to say a word then I'm going to ask you where you hear a certain sound in that word. Is it at the beginning of the word, the middle, or at the end of the word? You will show me by _____ (physically or on a graphic).

Assessment Strategy:
The teacher will be able to observe whether each student can identify where the targeted sound is located in each word.

Variations of the Game:
Use CVCe words or CCVC, CVCC words

Name of Game:	**TAP IT OUT**

Author: Shauna Lothrop

Targeted Skill: Identifying and Counting Syllables

Anticipated Outcome: The students will be able to tap out and count syllables in words.

Grade Level: Kindergarten, Grade 1

Resources Required:
Rhythm sticks or some other object that the students can tap together (i.e. popsicle sticks, wooden blocks)

Explanation to Teacher (game construction):
Collect rhythm sticks (check with your Music Teacher to see if they have a class set they can share with you) or other object that students will use to tap out the syllables in words.

Explanation to Teacher (how game works):
The teacher will identify a word and students will 'Tap-it-Out' with the rhythm sticks. It may be necessary to tap it out several times in order for the students to count how many syllables are in the target word. As students get familiar with the task move them about the classroom or school to identify and tap out the sounds in words you encounter as you move (i.e. hallway, office, doorway).

Directions to Children:
We are going to practice tapping out syllables with these rhythm sticks. I am going to say a word and then you are going to tap once for each syllable of the word. When we get really good at this we are going to start moving around the classroom looking for new words to tap and maybe even go around the school to find other words we can tap.

Assessment Strategy:
The teacher will observe as students tap out the syllables in words. The teacher may ask students to tap the syllables individually or as a group together.

Variations of the Game:
Instead of using rhythm sticks the students could clap their hands, tap their shoulders, pat their tummies, honk their nose, stomp their feet, jump up, etc.

Sight-Word Games

Name of Game:	## STAMP YOUR WORDS

Author: Shauna Lothrop

Targeted Skill: Sight-word recognition and spelling.

Anticipated Outcome: Students will be able to correctly stamp sight words they have been taught onto paper or in Play-Doh.

Grade Level: Kindergarten, Grade 1, Grade 2

Resources Required:
Alphabet stamps, paper or Play-Doh, list of sight words that have been taught/introduced.

Explanation to Teacher (game construction):
Gather the required resources.

Explanation to Teacher (how the game works):
Students will refer to a list of sight words and stamp them on their paper or into Play-Doh using alphabet stamps. Encourage the students to name the letters as they stamp and read the word once all the letters have been stamped.

Directions to Children:
You are going to practice stamping and spelling the sight words you know. Here is a list of the sight words you know. Stamp all the letters for the first sight word onto the paper/Play-Doh. Say each letter as you stamp it. When you have stamped all the letters, read the word. Now go on to the next word.

Assessment Strategy:
The teacher can ask individual students to read the sight words they have stamped. The teacher can quickly review the list of sight words with individual students as they are working in order to see which words they know and which words need further practice.

Variations of the Game:
This game is perfect for differentiating instruction. Each student could have a list of words tailored to them; some they know, some they've been introduced to, and one or two new words to practice.

The students could print a sentence under the stamped word (on paper) that includes that sight word. Students could work with a partner to say a sight word, the partner stamps it and checks it against the sight-word card their friend is holding.

Name of Game:	**POOL NOODLE TOWER SPELLING**
Author:	Shauna Lothrop
Targeted Skill:	Sight-word recognition and spelling.
Anticipated Outcome:	Students will be able to correctly spell sight words that they have been introduced to using pool noodle pieces with alphabet letters on them.
Grade Level:	Kindergarten, Grade 1, Grade 2

Resources Required:
Pool noodles; approximately three (at least two different colors is best), list of sight words.

Explanation to Teacher (game construction):
Use a serrated knife (or electric carving knife) to cut the pool noodle into two- to four-inch lengths. Using a permanent marker, print one alphabet letter on each length of pool noodle. I'd suggest using a different color of pool noodle for the vowels. Print letters that occur more frequently, such as s, t, m, r, etc. on several different lengths of pool noodle. It is best to store all the pieces in a big bucket or plastic bag.

Explanation to Teacher (how game works):
Students build sight word towers from a given list using the pool noodle pieces. They are building a pool noodle tower for each word (first letter at the top of the tower then moving down). Once they have built several words, the students can read the words to a friend/teacher before knocking over their towers and starting to build new words.

Directions to Children:
You are going to use pool noodle pieces to build towers that spell your sight words. First you need to pick a word to spell, then you need to find pool noodle pieces that have the letters for that word on them. When you go to put the tower together think about the first letter of the word as being at the top of your tower. Once you have built 'x'-number of sight words, find a friend/teacher, read them your words, then knock down your sight-word towers and start building new words.

Assessment Strategy:
The teacher can observe as students build their towers to see whether they recognize the sight words on the list and are able to correctly rebuild that word in a tower. The teacher can listen to individual students read their towers before knocking them down.

Variations of the Game:
Use different building materials as long as they have alphabet letters on the sides. Students could practice spelling their own names or names of friends.

Name of Game:	**SIGHT WORD SNAKES AND LADDERS**

Adapted From: www.sightwords.com

Targeted Skill: Recognition of Sight Words

Anticipated Outcome: Students will be able to

Grade Level: Kindergarten, Grade 1, Grade 2

Resources Required:
Game board that can be created and printed off from the website, die, token for each student to move around the game board.

Explanation to Teacher (game construction):
Go to the website and either pick the list of sight words from the lists provided or enter the sight words you want your students to practice while playing the game. Print out the game board (it will print out on four letter size pieces of paper). Glue the four pieces of paper together to create the game board. If possible, laminate the game board for durability. Gather a die and the tokens for students use.

Explanation to Teacher (how game works):
Students roll the die and move their token that many spaces forward. If they can read the sight word on the space they land on they can stay there. If the bottom of a ladder is on the square, they get to climb the ladder. They must also read the word at the top of the ladder. If a snake's head is on the square they land on they must slide down the snake to its tail. The game continues until one student reaches the final spot on the game board.

Directions to Children:
We are going to play a game of Snakes and Ladders. You will take turns rolling the die and moving forward on the game board. Whatever square you land on you must read out that word. If you can't read the word you move back to your last spot. If you land on a square that has the bottom of a ladder, you get to climb to the top of the ladder and read the word at the top. If you land on a square that has a snake's head you have to slide down the snake until you get to his tail. The first person to make it to the last box on the board is the winner.

Assessment Strategy:
The teacher can observe the ease with which students can read the words on the spaces they land on.

Variations of the Game:
This game is easy to differentiate for students' needs. Customize the words on the game board according to what words groups of students are working on.

Name of Game: **BOOM!**

Author: Shauna Lothrop

Targeted Skill: Sight Word Recognition

Anticipated Outcome: Students will read sight words with increasing accuracy and fluency

Grade Level: Kindergarten, Grade 1, Grade 2

Resources Required:
Popsicle Sticks with 1 sight word written on each, round container to hold all the popsicle sticks

Explanation to Teacher (game construction):
Print 1 sight word on each popsicle stick, Print BOOM! on 3-4 popsicle sticks. Place all popsicle sticks with the word at the bottom into the round container.

Explanation to Teacher (how game works):
Students can work individually, in pairs, or in small groups to play this game. When playing with a partner one student begins the game by pulling a popsicle stick and reading the word. If they read the word accurately they get to keep the popsicle stick. If they are unable to read the word they can ask their friend for help and then put the popsicle stick back in the container. Then the next student takes a turn. If a student pulls out a popsicle stick that says 'BOOM!' they have to put all the popsicle sticks they've gathered back into the container. The game continues until there are no popsicle sticks left in the container.

Directions to Children:
You are going to play a game called 'BOOM!'. You will take turns to pull a popsicle stick out of the container. There is a sight word printed on the popsicle stick. You read it out loud. If you are correct you get to keep the stick. If you don't know the word you can ask a friend for help and then put the stick back in the container. Then it's your friend's turn. If you pull out a popsicle stick that says 'BOOM!' you lose all the popsicle sticks you've collected and have to put them all back in the container. The game will end when there are no popsicle sticks left in the container.

Assessment Strategy:
The teacher will observe the ease with which each student is able to read the words they pull from the container. Words that a student is not able to read can be noted by the teacher for future practice and reinforcement.

Variations of the Game:
If students are working on a limited amount of sight words then print them on several popsicle sticks and let the students practice with just the words that have been introduced.

Janet's Comments

Dear Reader:

I am proud to introduce you to my colleague **Darci Dheensaw**, kindergarten teacher, from the Lauwelnew Tribal School in Saanich, British Columbia. Darci has excelled with her kindergarten class of 100% aboriginal children who have historically entered school with high vulnerabilities. Darci's children made exceptional progress in the past two years of the Joyful Literacy Intervention program: Almost all children learned more than 40 sight words by the end of the school year and began to read at or above grade level according to PM Benchmark measures. She credits her daily Blitz of games as her highest-priority strategy and is pleased to share her favorite games with you.

Darci Dheensaw

Janet

On the wings of an eagle!

These games have been developed to be used with the grade(s) level indicated; however, each game could be adapted for use at any primary grade level depending on the skill or skill level being targeted.

Here are some examples that I use in the classroom:

Alphabet Games

Name of Game: **ABC BALLOON GAME**

Author: Darci Dheensaw

Adapted From: giftblooms.com

Targeted Skill: Improve letter recognition

Anticipated Outcome: Students will be able to practice the alphabet while trying to keep balloons up in the air.

Grade Level: Kindergarten, Grade 1

Resources Required:
Balloons, black permanent marker.

Explanation to Teacher (game construction):
Inflate 5+ balloons. Write one letter on each balloon.

Explanation to Teacher (how game works):
Have the students form a circle. Toss balloon A into the circle, shouting "A" as you do. Have the students shout "A" back. The students are to say "A" every time they touch the balloon. The object of the game is to keep the balloon in the air and prevent it from touching the ground. Let the kids toss balloon A around a bit, then add balloon B to the mix. Make sure you shout out the letter name. Continue adding the rest of the balloons, shouting out each letter as you do. It may get chaotic but keep going until 5 or more balloons are in the air. The more balloons, the better! Once a balloon hits the ground, have everyone stop and recite the alphabet then resume playing. See how many balloons you can keep in play!

Directions to Children:
Stand in a circle. The teacher will toss in a balloon with the letter "A" on it. Every time you hit the balloon you say "A". Then the teacher will toss in a balloon with the letter "B" on it. Then you say "B" when you hit it. If the balloon hits the ground then you stop and everyone sings the Alphabet song. After you sing the song, the game continues again.

Assessment Strategy:
Teacher observes to see what letters are difficult for the students to say when they hit the balloons.

Variations of the Game:
Use alphabet balloons and ask students to name the letter and identify something that starts with that letter.

Alphabet/ Phonemic Awareness Games

Name of Game: **GUMBALLS**

Author: Darci Dheensaw

Adapted From: Play-Doh to Plato

Targeted Skill: Improve alphabet recognition

Anticipated Outcome: Students will be able to correctly name the letter and cover it on the gumball machine.

Grade Level: Kindergarten, Grade 1

Resources Required:
Alphabet cards, Bingo chips, gumball machine.

Explanation to Teacher (game construction):
Print a gumball machine for each student in the group. For extra durability laminate the machines. If gumball machines are laminated the letters can be individualized. Choose the letters you want to work on. Print these letters onto the gumball machine.

Explanation to Teacher (how game works):
Place the alphabet cards in a pile face down next to the gumball machine. Give each student a handful of bingo chips (tokens). The student turns over the top card in the pile and reads it out loud. The student uses the bingo chip to cover the letter on the gumball machine then says a word that starts with that letter. Play continues when all the gumballs are covered.

Directions to Children:
Turn over the top card in the pile and read it out loud. Use one of the tokens to cover the matching alphabet letter gumball. Name a word that starts with that letter. Play continues until all gumballs have been covered.

Assessment Strategy:
Teacher observes to see what letters are difficult for the students to name. Once complete the teacher can ask individual students to name the letters covered on their gumball machine.

Variations of the Game:
Use uppercase letters, lowercase letters or sight words. Mix upper and lowercase letters. If working on identifying certain letters only print those letters onto the gumball machine.

Name of Game:	**CROCODILE SNAP**
Author:	Darci Dheensaw
Adapted From:	Growing Kinders and makelearningfun.com
Targeted Skill:	Improve alphabet recognition
Anticipated Outcome:	Students will be able to correctly name the letter and its sound when they pull the letter out of the crocodile's mouth.
Grade Level:	Kindergarten, Grade 1

Resources Required:
Alphabet cards, snap cards and a crocodile. Make the crocodile using an empty Cascade detergent container or any container that snaps shut.

Explanation to Teacher (game construction):
Print the alphabet letters and poem. For extra durability laminate the letters. Choose the letters you want to work on. Make a crocodile.

Explanation to Teacher (how game works):
Say the poem and have the students reach into the crocodile's mouth and pull out a card. Have them show the card to the group and identify the letter and its sound. If they are correct it goes in the center of the table. If they are incorrect they can 'call a friend' for help! If a student pulls out a 'snap' card, students put their arms out like a crocodile and say, "Snap! Snap!" and all of the cards go back into the crocodile and play continues.

Directions to Children:
After the teacher has read the poem, reach carefully into the crocodile's mouth and pull out a card. Show the card to your friends and say the letter and the sound it makes. If you get it correct, it goes in the center of the table. If you need help with naming the letter or its sound, you can 'call a friend' for help! If a 'snap' card is pulled out then all the cards go back into the crocodile.

Assessment Strategy:
Teacher observes to see what letters or sounds are difficult for the students to name.

Variations of the Game:
Use uppercase letters, lowercase letters or sight words. Mix upper and lowercase letters.

Phonemic Awareness Game

Name of Game: **LETTER-SOUND HOPSCOTCH**

Author: Darci Dheensaw

Adapted From: Picture from Google images

Targeted Skill: Improve letter recognition and initial sounds

Anticipated Outcome: Students will be able to correctly name the letter and sound associated with that letter.

Grade Level: Kindergarten, Grade 1

Resources Required:
Sidewalk chalk, rock/beanbag as a marker, flat piece of pavement (e.g. sidewalk, playground).

Explanation to Teacher (game construction):
Use the chalk to draw 10 large squares in hopscotch formation. Write a different letter in each box.

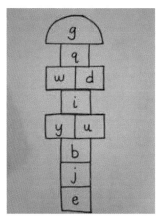

Explanation To Teacher (how game works):
Kids start by hopping on one foot at a time, and say the name of the letter they land on. When they land on the squares that go two across, one foot goes on each square. Once they have the hang of it, they are ready to play with the rock/beanbag. The child throws the beanbag into the 1st box. They try to hop around it while saying the sounds of the letters in the other boxes and then try to pick up the beanbag on their way back to the 1st box without losing their balance.

Directions to Children:
Throw your beanbag into the 1st square on the hopscotch. You are to hop over the first square then say the sound of the letters in the other boxes. When you get to the end of the squares, turn around and hop back until you get to the 1st square where your beanbag is. Pick it up saying the sound of the letter in the box. Repeat the process by throwing your beanbag into the 2nd square.

Assessment Strategy:
Teacher observes to see what letters/sounds are difficult for the students to name.

Variations of the Game:
This game has many variations. 1) As the children hop onto a letter they could say a word that begins with the letter. 2) Sight words could also be put in the hopscotch squares. 3) Word families - for example if you are working on 'at' words then the children can brainstorm 10 'at' words to put into the squares.

Name of Game:	**BUBBLE LETTERS**
Author:	Darci Dheensaw
Targeted Skill:	Improve letter recognition and letter sounds
Anticipated Outcome:	Students will be able to correctly name the letter and sound associated with that letter.
Grade Level:	Kindergarten, Grade 1

Resources Required:
Large alphabet letters. Plastic pointer with a finger for poking the bubbles. Bottle of bubbles and a wand.

Explanation to Teacher (game construction):
Make or buy bubbles.

Explanation to Teacher (how game works):
The teacher holds up a letter card and a student reads it. The teacher blows bubbles if the letter is read correctly. The children then try to pop the bubbles with the pointer while they are calling out the sound of the letter. For example if the letter is "B" the children will say "Buh, buh" for every bubble they pop.

Directions to Children:
When it's your turn, read the letter card that the teacher holds up. The teacher will blow bubbles when the letter is read correctly. You can ask a friend for help. Try to pop each bubble with the pointer while you are calling out the sound of the letter.

Assessment Strategy:
Teacher observes to see what letters/sounds are difficult for the students to name.

Variations of the Game:
The teacher can hold up sight words.

Sight Word Games

Name of Game:	**FLY SWATTER GAME**
Author:	Darci Dheensaw
Adapted From:	maketaketeach.com
Targeted Skill:	Improve sight word vocabulary
Anticipated Outcome:	Students will be able to correctly name the sight word before swatting it.
Grade Level:	Kindergarten, Grade 1, and Grade 2

Resources Required:
Dolch Pre-Primer flashcards. Fly swatters with Velcro dots on them. Insect cards with Velcro dots on them.

Explanation to Teacher (game construction):
 Print out the insects you plan to use. Put a sight word label on each insect. Also put Velcro dots on the insects so that when the insect is swatted it will be picked up by the fly swatter.

Explanation to Teacher (how game works):
Choose which words you wish to work with and pick out the corresponding insects. Set up the game by placing the insect cards out on a table, well-spaced out, and word side up. Have the students take turns swatting insects (catching them with the fly swatter) and reading the words. If the word is read correctly, the student can keep the insect. Continue play until all the insects are gone. The student with the most insects at the end of the session wins the game.

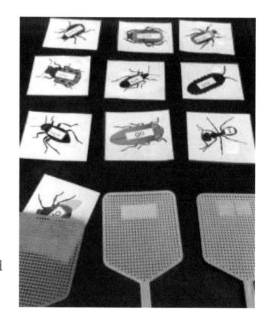

Directions to Children:
With your fly swatter, swat as many insects that you can after reading the word on it. The person with the most insects at the end of the game is the winner.

Assessment Strategy:
Teacher observes the words the child correctly and incorrectly recognizes in the game to track how they are progressing and the words that may need more attention.

Variations of the Game:
The teacher calls out one word at a time. The child must find the word among the insect cards on the table and then "splat" the word with their fly swatter while repeating the word. If they splat it they keep it for 1 point. Continue play until all the insects are gone. The student with the most insects at the end of the session wins the game.

Name of Game:	**GOING FISHING**
Author:	Darci Dheensaw
Adapted From:	maketeateach.com
Targeted Skill:	Improve sight word vocabulary
Anticipated Outcome:	Students will be able to correctly name the sight word that they catch on their fishing rod.
Grade Level:	Kindergarten, Grade 1, and Grade 2

Resources Required:
Dolch Pre-Primer words written on the back of fish. Paper clip fastened to the fish. A fishing pole either from the dollar store or made from dowel and string and a button magnet.

Explanation to Teacher (game construction):
Make or Xerox the fish. Laminate the fish for durability. Glue gun a paperclip onto each fish. Tie string on the dowel rod and glue a magnet at the end of the string.

Explanation to Teacher (how game works):
Differentiate this activity by choosing which and how many fish to use. Scatter the fish on the table with the word side down. Have the students take turns catching fish with the rod and reading the word on the fish. If the word is read correctly, the student can keep the fish. The student with the most fish at the end wins the game.

Directions to Children:
Catch a fish with your fishing rod. Read the word on the fish. If the word is read correctly you can keep the fish. The person with the most fish at the end of the game wins.

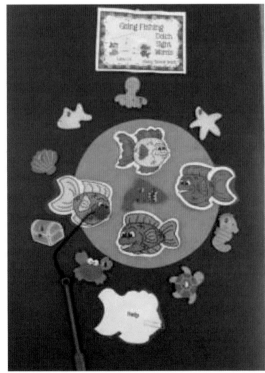

Assessment Strategy:
Teacher observes the words the child correctly and incorrectly recognizes in the game to track how they are progressing and the words that may need more attention.

Variations of the Game:
Use alphabet letters on the back of the fish for a letter recognition game.

Name of Game:	**SOCCER GAME**
Author:	Darci Dheensaw
Adapted From:	Playdoh to Plato
Targeted Skill:	Improve sight word vocabulary
Anticipated Outcome:	Students will be able to correctly name the sight word and they will then shoot the soccer ball into the net.
Grade Level:	Kindergarten, Grade 1

Resources Required:
Print off the soccer field. Print Dolch Pre-Primer words on the back of soccer balls. Put a soccer ball into a milk lid. To make a goal you can use a small fruit basket and cut off the bottom or use an 8 cm long rectangular block piece like in the picture.

Explanation to Teacher (game construction):
Have a soccer field laminated for each student in the group. They get a soccer ball "milk lid with a laminated mini soccer ball inside it". Each student gets a goal. Print Dolch sight words on the back of soccer balls.

Explanation to Teacher (how game works):
Each student sets up the soccer field with the goal post. I give each student their own pile of sight words that they are working on. The student turns over the soccer ball and reads the sight word. After they read it they may shoot (flick) the "milk lid" soccer ball toward the goal. If they get it into the goal then they get a point and keep the sight word ball. They also tell me the sight word in a sentence. They could then print the sentence while they wait for their friends to take their turns. The student with the most soccer balls is the winner.

Directions to Children:
Set up your soccer field and goal post. Turn over the ball and read the sight word. If you get it correct then you can shoot (flick) the "milk lid" soccer ball towards the goal. If you get a goal you keep the sight word soccer ball and have 1 point. If you miss your shot you can shoot again. Tell your teacher a sentence with the word in it and then print the sentence.

Assessment Strategy:
Teacher observes to see what sight words are difficult for the students to name.

Variations of the Game:
You could add "red cards" to the back of some soccer balls. If a student chooses a soccer ball with a red card sign on the back, all the cards must be put back in the pile and play continues. This game can be played with letters as well.

Name of Game:	**POP!**
Author:	Darci Dheensaw
Adapted From:	Deanna Jump
Targeted Skill:	Improve sight word vocabulary
Anticipated Outcome:	Students will be able to correctly name and spell the sight words.
Grade Level:	Kindergarten, Grade 1

Resources Required:
Dolch Pre-Primer flashcards, game board and token (penny).

Explanation to Teacher (game construction):
Print out the game board and the bubble gum word cards.

Explanation to Teacher (how game works):
Place the bubble gum word cards and POP cards in a bag. Place the penny on the start. The students take turns pulling a card from the bag. If they can read the word and spell it correctly they get to move their game piece the same number of letters in the word. For example, "come c-o-m-e come". They should move 4 spaces. If they pull out a POP card they go back 3 spaces. (P-O-P).

Directions to Children:
Pull 1 word out of the bag. Read the word then spell the word. (e.g. Come C-O-M-E). If the word has 4 letters then you move 4 spaces. If you pull out a POP card then you go back 3 spaces.

Assessment Strategy:
Teacher observes to see what sight words are difficult for the students to read and spell.

Variations of the Game:
Have the student make up a sentence with the word in it.

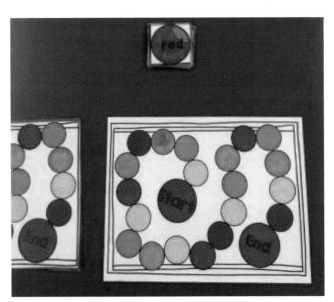

Name of Game: # PARK THAT WORD

Author: Darci Dheensaw

Adapted From: Monica House 2013

Targeted Skill: Improve sight word vocabulary

Anticipated Outcome: Students will be able to correctly name the sight word and then "park" their car in the corresponding spot.

Grade Level: Kindergarten, Grade 1, and Grade 2

Resources Required:
Dolch Pre-Primer flashcards. A box of Hot Wheel cars (I put about 20 cars on the table). Dolch Pre-Primer parking lots.

Explanation to Teacher (game construction):
Print a parking lot mat for each student in the group with a sight word in each stall. For extra durability laminate the mats. If a blank mat is made then you can individualize each parking lot. Print Pre-Primer Dolch cards.

Explanation to Teacher (how game works):
Place the sight word cards in a pile face down next to the parking lot mats. The student turns over the top card and reads it. If it is read correctly then he parks his car in the parking lot. (He can get help from a friend if he does not know the word.)

Directions to Children:
Read the word that is on the pile. Park your car in the corresponding parking spot. When your parking lot is full the game is over.

Assessment Strategy:
Teacher observes to see what sight words are difficult for the students to name.   Once complete the teacher can ask individual students to name a few words on their parking lot.

Variations of the Game:
Use only uppercase letters or only lowercase letters in the parking lot.

Sometimes, I control the pile of sight words and flip over a sight word. If a student has that word in their parking lot, they drive the car and park it in that stall. The first child with all their stalls filled with cars is the winner.

Name of Game:	**PIZZA BINGO**

Author: Darci Dheensaw

Adapted From: Beverly Close

Targeted Skill: Improve sight word vocabulary

Anticipated Outcome: Students will be able to correctly name the sight word card.

Grade Level: Kindergarten, Grade 1,

Resources Required:
Pizza mat. Dolch Pre-Primer cards. Pepperoni markers to cover the sight words on the pizza.

Explanation to Teacher (game construction):
Print and laminate pizzas. On the laminated pizzas print sight words. Cut out pepperoni markers.

Explanation to Teacher (how game works):
Place the sight word cards face down next to the pizzas. Turn over the card. Have the child read the sight word. If they have the sight word on their pizza then they cover it with a pepperoni slice. They can also say the word in a sentence. The first person to cover all the sight words on the pizza is the winner and calls out, "I've got a pizza!" They then read the words on their card to the group.

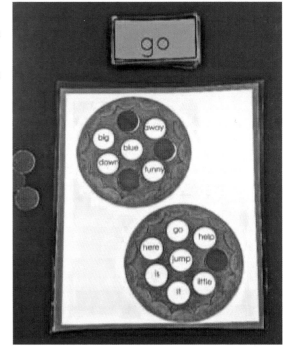

Directions to Children:
Put your pizza mat in front of you. Turn over the sight word card in the pile. Read the card. If you have that word, cover it with a pepperoni slice. The first person to cover all the sight words on the pizza is the winner.

Assessment Strategy:
Teacher observes to see what sight words are difficult for the students to name.

Variations of the Game:
On the four laminated pizzas I have about 10 circles where I write in sight words. I then have pepperoni slices that are in a pile and the children turn over the pepperoni to read a sight word. If they have the sight word on their pizza then they cover it with a red bingo chip. The first person to cover all their circles on the pizza is the winner.

Teacher-designed Blitz Games

Janet's Comments

Dear Reader:

I am proud to introduce you to **Nancy Eassie**, Learning Assistance teacher at the Lauwelnew Tribal School in Saanich, British Columbia. When we began the Joyful Literacy Intervention program two years ago Nancy found grade two children who still did not know the alphabet, and children at the end of grade one who had not yet begun to read. Nancy began a school-wide Blitz program four days a week; she began with the grade twos until they were caught up, then designed an Alphabet and Sight Word Blitz program to escalate the pace of skill learning – all based on fun games. Enjoy them with your children!

Janet

Nancy Eassie

These games have been developed to be used with the grade(s) level indicated; however, each game could be adapted for use at any primary grade level depending on the skill or skill level being targeted.

The games that are listed below are just a few that have been designed in the past two years. As with many schools, budgets are minimal or non-existent for many. This is where imagination and repurposing what we already have is very important. In many cases they become the most loved games.

One of my first games was simply an egg carton and a plastic flip frog I found in the prize box. In each egg spot I put a letter and when the kids flipped the frog, they needed to tell me about the letter it landed on. It was simple and cost me nothing.

The following games cost me $20. That's it. The trick is to look at material and use it for something else. The best advice I can give you is to scour through the clearance section in craft stores and visit the local bargain store seasonally so that games can rotate. If you think something is boring, chances are the students will think so too. Please note that the games are intended to be fun. Assessment of the games can be done weekly with simple flash cards and *Circle Charts*, but it is important to allow students to enjoy the moment and become familiar with the words through play and context. If it is always about the assessment, the joy of reading will be a hard place to get to. Remember what Dr. Mort keeps referring to: **"The joy of literacy."**

Name of Game:

NAME THAT HOLE IN ONE!
(INDOOR/OUTDOOR GOLF)

Author: Nancy Eassie

Targeted Skill: Level 2 Sight Words.

Anticipated outcome: To be able to identify words that students are struggling with, so that recall is easier.

Grade Level: Although these are level 2 sight words (Grade 2 students), I found this works for all grades.

Resources Required:

Bucket, 46 ping pong balls, 2 plastic golf putters, permanent felt pens, list of sight words of choice.

Explanation to Teacher (game construction):

Print each word on each ping-pong ball.

Explanation to Teacher (how to play the game):

Dump ping-pong balls between two students. Each student will have a plastic golf putter. Place the bucket about three feet away from the students. The student then picks up a ping-pong ball and identifies the word. If they know the word they place the ball on the floor and try to get it in the bucket. The more words they know, the more often they get the opportunity to putt the ball.

Assessment Strategy:

This game is solely for the purpose of getting comfortable with the words. Assessment can be done with basic flash cards.

Variation of the Game:

This game can be used for any of the set of list words or alphabet. I would suggest however that each set of words be color coded for each level so it is easier to separate them. As the students get more comfortable with the words, I find that timing them gave a competitive edge to the game.

Personal note:

If you have students who need to move, this may help because learning by doing works better. This is a moving game that has busy voices and also helps with hand-eye coordination and communication with peers. It can be played indoors or outdoors.

| Name of Game: | **AIR PRESSURE** |

Author: Nancy Eassie

Targeted Skill: Level 2 Sight Words.

Anticipated Outcome: To identify words that students are struggling with so that recall is easier.

Grade Level: Although these are level 2 sight words (Grade 2 students), I found this works for all grades.

Resources Required:

Ping-pong balls from "Name That Hole in One" game, hula-hoops, straws.

Explanation to Teacher (construction of game):

List words printed on ping-pong balls.

Direction to Children:

Randomly pick a ping-pong ball out of the bucket or bowl, say the word, place on the table or floor and use a straw to blow the ping-pong ball from one end of the hula-hoop to the other. The hula-hoop is basically a way to contain the ping-pong balls.

Assessment Strategy:

This game is solely for the purpose of getting comfortable with the words. Assessment can be done with basic flash cards.

Variation of the Game:

This game can be used for any of the set of list words or alphabet. I would suggest however that each set of words be color coded for each level so it is easier to separate them.

Personal note:

Kids love anything that has to do with a race. It is not about winning and losing, it's about the rush. If you are inclined to work on speech at the same time, get your student to place the straw in between the front of their lips and say words that have 's' sounds. My girlfriend, who's in radio, was given this little task. It was to help prevent the high pitch 's' sounds that sound whistly, similar to the gopher in the Winnie the Pooh series.

Name of Game:	**SNOWBALLS**
Author:	Nancy Eassie
Targeted Skill:	Level 2 Sight Words.
Anticipated Outcome:	To be able to identify words that students are struggling with, so that recall is easier.
Grade Level:	Although these are level 2 sight words (Grade 2 students), I found this works for all grades.

Resources Required:
Ping-pong balls, plastic bowl, plastic tongs.

Explanation to Teacher (construction of game):
List words printed on ping-pong balls.

Explanation to Teacher (how to play game):
Students will use the tongs to pick up the ping-pong balls and say the word. If the student does not know the word they put the ball back. This is a good game to allow students to use their fine motor skills with the tongs as well as cooperation skills. Many students will ask their peer for help for what the word is or they will work on it together.

Direction to Children:
Use tongs to pick up balls from the bowl and say the word. If you know the word you can keep the "snowball," if not, put it back in the bowl.

Assessment Strategy:
Teachers can quickly look at words on ping-pong balls near them and ask students to recite them again.

Variation of the Game:
This game can be used for any of the set of list words or alphabet. I would suggest however that each set of words be color coded for each level so it is easier to separate them.

Personal note:
There is rarely any snow where we live so the idea of a snowball is exciting for most of our students. Also, with so many of our students who are struggling with reading and have other issues, it is nice to have one task to help in many areas.

Name of Game:	SOUNDS THAT MAKE YOU GO HMMM...
Author:	Nancy Eassie
Targeted Skill:	Level 2 Sight Words.
Anticipated Outcome:	To have students identify the similarities and differences in words and sounds.
Grade Level:	Although these are level 2 sight words (Grade 2 students), I found this works for all grades.

Resources Required:
Hula-hoops, ping-pong balls, plastic bowl.

Explanation to Teacher (construction of game):
List words on ping-pong balls.

Explanation to Teacher (how to play game):
Ask students to separate some of the words in groups. This is where the instructor needs to know where the difficulties may be and have students work on pronunciation and phonological awareness.

Direction to Children:
Ask students to separate words into groups that you have previously identified.

Assessment Strategy:
This is a perfect opportunity to watch your students after you have given them directions of how you want them to separate the words. You will probably find the thing that is giving them grief and help them over the hump.

Variation of the Game:
This game can be used for any of the set of list words or alphabet. I would suggest however that each set of words be color coded for each level so it is easier to separate them. Any of the words can be separated according to what the student is having difficulty with. For example, it could be all words with 'th' or all with the same first sound 'd' or 'w'. If you lay the hula-hoops slightly over each other you now have a 3D Venn diagram. The possibilities are endless!

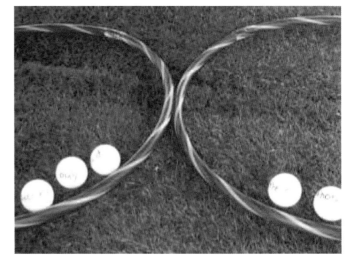

Personal note:
The hula-hoops also help me in my reading groups. The 3D Venn diagrams make it very useful. I have students write on strips of paper so that story statements can be easily rearranged and discussed.

Name of Game:	**GONE FISHIN'**

Author: Nancy Eassie (adapted from Ice Fishing for Sight Words (Editable Freebies) at Differentiated Kindergarten: differentiatedkindergarten.com)

Targeted Skill: Level 2 sight words.

Anticipated Outcome: To identify words that students are struggling with, so that recall is easier.

Grade Level: Although these are level 2 sight words (Grade 2 students), I found this works for all grades.

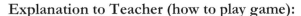

Resources Required:
Colored paper, laminator, paper fasteners, plastic bucket, 2 magnets, string and 1 pair of chopsticks.

Explanation to Teacher (construction of game):
Head to web site at Differentiated Kindergarten and look up Ice Fishing for Sight Words. Here is the direct link:

http://differentiatedkindergarten.com/colonize-your-classroom-with-editable-sight-word-fishing-fun/?m

Print the sight words, cut out fish, laminate, place fasteners through the eye of each fish. Tie string around one end of chopstick and at other end fasten magnet. Repeat for other chopstick. Place fish into bucket.

Explanation to Teacher (how to play game):
Have students go "fishing" in the bucket. The magnet will stick to a fish. Once the student has the fish out, they need to say the word. If they catch a shark, they must re-read each sight word fish and place them back into the bucket.

Direction to Children:
Once you catch a fish you must say the word. If you catch a shark you need to re-read all the fish you have already caught and put them back in the bucket to be caught again.

Assessment Strategy:
This game is solely for the purpose of getting comfortable with the words. Assessment can be done with basic flash cards.

Variation of the Game:
This game can be used for any of the set of list words or alphabet. I would suggest however that each set of words be color coded for each level so it is easier to separate them. Please note that this bucket has Level 1 sight words printed. This is a fun way to get kids playing at any level.

Personal note:
In the community where I currently work, fishing is cultural. If I were a better artist I would have made salmon, crab, and killer whales for the game. Look in the community and find what is personal. The only thing I changed in this game was having it as a basic fishing game vs. ice fishing. Ice fishing does not mean anything to my students and I want them to connect to their everyday reality.

| Name of Game: | **CONNECT 4 SIGHT WORDS** |

Authors: Nancy Eassie and Scott Eassie (adapted from Connect4 by Milton Bradley)

Targeted Skill: Level 2 Sight Words.

Anticipated Outcome: To identify words that students are struggling with, so that recall is easier.

Grade Level: Although these are level 2 sight words (Grade 2 students), I found this works for all grades.

Resources Required:
14 X 11 canvas (from Dollar Store or Michael's Craft Store), 1 ½ inch diameter discs in two colors (I used expansion discs from arc – available at Staples), magic cover removable sticky paper (Dollar Store), left over paint from home or school.

Explanation to Teacher (construction of game):
Color wash canvas. Once it's dry measure out a 7 X 6 grid, paint lines with paint or puffy paint. Cut out magic cover paper and cut out circles to fit inside discs. Print sight words on the paper that is on the discs. One full set for each color. The reasoning for putting the paper on the discs is that I found that the marker always rubs off. Also, if needed, it is easy to replace words or use for another purpose.

Explanation to Teacher (how to play game):
Students pick the color of discs. Students will then pick a random disc. Students must say the word and then place it on a square on the grid. The first student to place four colored discs in a row wins.

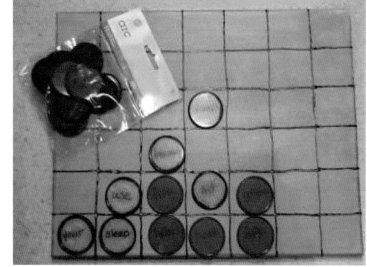

Direction to Children:
Same directions as original Connect4. Having four in a row with your color disc wins. Remember to try to block your opponent.

Assessment Strategy:
This game is solely for the purpose of getting comfortable with the words. Assessment can be done with basic flash cards.

Variation of the Game:
If it is difficult to find the discs, another way would be to collect milk caps in different colors and print words on the caps. This game can be used for any of the set of list words or alphabet. I would suggest however that each set of words be color coded for each level so it is easier to separate them.

Name of Game:	**I SPY A SIGHT WORD**

Author: Nancy Eassie

Targeted Skill: Level 2 Sight Words.

Anticipated Outcome: To be able to identify words that students are struggling with, so that recall is easier.

Grade Level: Although these are level 2 sight words (Grade 2 students), I found this works for all grades.

Resources Required:
All resources from Connect4 Sight Words.

Explanation to Teacher (construction of game):
Fill a board with all the sight words that the student needs help with or the whole board. It's basic 'I spy' wording. For example: you or another student can say, "I spy with my little eye a word that starts with the letter 'f' or makes the sound 'fff.'" Other students will have to think of all the words they know on the board to figure out it is the word 'five.'

Explanation to Teacher (how to play game):
Most students know how to play 'I spy.' It can be as easy or as difficult as you want. For example: you or another student can say, "I spy with my little eye a word that starts with the letter 'f' or makes the sound 'fff.'.Other students will have to think of all the words they know on the board to figure out it is the word 'five.'

Direction to Children:
Explain to students that they are going to be playing 'I spy' but it will only be with the words on the board. Have them take turns or play it with them. Start with, "I spy with my little eye the word that starts with the letter 's' (sleep), or "I spy with my little eye a word that rhymes with bit" (sit).

Assessment Strategy:
This game is solely for the purpose of getting comfortable with the words. Assessment can be done with basic flash cards.

Variation of the Game:
This game can be used for any of the set of list words or the alphabet. I would suggest however that each set of words be color coded for each level so it is easier to separate them. If all else fails, play it on an open page in a leveled reader. Just open a page and play by the same rules.

Game or Strategy?

The next two games are considered strategies rather than games. It is important that even though students are getting to know the sight words they need to see the words in context. It is sometimes really difficult to get kids 'hooked.' I have found that making it fun is really important. These are Dollar Store finds and I am always on the look-out for something that I can use. It is not always conventional, as you will see.

Name of Game: **SWAT A WORD**

Author: Nancy Eassie

Targeted skill: To have fun outlining words in leveled readers.

Anticipated Outcome: Students will WANT to sit with their books and find words.

Grade Level: All.

Resources Required:
Fly swatters, scissors.

Explanation to Teacher (construction of game):
Cut out areas of the fly swatter to single out a word or phrase.

Explanation to Teacher (how to play game):
Give student a swatter to hold while reading.

Direction to Children:
It is important to tell students that the swatter is only for reading. It is not intended for swatting objects or friends. Have them understand that the swatter is a privilege and it can be taken away.

Variation of the Game:
If students are ready to tackle reading more quickly, a small wand (found in the party section of your local Dollar Store) is fun as well.

Book: Step into Reading, Step 2, *P.J. Funnybunny Camps out*, by Marilyn Sadler and illustrated by Roger Bollen.

Name of Game:	## LOOKING GLASSES

Author: Nancy Eassie

Targeted Skill: To make reading something that can be looked forward to.

Anticipated Outcome: Students will WANT to sit with their books and LOOK through their glasses.

Grade Level: All.

Resources Required:
Fun glasses in all sections at the local Dollar Store.

Explanation to Teacher (construction of game):
You can find all sorts of crazy glasses now. Some are plain, some look like cake, some looked like sports or musical instruments.

Explanation to Teacher (how to play game):
Students put on their glasses and read. Sometimes it takes something small to boost self-confidence and sometimes being silly helps being comfortable with the written words.

Direction to Children:
Tell students that these are their Looking Glasses. Please respect them. They are only for reading.

Personal note:
This idea really was a result of watching my youngest child. She wouldn't take a shower because she said it hurt her eyes. My husband and I put on her swimming goggles and the problem was solved. I simply related the idea back to reading. It had to do with comfort and believing. Self-esteem is huge when they start to understand what words are. This is a gimmick and the hook that students can buy into.

Janet's Summary

I have visited hundreds of classrooms that are implementing Joyful Literacy Interventions. The joy is palpable and it is like nothing I have seen before. Children line up to be assessed for the *Circle Charts*. They are eager to be affirmed in their learning and insist they are ready for the next set of skills. They want to participate in their *Circle Charts*,challenging their teachers to take them further – they want to finish that list. Children choose literacy activities during free play time in spite of encouragement to relax and try something different. They call out to classroom visitors, "Come and see what I can do!"

Teachers beam with pride! Never before have they been able to take so many children so far, so quickly. Even the most vulnerable children are making progress faster than ever previously imagined.

When I began to design my well-researched dream of how to reach 90% of all children and have them reading and writing at grade level, I never imagined it would happen so quickly. The implementation of the Blitz, combined with the *Circle Charts* and implemented with determination and integrity by our incredible professional staff, offers new hope for 30% of the children who have never had this golden opportunity.

We are saving the lives of many children and providing them with new possibilities in their adult years. Join us in our Joyful Literacy Intervention dream. It will change your life, too!

Sincerely,

The Joy of Learning!

References

Allington, R. L. (2006). What really matters for struggling readers (2nd ed.). Boston, MA: Allyn & Bacon.

Allington, R. L. (2009). What really matters for RTI (Response to Intervention). Boston, MA: Allyn & Bacon.

Allington, R. L. (2012). What really matters for struggling readers: Designing research-based programs. Boston, MA: Pearson.

Allington, R. L. (2014, May). Early Intervention. Paper presented at the meeting of Summit 5, Victoria, BC

Allington, R. L., & Cunningham, P. (1996). Schools that work: Where all children read and write. Scarborough, ON: Harper-Collins.

Allington, R. L., & Cunningham, P. (2007). Classrooms that work: They can all read and write (4th ed.). Scarborough, ON: Harper-Collins.

Allington, R. L., & McGill-Franzen, A. (2013). Summer Reading: Closing the rich/poor reading achievement gap. New York, NY: Teacher's College Press.

Bear, D., Invernizzi, M., Templeton, S., & Johnston, F. (2012). Words their way: Word study for phonics, vocabulary, and spelling instruction (5th ed.). Boston, MA: Pearson.

Beatty, J. J., & Pratt, L. (2012). Early literacy in preschool and kindergarten: A multicultural perspective (3rd ed.). Boston, MA: Pearson.

Burkey, L. C., Lenhart, L. A., & McKeon, C. A. (2008). Developing early literacy: Report of the national early literacy panel. Washington, DC: National Institute for Literacy. Retrieved from http://lincs.ed.gov/publications/pdf/NELPReport09.pdf

Canadian Council of Learning. (2006). Let the children play. Retrieved from http://www.ccl-cca.ca/pdfs/LessonsInLearning/Nov-08-06-Let-the-Children-Play.pdf Cunningham, A., & Zibulsky, J. (2014). Book smart. New York, NY: Oxford University Press.

Curtis, D., & Carter, M. (2003). Designs for learning and living. St. Paul, MN: Redleaf Press. Diller, D. (2003). Literacy work stations: Making centers work. Portland, ME: Stenhouse.

Diller, D. (2005). Practice with purpose. Portland, ME: Stenhouse.

Diller, D. (2008). Spaces and places: Designing classrooms for literacy. Portland, ME: Stenhouse.

Early Learning Profile (2012). School District No. 23 Central Okanagan.

Edwards, C., Gandini, L., & Foreman, G. (Eds.). (1998). The hundred languages of children (2nd ed.). London, ON: Ablex.

Flemington, K., Hewins, L., & Villiers, U. (2011). Journey to literacy: No worksheets required. Markham, ON: Pembroke.

Fountas, I. C., & Pinnell, G. S. (2011). Literacy beginnings: A prekindergarten handbook. Portsmouth, NH: Heinemann.

Johnson, J., & Keier, K. (2010). Catching readers before they fall: Supporting readers who struggle, K-4. Portland, MA: Stenhouse.

Lyons, C. A. (2012). Teaching struggling readers: How to use brain-based research to maximize learning. Portsmouth, NH: Heinemann.

McGee, L., & Morrow, L. M. (2005). Teaching literacy in kindergarten. New York, NY: The Guildford Press. McGill-Franzen, A. (2006). Kindergarten literacy: Matching assessment and instruction in kindergarten. New York, NY: Scholastic.

Middendorf, C. (2009). Building oral language skills. New York, NY: Scholastic.

Morrow, L. M. (2012). Literary development in the early years: Helping children read and write (7th ed.). Boston, MA: Pearson.

Mort, J. (1983). Teaching with the winning touch. Carthage, IL: Good Apple.

Mort, J. (2015) Joyful Literacy Interventions Part One: Early Learning Classroom Essential.

National Association for the Education of Young Children. (2003). Chopsticks and counting chips: Do play and foundational skills need to compete for the teacher's attention in an early childhood classroom? Retrieved from https://www.ccl-cca.ca/pdfs/LessonsInLearning/Nov-08-06-Let-the-children-play.pdf

National Early Learning Panel. (2009). Developing early literacy: Report of the early learning panel. National Center for Family Literacy. Retrieved from http://lincs.ed.gov/publications/pdf/NELPReport09.pdf

National Strategy for Early Literacy. (2009). The Canadian Language and Literacy Research Network. Retrieved from http://research4children.com/data/documents/ NationalStrategyforEarlyLiteracyReportsandRecommendationspdf.pdf

Payne, C. D., & Schulman, M. B. (1998). Getting the most out of morning message and other shared writing lessons. New York, NY: Scholastic.

Pinnell, G. S., & Fountas, I. C. (2009). When readers struggle: Teaching that works. Portsmouth, NH: Heinemann.

Rog, L. J. (2001). Read, write, play, learn: Literacy instruction in today's kindergarten.   Newark, DE: International Reading Association.

Routman, R. (2003). Reading essentials. Portsmouth, NH: Heinemann. Routman, R. (2005). Writing essentials. Portsmouth, NH: Heinemann. Routman, R. (2014). Read, write, lead. Alexandria, VA: ASCD

Schultze, B. (2008). Basic tools for beginning writers. Markham, ON: Pembroke.

Sousa, D. A., & Tomlinson, C. A. (2011). How neuroscience supports the learner-friendly classroom: Differentiation and the brain. Bloomington, IN: Solution Tree Press.

Trehearne, M. (2011). Learning to write and loving it. Thousand Oaks, CA: Corwin.

Vacca, J., Vacca, R. T., & Gove, M. K. (2012). Reading and learning to read (8th ed.). Boston, MA: Pearson. Weisman, C., Gandini, L., & Gandini, T. (1999). Beautiful stuff: Learning with found materials. Worcester, MA: Davis.

Wikipedia. Dolch Word List. Retrieved from en.wikipedia.org/wiki/Dolch_word_list

www.google.ca/search?q=Free+bubble+blowing+images&biw=1203&bih=663&tbm=isch&tbo=u&source=univ&sa=X&ved=0ahUKEwixv62Gg_bOAhUN9WMKHdf5DLQQ7AkIQw

Appendix: The Circle Charts

A Powerful Assessment and Tracking Tool: Foundational Skills K to 3

Circle Chart Template

THE ALPHABETIC PRINCIPLE
Letter-sound Recognition (K/1) – LOWER CASE

- Name lower case letters
- Produce letter sounds
- Produce a word beginning with the letter/sound
- Find the letter in text

Teacher's Chart

Class _____

Date _____

STUDENT'S NAME

b	c	d	f	g	h	j	k	l	m	n	p	q	r	s	t	v	w	x	y	z

Janet N. Mort PhD • jnmort@shaw.ca
Early Learning Inc.
A First Class Beginning

Skill Mastery Progress
Black – Sept/Oct/Nov
Green – Dec/Jan
Yellow – Jan/Feb/Mar
Red – Apr/May/Jun

Degree of Skill Mastery
- ● Skill Mastery
- ◑ Skill Review Required
- ○ Skill Instruction Required

Teacher's Chart

Class _____

Date _____

THE ALPHABETIC PRINCIPLE
Letter-sound Recognition (K/1) – UPPER CASE

- Name upper case letters   • Produce letter sounds
- Sequence uppercase letters

Degree of Skill Mastery
● Skill Mastery
◑ Skill Review Required
○ Skill Instruction Required

Skill Mastery Progress
Black – Sept/Oct/Nov
Green – Dec/Jan
Yellow – Jan/Feb/Mar
Red – Apr/May/Jun

EL Early Learning INC.
A First Class Beginning.

Janet N. Mort PhD • jnmort@shaw.ca

© 2015 Early Learning Inc.

STUDENT'S NAME	B	C	D	F	G	H	J	K	L	M	N	P	Q	R	S	T	V	W	X	Y	Z
	○	○	○	○	○	○	○	○	○	○	○	○	○	○	○	○	○	○	○	○	○
	○	○	○	○	○	○	○	○	○	○	○	○	○	○	○	○	○	○	○	○	○
	○	○	○	○	○	○	○	○	○	○	○	○	○	○	○	○	○	○	○	○	○
	○	○	○	○	○	○	○	○	○	○	○	○	○	○	○	○	○	○	○	○	○
	○	○	○	○	○	○	○	○	○	○	○	○	○	○	○	○	○	○	○	○	○
	○	○	○	○	○	○	○	○	○	○	○	○	○	○	○	○	○	○	○	○	○
	○	○	○	○	○	○	○	○	○	○	○	○	○	○	○	○	○	○	○	○	○
	○	○	○	○	○	○	○	○	○	○	○	○	○	○	○	○	○	○	○	○	○
	○	○	○	○	○	○	○	○	○	○	○	○	○	○	○	○	○	○	○	○	○
	○	○	○	○	○	○	○	○	○	○	○	○	○	○	○	○	○	○	○	○	○
	○	○	○	○	○	○	○	○	○	○	○	○	○	○	○	○	○	○	○	○	○
	○	○	○	○	○	○	○	○	○	○	○	○	○	○	○	○	○	○	○	○	○
	○	○	○	○	○	○	○	○	○	○	○	○	○	○	○	○	○	○	○	○	○
	○	○	○	○	○	○	○	○	○	○	○	○	○	○	○	○	○	○	○	○	○

THE ALPHABETIC PRINCIPLE
Letter-sound Recognition (K/1) – VOWELS

Teacher's Chart

Class _____

Date _____

Janet N. Mort PhD • Jnmort@shaw.ca

Early
Learning INC.

A First Class Beginning

Skill Mastery Progress

Black – Sept/Oct/Nov
Green – Dec/Jan
Yellow – Jan/Feb/Mar
Red – Apr/May/Jun

Degree of Skill Mastery

● Skill Mastery
◑ Skill Review Required
○ Skill Instruction Required

STUDENT'S NAME	a	e	i	o	u		A	E	I	O	U														
	○	○	○	○	○	○	○	○	○	○	○	○	○	○	○	○	○	○	○	○	○	○	○	○	○
	○	○	○	○	○	○	○	○	○	○	○	○	○	○	○	○	○	○	○	○	○	○	○	○	○
	○	○	○	○	○	○	○	○	○	○	○	○	○	○	○	○	○	○	○	○	○	○	○	○	○
	○	○	○	○	○	○	○	○	○	○	○	○	○	○	○	○	○	○	○	○	○	○	○	○	○
	○	○	○	○	○	○	○	○	○	○	○	○	○	○	○	○	○	○	○	○	○	○	○	○	○
	○	○	○	○	○	○	○	○	○	○	○	○	○	○	○	○	○	○	○	○	○	○	○	○	○
	○	○	○	○	○	○	○	○	○	○	○	○	○	○	○	○	○	○	○	○	○	○	○	○	○
	○	○	○	○	○	○	○	○	○	○	○	○	○	○	○	○	○	○	○	○	○	○	○	○	○
	○	○	○	○	○	○	○	○	○	○	○	○	○	○	○	○	○	○	○	○	○	○	○	○	○
	○	○	○	○	○	○	○	○	○	○	○	○	○	○	○	○	○	○	○	○	○	○	○	○	○
	○	○	○	○	○	○	○	○	○	○	○	○	○	○	○	○	○	○	○	○	○	○	○	○	○
	○	○	○	○	○	○	○	○	○	○	○	○	○	○	○	○	○	○	○	○	○	○	○	○	○
	○	○	○	○	○	○	○	○	○	○	○	○	○	○	○	○	○	○	○	○	○	○	○	○	○

PHONOLOGICAL AWARENESS (K/1)

Teacher's Chart

Class _____

Date _____

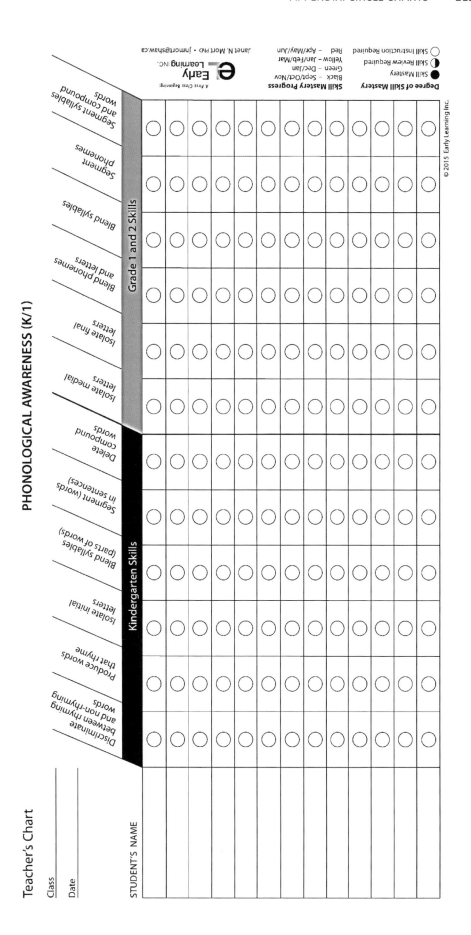

WORD STUDY (1/2)

Teacher's Chart

Class _____

Date _____

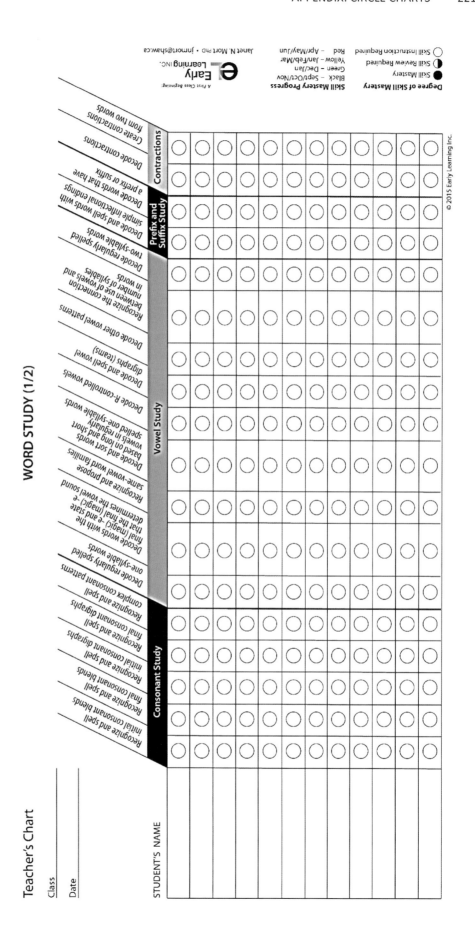

© 2015 Early Learning Inc.

Janet N. Mort PhD • jnmort@shaw.ca

E. Early Learning INC.

A First Class Beginning

Degree of Skill Mastery

● Skill Mastery
◐ Skill Review Required
○ Skill Instruction Required

Skill Mastery Progress

Black – Sep/Oct/Nov
Green – Dec/Jan
Yellow – Jan/Feb/Mar
Red – Apr/May/Jun

Column headers:

Consonant Study
- Recognize and spell initial consonant blends
- Recognize and spell final consonant blends
- Recognize and spell initial consonant digraphs
- Recognize and spell final consonant digraphs
- Recognize and spell complex consonant patterns

Vowel Study
- Decode regularly spelled one-syllable words
- Decode words with the final (magic) -e and state that the final (magic) -e determines the vowel sound
- Recognize and propose same-vowel word families
- Decode and sort words based on long and short vowels in regularly spelled one-syllable words
- Decode R-controlled vowels
- Decode and spell vowel digraphs (teams)
- Decode other vowel patterns
- Recognize the connection between use of vowels and number of syllables in words

Prefix and Suffix Study
- Decode regularly spelled two-syllable words
- Decode and spell words with simple inflectional endings
- Decode words that have a prefix or suffix

Contractions
- Decode contractions
- Create contractions from two words

STUDENT'S NAME

CONCEPTS OF PRINT (K/1)

Class _____

Date _____

(INSTRUCTIONS: Use a predictable book of about 8 pages where pictures support text, with periods and question marks. Hand the book to the child closed with the spine facing the child. Begin. Read the book a page or two at a time pausing to ask the next few questions in the list as appropriate to the text.)

Skill Mastery Progress

Black – Sept/Oct/Nov
Green – Dec/Jan
Yellow – Jan/Feb/Mar
Red – Apr/May/Jun

Degree of Skill Mastery

● Skill Mastery
◑ Skill Review Required
○ Skill Instruction Required

Janet N. Mort PhD • Jnmort@shaw.ca

E Early Learning INC.
A First Class Beginning

© 2015 Early Learning Inc.

STUDENT'S NAME	Book Concepts			Directionality			Word Concepts				Letter Concepts			Punctuation Marks	
	Front cover	Title	Print carries message (not the illustrations)	Beginning of text	Left to right sequence	Return sweep	One word	First word	Last word	Spaces between words	First letter in word	Last letter in word	Period	Capital letter	Question mark	Exclamation mark

DOLCH HIGH FREQUENCY WORDS: (PRE-PRIMER 1)

Teacher's Chart

Class _____

Date _____

Degree of Skill Mastery
- ● Skill Mastery
- ◐ Skill Review Required
- ○ Skill Instruction Required

Skill Mastery Progress
- Black – Sept/Oct/Nov
- Green – Dec/Jan
- Yellow – Jan/Feb/Mar
- Red – Apr/May/Jun

EL Early Learning INC.
A First Class Beginning
Janet N. Mort PhD • jnmort@shaw.ca

© 2015 Early Learning Inc.

STUDENT'S NAME	1. a	2. and	3. away	4. big	5. blue	6. can	7. come	8. down	9. find	10. for	11. funny	12. go	13. help	14. here	15. I	16. in	17. is	18. it	19. jump	20. little

DOLCH HIGH FREQUENCY WORDS (PRE-PRIMER 2)

Teacher's Chart

Class

Date

Degree of Skill Mastery

● Skill Mastery
◐ Skill Review Required
○ Skill Instruction Required

Skill Mastery Progress

Black – Sept/Oct/Nov
Green – Dec/Jan
Yellow – Jan/Feb/Mar
Red – Apr/May/Jun

ℓ· Early Learning INC.

A First Class Beginning

Janet N. Mort PhD • jnmort@shaw.ca

© 2015 Early Learning Inc.

STUDENT'S NAME	21. look	22. make	23. me	24. my	25. not	26. one	27. play	28. red	29. run	30. said	31. see	32. the	33. three	34. to	35. two	36. up	37. we	38. where	39. yellow	40. you
	○	○	○	○	○	○	○	○	○	○	○	○	○	○	○	○	○	○	○	○
	○	○	○	○	○	○	○	○	○	○	○	○	○	○	○	○	○	○	○	○
	○	○	○	○	○	○	○	○	○	○	○	○	○	○	○	○	○	○	○	○
	○	○	○	○	○	○	○	○	○	○	○	○	○	○	○	○	○	○	○	○
	○	○	○	○	○	○	○	○	○	○	○	○	○	○	○	○	○	○	○	○
	○	○	○	○	○	○	○	○	○	○	○	○	○	○	○	○	○	○	○	○
	○	○	○	○	○	○	○	○	○	○	○	○	○	○	○	○	○	○	○	○
	○	○	○	○	○	○	○	○	○	○	○	○	○	○	○	○	○	○	○	○
	○	○	○	○	○	○	○	○	○	○	○	○	○	○	○	○	○	○	○	○
	○	○	○	○	○	○	○	○	○	○	○	○	○	○	○	○	○	○	○	○
	○	○	○	○	○	○	○	○	○	○	○	○	○	○	○	○	○	○	○	○
	○	○	○	○	○	○	○	○	○	○	○	○	○	○	○	○	○	○	○	○
	○	○	○	○	○	○	○	○	○	○	○	○	○	○	○	○	○	○	○	○

DOLCH HIGH FREQUENCY WORDS: (PRIMER 1)

Janet N. Mort PhD • Jnmort@shaw.ca

e. Early
Learning INC.

A First Class Beginning

© 2015 Early Learning Inc.

Skill Mastery Progress

Black – Sept/Oct/Nov
Green – Dec/Jan
Yellow – Jan/Feb/Mar
Red   – Apr/May/Jun

Degree of Skill Mastery

● Skill Mastery
◑ Skill Review Required
○ Skill Instruction Required

Teacher's Chart

Class

Date

STUDENT'S NAME

41. all	42. am	43. are	44. at	45. ate	46. be	47. black	48. brown	49. but	50. came	51. did	52. do	53. eat	54. four	55. get	56. good	57. have	58. he	59. into	60. like

DOLCH HIGH FREQUENCY WORDS: (PRIMER 2)

Teacher's Chart

Class _____

Date _____

STUDENT'S NAME

Word list (column headers):

61. must
62. new
63. no
64. now
65. on
66. our
67. out
68. please
69. pretty
70. ran
71. ride
72. saw
73. say
74. she
75. so
76. soon
77. that
78. there
79. they
80. this

Degree of Skill Mastery
- ● Skill Mastery
- ◐ Skill Review Required
- ○ Skill Instruction Required

Skill Mastery Progress
- Black – Sept/Oct/Nov
- Green – Dec/Jan
- Yellow – Jan/Feb/Mar
- Red – Apr/May/Jun

Early Learning INC.
A First Class Beginning
Janet N. Mort PhD • Jnmort@shaw.ca

© 2015 Early Learning Inc.

DOLCH HIGH FREQUENCY WORDS: (PRIMER 3)

Teacher's Chart

Class

Date

STUDENT'S NAME

81. too
82. new
83. under
84. want
85. was
86. well
87. went
88. what
89. white
90. who
91. with
92. yes

ℰ Early Learning INC.

A First Class Beginning

Janet N. Mort PhD • Jnmort@shaw.ca

Skill Mastery Progress

Black – Sept/Oct/Nov
Green – Dec/Jan
Yellow – Jan/Feb/Mar
Red – Apr/May/Jun

Degree of Skill Mastery

● Skill Mastery
◐ Skill Review Required
○ Skill Instruction Required

DOLCH HIGH FREQUENCY WORDS: (GRADE ONE 1)

Degree of Skill Mastery

● Skill Mastery

◐ Skill Review Required

○ Skill Instruction Required

Skill Mastery Progress

Black – Sept/Oct/Nov

Green – Dec/Jan

Yellow – Jan/Feb/Mar

Red – Apr/May/Jun

ə Early Learning INC.

A First Class Beginning

Janet N. Mort PhD • Jnmort@shaw.ca

© 2015 Early Learning Inc.

Teacher's Chart

Class _____

Date _____

STUDENT'S NAME	93. after	94. again	95. an	96. any	97. ask	98. as	99. by	100. could	101. every	102. fly	103. from	104. give	105. going	106. has	107. had	108. her	109. him	110. his	111. how	112. just
	○	○	○	○	○	○	○	○	○	○	○	○	○	○	○	○	○	○	○	○
	○	○	○	○	○	○	○	○	○	○	○	○	○	○	○	○	○	○	○	○
	○	○	○	○	○	○	○	○	○	○	○	○	○	○	○	○	○	○	○	○
	○	○	○	○	○	○	○	○	○	○	○	○	○	○	○	○	○	○	○	○
	○	○	○	○	○	○	○	○	○	○	○	○	○	○	○	○	○	○	○	○
	○	○	○	○	○	○	○	○	○	○	○	○	○	○	○	○	○	○	○	○
	○	○	○	○	○	○	○	○	○	○	○	○	○	○	○	○	○	○	○	○
	○	○	○	○	○	○	○	○	○	○	○	○	○	○	○	○	○	○	○	○
	○	○	○	○	○	○	○	○	○	○	○	○	○	○	○	○	○	○	○	○
	○	○	○	○	○	○	○	○	○	○	○	○	○	○	○	○	○	○	○	○
	○	○	○	○	○	○	○	○	○	○	○	○	○	○	○	○	○	○	○	○
	○	○	○	○	○	○	○	○	○	○	○	○	○	○	○	○	○	○	○	○
	○	○	○	○	○	○	○	○	○	○	○	○	○	○	○	○	○	○	○	○

DOLCH HIGH FREQUENCY WORDS: (GRADE ONE 2)

Teacher's Chart

Class _____

Date _____

STUDENT'S NAME

113. know	114. let	115. live	116. may	117. of	118. old	119. once	120. open	121. over	122. put	123. round	124. some	125. stop	126. take	127. thank	128. them	129. then	130. think	131. walk	132. were

Degree of Skill Mastery
● Skill Mastery
◑ Skill Review Required
○ Skill Instruction Required

Skill Mastery Progress
Black – Sept/Oct/Nov
Green – Dec/Jan
Yellow – Jan/Feb/Mar
Red – Apr/May/Jun

A First Class Beginning:
ǝ Early Learning INC.
Janet N. Mort PhD • Jnmort@shaw.ca

© 2015 Early Learning Inc.

DOLCH HIGH FREQUENCY WORDS: (GRADE TWO 1)

Teacher's Chart

Class

Date

STUDENT'S NAME

Column headings (words):
133. always
134. around
135. because
136. been
137. before
138. best
139. both
140. buy
141. call
142. cold
143. does
144. don't
145. fast
146. first
147. five
148. found
149. gave
150. goes
151. green
152. its

Degree of Skill Mastery
● Skill Mastery
◗ Skill Review Required
○ Skill Instruction Required

Skill Mastery Progress
Black – Sept/Oct/Nov
Green – Dec/Jan
Yellow – Jan/Feb/Mar
Red – Apr/May/Jun

A First Class Beginning

e Early
Learning INC.

Janet N. Mort PhD • Jnmort@shaw.ca

© 2015 Early Learning Inc.

DOLCH HIGH FREQUENCY WORDS: (GRADE TWO 2)

Teacher's Chart

Class

Date

Degree of Skill Mastery

● Skill Mastery

◖ Skill Review Required

○ Skill Instruction Required

Skill Mastery Progress

Black – Sept/Oct/Nov

Green – Dec/Jan

Yellow – Jan/Feb/Mar

Red – Apr/May/Jun

A First Class Beginning

e. **Early**
Learning INC.

Janet N. Mort PhD • jnmort@shaw.ca

© 2015 Early Learning Inc.

STUDENT'S NAME	153. made	154. many	155. off	156. or	157. pull	158. read	159. right	160. sing	161. sit	162. sleep	163. tell	164. their	165. these	166. those	167. upon	168. us	169. use	170. very	171. wash	172. why
	○	○	○	○	○	○	○	○	○	○	○	○	○	○	○	○	○	○	○	○
	○	○	○	○	○	○	○	○	○	○	○	○	○	○	○	○	○	○	○	○
	○	○	○	○	○	○	○	○	○	○	○	○	○	○	○	○	○	○	○	○
	○	○	○	○	○	○	○	○	○	○	○	○	○	○	○	○	○	○	○	○
	○	○	○	○	○	○	○	○	○	○	○	○	○	○	○	○	○	○	○	○
	○	○	○	○	○	○	○	○	○	○	○	○	○	○	○	○	○	○	○	○
	○	○	○	○	○	○	○	○	○	○	○	○	○	○	○	○	○	○	○	○
	○	○	○	○	○	○	○	○	○	○	○	○	○	○	○	○	○	○	○	○
	○	○	○	○	○	○	○	○	○	○	○	○	○	○	○	○	○	○	○	○
	○	○	○	○	○	○	○	○	○	○	○	○	○	○	○	○	○	○	○	○
	○	○	○	○	○	○	○	○	○	○	○	○	○	○	○	○	○	○	○	○
	○	○	○	○	○	○	○	○	○	○	○	○	○	○	○	○	○	○	○	○
	○	○	○	○	○	○	○	○	○	○	○	○	○	○	○	○	○	○	○	○

DOLCH HIGH FREQUENCY WORDS: (GRADE TWO 3)

Teacher's Chart

Class _____

Date _____

STUDENT'S NAME

173. which
174. wish
175. work
176. would
177. write
178. your

Janet N. Mort PhD • jnmort@shaw.ca

Early Learning INC.

A First Class Beginning

© 2015 Early Learning Inc.

Skill Mastery Progress

Black – Sept/Oct/Nov
Green – Dec/Jan
Yellow – Jan/Feb/Mar
Red – Apr/May/Jun

Degree of Skill Mastery

● Skill Mastery
◑ Skill Review Required
○ Skill Instruction Required

DOLCH HIGH FREQUENCY WORDS: (GRADE THREE 1)

Teacher's Chart

Class _____

Date _____

e. Early
Learning Inc.

A First Class Beginning

Janet N. Mort PhD • Jnmort@shaw.ca

© 2015 Early Learning Inc.

Skill Mastery Progress

Black – Sept/Oct/Nov
Green – Dec/Jan
Yellow – Jan/Feb/Mar
Red – Apr/May/Jun

Degree of Skill Mastery

● Skill Mastery
◐ Skill Review Required
○ Skill Instruction Required

STUDENT'S NAME	179. about	180. better	181. bring	182. carry	183. clean	184. cut	185. done	186. draw	187. drink	188. eight	189. fall	190. far	191. full	192. got	193. grow	194. hold	195. hot	196. hurt	197. if	198. keep

DOLCH HIGH FREQUENCY WORDS: (GRADE THREE 2)

Teacher's Chart

Class _____

Date _____

Degree of Skill Mastery

● Skill Mastery
◐ Skill Review Required
○ Skill Instruction Required

Skill Mastery Progress

Black – Sept/Oct/Nov
Green – Dec/Jan
Yellow – Jan/Feb/Mar
Red – Apr/May/Jun

Early Learning INC.
A First Class Beginning

Janet N. Mort PhD • jnmort@shaw.ca

© 2015 Early Learning Inc.

STUDENT'S NAME	199. kind	200. laugh	201. light	202. long	203. much	204. myself	205. never	206. only	207. own	208. pick	209. seven	210. show	211. six	212. small	213. start	214. ten	215. today	216. together	217. try	218. warm
	○	○	○	○	○	○	○	○	○	○	○	○	○	○	○	○	○	○	○	○
	○	○	○	○	○	○	○	○	○	○	○	○	○	○	○	○	○	○	○	○
	○	○	○	○	○	○	○	○	○	○	○	○	○	○	○	○	○	○	○	○
	○	○	○	○	○	○	○	○	○	○	○	○	○	○	○	○	○	○	○	○
	○	○	○	○	○	○	○	○	○	○	○	○	○	○	○	○	○	○	○	○
	○	○	○	○	○	○	○	○	○	○	○	○	○	○	○	○	○	○	○	○
	○	○	○	○	○	○	○	○	○	○	○	○	○	○	○	○	○	○	○	○
	○	○	○	○	○	○	○	○	○	○	○	○	○	○	○	○	○	○	○	○
	○	○	○	○	○	○	○	○	○	○	○	○	○	○	○	○	○	○	○	○
	○	○	○	○	○	○	○	○	○	○	○	○	○	○	○	○	○	○	○	○
	○	○	○	○	○	○	○	○	○	○	○	○	○	○	○	○	○	○	○	○
	○	○	○	○	○	○	○	○	○	○	○	○	○	○	○	○	○	○	○	○
	○	○	○	○	○	○	○	○	○	○	○	○	○	○	○	○	○	○	○	○

READING FLUENCY AND COMPREHENSION (K/1/2)

Teacher's Chart

Class _____

Date _____

Degree of Skill Mastery

● Skill Mastery
◐ Skill Review Required
○ Skill Instruction Required

Skill Mastery Progress

Black – Sept/Oct/Nov
Green – Dec/Jan
Yellow – Jan/Feb/Mar
Red   – Apr/May/Jun

ᗱ Early Learning INC.

A First Class Beginning

Janet N. Mort PhD • jnmort@shaw.ca

© 2015 Early Learning Inc.

STUDENT'S NAME	Reads text with accuracy and fluency	Reads text with expression and volume	Reads text with phrasing	Reads text with pace	Engages in stories independently	Engages in story reading in groups	Responds to stories with questions or comments	Retells stories including setting, theme, plot and conclusion	Summarizes the reading	Participates in extension activities post-reading	Recognizes text features such as table of contents, author's notes/biography and introduction
	○	○	○	○	○	○	○	○	○	○	○
	○	○	○	○	○	○	○	○	○	○	○
	○	○	○	○	○	○	○	○	○	○	○
	○	○	○	○	○	○	○	○	○	○	○
	○	○	○	○	○	○	○	○	○	○	○
	○	○	○	○	○	○	○	○	○	○	○
	○	○	○	○	○	○	○	○	○	○	○
	○	○	○	○	○	○	○	○	○	○	○
	○	○	○	○	○	○	○	○	○	○	○
	○	○	○	○	○	○	○	○	○	○	○
	○	○	○	○	○	○	○	○	○	○	○
	○	○	○	○	○	○	○	○	○	○	○
	○	○	○	○	○	○	○	○	○	○	○

Fluency: Reads text with accuracy and fluency; Reads text with expression and volume; Reads text with phrasing; Reads text with pace

Comprehension: Engages in stories independently; Engages in story reading in groups; Responds to stories with questions or comments; Retells stories including setting, theme, plot and conclusion; Summarizes the reading; Participates in extension activities post-reading; Recognizes text features such as table of contents, author's notes/biography and introduction

EMERGENT WRITING (K)

Teacher's Chart

Class

Date

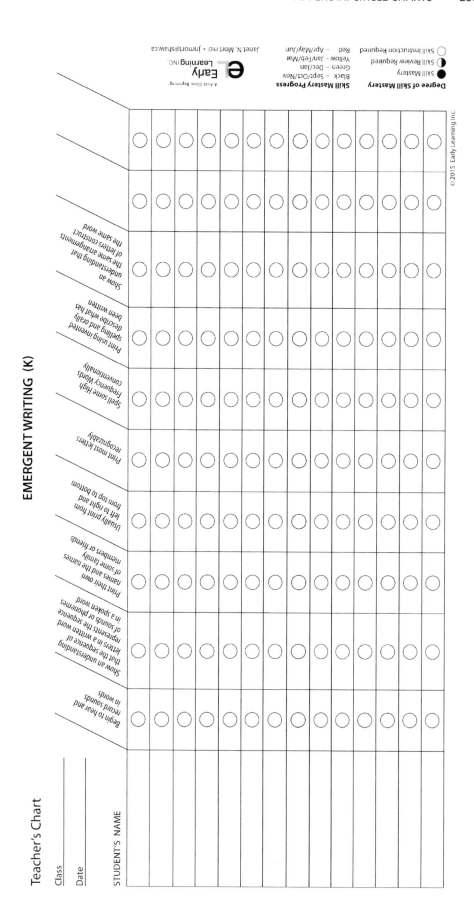

Degree of Skill Mastery
● Skill Mastery
◐ Skill Review Required
○ Skill Instruction Required

Skill Mastery Progress
Black – Sept/Oct/Nov
Green – Dec/Jan
Yellow – Jan/Feb/Mar
Red – Apr/May/Jun

e Early Learning INC.
A First Class Beginning!
Janet N. Mort PhD · jnmort@shaw.ca

Chart columns:
- STUDENT'S NAME
- Begin to hear and record sounds in words
- Show an understanding that the sequence of letters in a written word represents the sequence of sounds or phonemes in a spoken word
- Print their own names and the names of some family members or friends
- Usually print from left to right and from top to bottom
- Print most letters recognizably
- Spell some High Frequency Words conventionally
- Print using invented spelling and orally describe what has been written
- Show an understanding that the same arrangements of letters construct the same word

DEVELOPMENTAL WRITING (GRADE 1)

Teacher's Chart

Class _____

Date _____

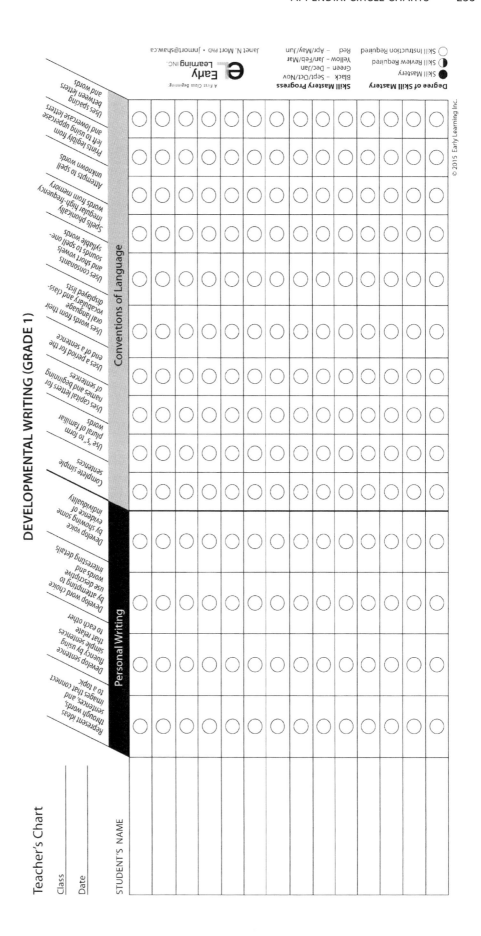

Conventions of Language

- Uses spacing between letters and words
- Prints legibly from left to using uppercase and lowercase letters
- Attempts to spell unknown words
- Spells phonetically irregular high-frequency words from memory
- Uses consonants and short vowels sounds to spell one-syllable words
- Uses words from their oral language vocabulary and class-displayed lists
- Uses a period for the end of a sentence
- Uses capital letters for names and beginning of sentences
- Use "s" to form plural of familiar words
- Complete simple sentences

Personal Writing

- Develop voice by showing some evidence of individuality
- Develop word choice by attempting to use descriptive words and interesting details
- Develop sentence fluency by using simple sentences that relate to each other
- Represent ideas through words, sentences, and images that connect to a topic

STUDENT'S NAME

e Early Learning Inc.

A First Class Beginning

Janet N. Mort PhD • jnmort@shaw.ca

© 2015 Early Learning Inc.

Skill Mastery Progress

- Black – Sept/Oct/Nov
- Green – Dec/Jan
- Yellow – Jan/Feb/Mar
- Red – Apr/May/Jun

Degree of Skill Mastery

- ● Skill Mastery
- ◐ Skill Review Required
- ○ Skill Instruction Required

DEVELOPMENTAL WRITING (GRADE 2)

Teacher's Chart

Class _____

Date _____

STUDENT'S NAME

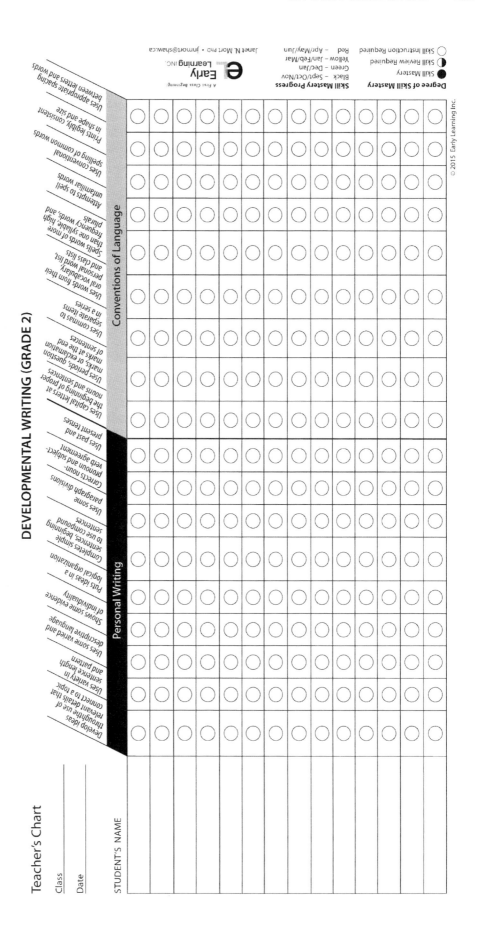

Conventions of Language

- Uses appropriate spacing between letters and words
- Prints legibly, consistent in shape and size
- Uses conventional spelling of common words
- Attempts to spell unfamiliar words
- Spells words of more than one syllable, high frequency words, and plurals
- Uses words from their oral vocabulary, personal word list, and class lists
- Uses commas to separate items in a series
- Uses periods, question marks, or exclamation marks at the end of sentences
- Uses capital letters at the beginning of proper nouns and sentences

Personal Writing

- Uses past and present tenses
- Corrects noun-pronoun and subject-verb agreement
- Uses some paragraph divisions
- Completes simple sentences, beginning to use compound sentences
- Puts ideas in a logical organization
- Shows some evidence of individuality
- Uses some varied and descriptive language
- Uses variety in sentence length and pattern
- Uses relevant details that connect to topic
- Develop ideas thoughtful use of

Degree of Skill Mastery

● Skill Mastery
◑ Skill Review Required
○ Skill Instruction Required

Skill Mastery Progress

Black – Sept/Oct/Nov
Green – Dec/Jan
Yellow – Jan/Feb/Mar
Red – Apr/May/Jun

E. Early Learning INC.

A First Class Beginning.

Janet N. Mort PhD • jnmort@shaw.ca

© 2015 Early Learning Inc.

ORAL LANGUAGE: SPEAKING AND LISTENING (K/1/2)

Teacher's Chart

Class

Date

STUDENT'S NAME

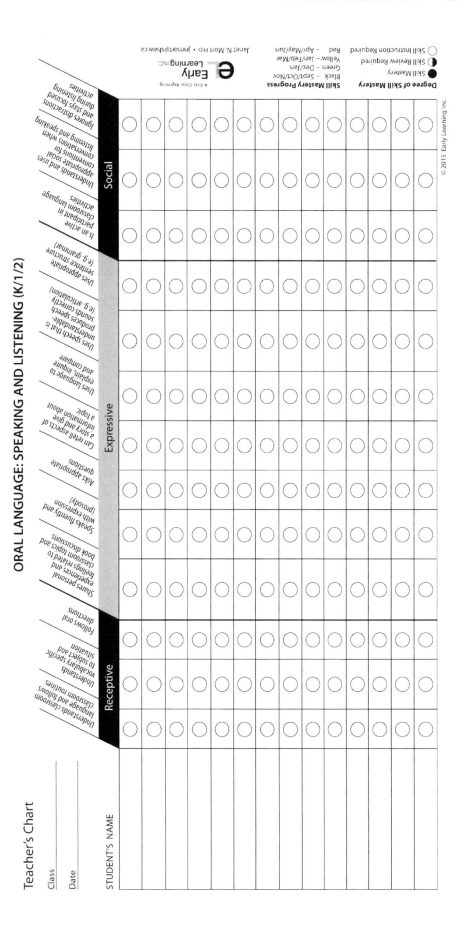

Degree of Skill Mastery
- ● Skill Mastery
- ◐ Skill Review Required
- ○ Skill Instruction Required

Skill Mastery Progress
- Black – Sep/Oct/Nov
- Green – Dec/Jan
- Yellow – Jan/Feb/Mar
- Red – Apr/May/Jun

e. Early Learning inc.
A First Class Beginning

Janet N. Mort PhD • jnmort@shaw.ca

© 2015 Early Learning Inc.

Receptive
- Understands classroom language and follows classroom routines
- Understands vocabulary specific to subject and situation
- Follows oral directions

Expressive
- Shares personal experiences and feelings related to classroom topics and book discussions
- Speaks fluently and with expression (prosody)
- Asks appropriate questions
- Can retell aspects of a story and give information about a topic
- Uses language to explain, inquire and compare
- Uses speech that is understandable–produces speech sounds correctly (e.g. articulation)
- Uses appropriate sentence structure (e.g. grammar)

Social
- Is an active participant in classroom language activities
- Understands and uses appropriate social conventions for conversations when listening and speaking
- Ignores distractions and stays focused during listening activities

LITERATURE AND INFORMATIONAL TEXT FOUNDATIONAL SKILLS (K/2)

Teacher's Chart

Class _____

Date _____

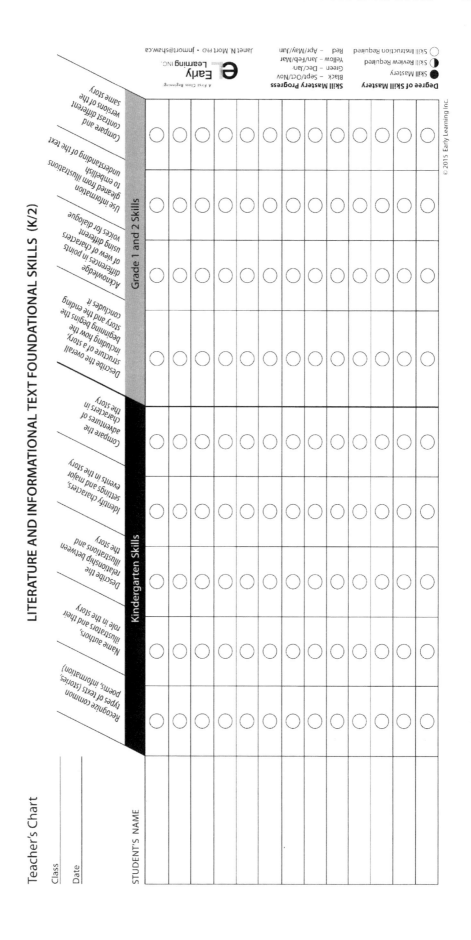

Degree of Skill Mastery

● Skill Mastery
◐ Skill Review Required
○ Skill Instruction Required

Skill Mastery Progress

Black – Sept/Oct/Nov
Green – Dec/Jan
Yellow – Jan/Feb/Mar
Red – Apr/May/Jun

e Early Learning INC.
A First Class Beginning

Janet N. Mort PhD • jnmort@shaw.ca

© 2015 Early Learning Inc.

Grade 1 and 2 Skills
- Compare and contrast different versions of the same story
- Use information gleaned from illustrations to embellish understanding of the text
- Acknowledge differences in points of view of characters using different voices for dialogue
- Describe the overall structure of a story, including how the beginning begins the story and the ending concludes it

Kindergarten Skills
- Compare the adventures of characters in the story
- Identify characters, settings and major events in the story
- Describe the relationship between illustrations and the story
- Name authors, illustrators and their role in the story
- Recognize common types of texts (stories, poems, information)

STUDENT'S NAME

LITERATURE AND INFORMATIONAL TEXT FOUNDATIONAL SKILLS (K/1/2)

Teacher's Chart

Class _____

Date _____

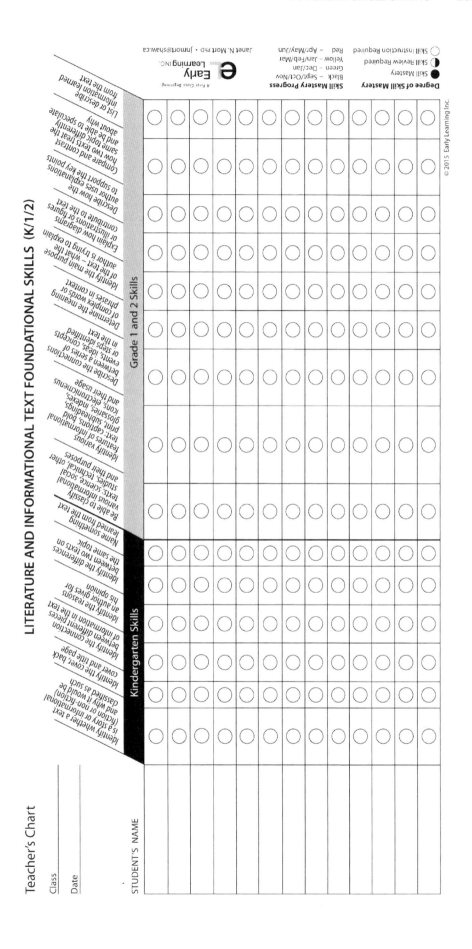

Teacher's Chart

Class _____

Date _____

STUDENT'S NAME

Janet N. Mort PhD • jnmort@shaw.ca

Early Learning INC.

A First Class Beginning

© 2015 Early Learning Inc.

Skill Mastery Progress

Black – Sept/Oct/Nov
Green – Dec/Jan
Yellow – Jan/Feb/Mar
Red – Apr/May/Jun

Degree of Skill Mastery

● Skill Mastery
◐ Skill Review Required
○ Skill Instruction Required

Made in the USA
Columbia, SC
04 March 2018